Towards Multilingual Education

BILINGUAL EDUCATION & BILINGUALISM
Series Editors: Nancy H. Hornberger, *University of Pennsylvania, USA,* and Colin Baker, *Bangor University, Wales, UK*

Bilingual Education and Bilingualism is an international, multidisciplinary series publishing research on the philosophy, politics, policy, provision and practice of language planning, global English, indigenous and minority language education, multilingualism, multiculturalism, biliteracy, bilingualism and bilingual education. The series aims to mirror current debates and discussions.

Full details of all the books in this series and of all our other publications can be found on http://www.multilingual-matters.com, or by writing to Multilingual Matters, St Nicholas House, 31-34 High Street, Bristol BS1 2AW, UK.

BILINGUAL EDUCATION & BILINGUALISM
Series Editors: Nancy H. Hornberger and Colin Baker

Towards Multilingual Education
Basque Educational Research from an International Perspective

Jasone Cenoz

MULTILINGUAL MATTERS
Bristol • Buffalo • Toronto

Nire mutilei, Iñigo eta Durk

Library of Congress Cataloging in Publication Data
A catalog record for this book is available from the Library of Congress.
Cenoz, Jasone
Towards Multilingual education: Basque Educational Research in International Perspective
Jasone Cenoz
Bilingual Education & Bilingualism:72
Includes bibliographical references and index.
1. Education, Bilingual—Spain—País Vasco. 2. Multicultural education—Spain—País Vasco. 3. Multilingualism—Spain—País Vasco. 4. Language and education—Spain—País Vasco. 5. Basque language—Study and teaching—Spain—País Vasco. 6. Spanish language—Study and teaching—Spain—País Vasco. 7. English language—Study and teaching—Spain—País Vasco. 8. Second language acquisition—Study and teaching—Spain—País Vasco. I. Title.
LC3736.S7C46 2009
370.117'509466–dc22 2009026144

British Library Cataloguing in Publication Data
A catalogue entry for this book is available from the British Library.

ISBN-13: 978-1-84769-193-4 (hbk)
ISBN-13: 978-1-84769-192-7 (pbk)

Multilingual Matters
UK: St Nicholas House, 31–34 High Street, Bristol BS1 2AW, UK.
USA: UTP, 2250 Military Road, Tonawanda, NY 14150, USA.
Canada: UTP, 5201 Dufferin Street, North York, Ontario M3H 5T8, Canada.

The policy of Multilingual Matters/Channel View Publications is to use papers that are natural, renewable and recyclable products, made from wood grown in sustainable forests. In the manufacturing process of our books, and to further support our policy, preference is given to printers that have FSC and PEFC Chain of Custody certification. The FSC and/or PEFC logos will appear on those books where full certification has been granted to the printer concerned.

Typeset by IDS Infotech.
Printed and bound in Great Britain by the MPG Books Group.

Contents

Preface

There is a long and fascinating history of case studies in language acquisition research. Perhaps the most well-known examples are Adam, Eve and Sarah – the famous children studied by Roger Brown and reported in his classic book *A First Language: The Early Stages* in 1973. The history of case study research on bilingual acquisition is even older, going back to the research of Ronjat on his bilingual son published in 1913 and, perhaps better known, the massive series of reports by Werner Leopold on his two daughters published between 1939 and 1949. One of the real values of a case study approach is the richness of understanding that comes from in depth and longitudinal analyses of single learners. Case studies are richly heuristic – they point to what can happen; they provide ample hypotheses for further research; and they provide the opportunity for multiple perspectives on development.

In this book *Towards Multilingual Education*, Jasone Cenoz presents a different kind of case study. It is the case study of a whole country, the Basque Country, and its development of multilingual forms of education. Like good case studies of monolingual and bilingual acquisition, the case study of the Basque Country is rich and insightful. There are three interwoven strands to this relatively short volume – one strand concerns itself with developments in the Basque Country itself as it evolves linguistically and seeks to develop educational programs that reflect the ever changing sociolinguistic realities of which it is a part; a second strand is concerned with theoretical contexts for studying bi and multilingual forms of education in international perspective; and the third strand addresses methodological issues implicated in doing multi-dimensional research on such a complex phenomenon as multilingual education. All of these strands are developed with reference to very diverse conceptual and theoretical perspectives, including typological considerations when describing multilingual education, content-based approaches to multilingual education; attitudes and motivations in multilingual education; outcomes of multilingual education; the age factor, a pervasive issue in most contexts that have bi- or multilingual forms of education; and third language acquisition. It is the in-depth analyses of the Basque experiments in multilingual education that makes this book so rich, pushing thinking beyond current frameworks.

Discussions of bilingualism and bilingual education have often tended to conceptualize issues somewhat categorically; for example, with reference to coordinate and compound bilingualism; elite and folk bilingualism; and additive versus subtractive forms of bilingual education, to name a few. Multilingualism and multilingual education challenge rigid binary classifications and even complex ones such as Mackey's typology of various forms of bilingual education that yielded 250 alternatives (Mackey, 1970). Cenoz proposes an alternative way of resolving this complexity by proposing *Continua of Multilingual Education*, inspired by Hornberger's Continua of Biliteracy. Cenoz's continua include educational variables (subject, language of instruction, teachers and school context), linguistic variables (linguistic distance among the languages involved) and sociolinguistic variables at the micro and macro levels. The continua of multilingual education provide a more realistic portrait of the dynamic complexities and interactions that characterize learners, educators and programs in multilingual education contexts. With Cenoz's continua, our view of multilingual education is kaleidoscopic, changing as the issues that motivate research change and as alternative research methodologies are adopted to examine specific issues.

With respect to educational variables, the Basque case study is truly rich, in large part because it is a country within a country (Spain). This means that there are Basque dominant and Spanish dominant schoolchildren to consider. This 'national' reality has resulted in the creation of alternative forms of multilingual education that respect the language dominance of the major language groups. At the same time, the Basque Country is, of course, part of the evolving European Union and, therefore, has immigrants who speak other languages that need to be considered. Like all other countries, the effects of globalization are also shaping Basque language policies. '*Europeanization*' and globalization have prompted parents to seek instruction in English as a third language so that their children have full access to seek possibilities in employment, science, technology and travel that are afforded by these internationalizing trends. Educational policies and issues are nuanced in the Basque Country and highly complex because, although Basque is a national language, it does not enjoy the full status of a majority language since it is in a demographic minority in comparison to Spanish. This has resulted in extraordinary measures to bolster Basque language development among both Basque dominant and Spanish dominant residents at the same time as policies are implemented to ensure that Basque schoolchildren also master Spanish. These efforts are seen at all levels of education, from pre-school to university. Few accounts of bi- or multi-lingual education include descriptions of bi- or multi-lingual programs at the university level. This is a truly original and important feature of this volume. The commitment to multilingual education is also evident in the extraordinarily rich programs of research that are being carried out at all levels of the educational system. Cenoz's narrative goes beyond the Basque Country to include discussions of multilingual forms of education in other countries so that the reader gains a broad perspective.

Cenoz's own research takes full advantage of the linguistic continua in her framework as she explores learner outcomes, age effects on learning, and the results of learning English as a third versus a second language. The Basque Country is a particularly interesting context for studying these issues because the three languages at the heart of her research are typologically distinct. This creates an interesting and somewhat unusual opportunity to look at cross-linguistic effects in language learning. This is fully explored in Chapter 7, *The Influence of Bilingualism on Third Language Acquisition*. Research by Cenoz and her colleagues demonstrates the positive effects that bilingualism can have on third language acquisition despite typological differences. At the same time, and in keeping with her continua of multilingual education framework, Cenoz illustrates how other factors, including metalinguistic and sociocultural factors, can mask such effects. A hallmark of this volume and the research conducted by the author as well as other researchers in the Basque Country is their keen attention to the potential importance and influence of other factors. Even when the focus of research attention is cognitive or linguistic in nature, the possible influences of sociocultural contextual factors is not far from the author's vantage point. Like all good case studies, the Basque researchers use a combination of quantitative and qualitative methodologies to great effect.

Learner factors are subsumed under sociolinguistic context factors at both macro- and micro-levels. Micro-level context factors include the general vitality of the languages involved which, in turn, is related to the number of speakers of the language, the status of each language, and its use or visibility in the linguistic landscape. Micro-level context factors include learners' use of language in the home and the role of language in their immediate social networks. Including learners as part of the sociolinguistic context expands our conceptualization of learners as primarily cognitive beings to their being both part of, and influenced by, micro- and macro-levels of the sociolinguistic context in which they live and learn. This makes eminent sense within Cenoz's continua framework and within the rich and complex sociolinguistic communities in which they live and learn. Viewed from this perspective, language learning is as much sociolinguistic as it is psycho-educational in nature.

Cenoz's case study of the Basque Country will appeal to many different audiences – linguistic, sociolinguistic and psycholinguistic students doing graduate work, educators and educational researchers who are interested in multilingual education for practical reasons, policy makers and language planners interesting in language planning, and, of course, researchers interested in multilingual education.

F. Genesee
McGill University

References

Brown, R. (1973) *A First Language: The Early Stages.* Harmondsworth. UK: Penguin.

Leopold, W.F (1939, 1947, 1949a, b) *Speech Development of a Bilingual Child: A Linguist's Record* (in four parts). Evanston, IL: Northwestern Press.

Mackey, W. (1970) A typology of bilingual education. *Foreign Language Annals* 3, 596–608.

Ronjat, J. (1913) *Le developpement du langage observé chez un enfant bilingue.* Paris: Champion.

Introduction

This volume focuses on bilingual and multilingual education and discusses the results of research conducted in the Basque educational system as related to other contexts. Basque is a language of unknown origin spoken in a small area in Western Europe and it is in contact with French and Spanish. The Basque language is extensively used in education in one of the areas of the Basque Country, the Basque Autonomous Community.

Bilingual and multilingual education in the Basque Country is interesting for an international audience for several reasons. First, the minority status of Basque and its revival as a language of instruction both as an L1 and L2 and its use along with Spanish and foreign language make Basque education an interesting combination of different processes. Language learning in the Basque educational system is linked to research on heritage, second and foreign languages as defined by Kramsch (2007: 5). In fact Basque can be considered a heritage language '*learned by members of an ethnic group desirous to reconnect with the culture of their ancestors*' because it is learned by Basque L1 speakers and by Basque students who no longer speak Basque and learn it at school. At the same time, speakers of Basque as a first language learn Spanish as a second language defined as '*a language other than the mother tongue learned in an environment in which that language is the dominant language or where the language is an international language of commerce and industry*'. All students in the Basque Autonomous community also learn a foreign language understood as '*a language that is learned in an instructional environment or during a temporary sojourn abroad as part of general education or for professional purposes*'.

Second, the spread of Basque as the language of instruction and the new multilingual and multicultural situation in the Basque Country have developed into situations which do not fit completely into the three categories of heritage, second and foreign language. It is very common for speakers of Spanish as a first language and for immigrants who speak other languages to be instructed through Basque even if this was not the language used by their ancestors. These situations cannot be considered heritage language learning in a strict way but it is difficult to consider them 'second language' because Basque is not the dominant language or an international language and it is not a foreign language either because it an official language in some parts of the Basque Country. These additional possibilities make the Basque educational system even more interesting but also show that it is difficult to fit educational and sociolinguistic realities within strict boundaries and that there is overlap between the scope of heritage, second and foreign languages.

Third, the Basque educational system provides interesting information on language learning but also on other aspects of bilingual and multilingual education. The Basque case blurs the boundaries between one of the dichotomies associated of bilingual education, the difference between elite and folk bilingualism (De Mejía, 2002). The Basque educational system cannot be considered elitist when it is aimed at the whole school population, it could rather be folk bilingualism. On the other hand the economic resources allocated to bilingual education are quite high and speakers of the minority language are not economically disadvantaged as compared to speakers of the majority. In this sense, it is not a typical situation of many other minorities.

Some other interesting aspects of bilingual and multilingual education in the Basque Country are that education through Basque extends all the way from kindergarten to university and that English has an increasing role. The use of Basque as the language of instruction at different levels of education faces different challenges and implies important differences regarding language planning. The increasing use of Basque at the university both for teaching and research explores new areas for minority languages which are more common in lower levels of education. The increasing need of English in society has changed its presence in the Basque educational system. The first important step was to introduce English as a third language in kindergarten. Further steps include the use of English to teach content, the use of English as an additional language of instruction and the development of an integrated syllabus for Basque, Spanish and English. The Basque educational system is innovative in using these approaches to teach English in combination with the maintenance and promotion of the minority language.

This volume discusses the Basque educational system and research conducted on the outcomes of bilingual and multilingual education. It is aimed at scholars working on bilingual and multilingual education, language acquisition in educational contexts, language policy and minority languages in different parts of the world. The volume can also be of interest for professionals in language planning and teachers and teacher educators working in these areas. The book is divided into 10 chapters and a chapter with the conclusions and future perspectives.

The first chapter, *Why Multilingualism in Education?*, discusses in a general way the main topics of the volume, the spread of English, the revival of minority languages and the role of education. It also introduces the Basque Autonomous Community (BAC) and the languages used in its educational system.

Chapter 2, *Towards a Typology of Multilingual Education*, reviews some typologies of bilingual and multilingual education and presents the '*Continua of Multilingual Education*' as a tool to accommodate different types of multilingual education in diverse sociolinguistic contexts. The final section of the chapter includes the different types of bilingual and multilingual programs in the BAC and discusses them according to the '*Continua of Multilingual Education*'.

Chapters 3 and 4 focus on the use of Basque, a minority language as the language of instruction in the BAC. Chapter 3, *Using the Minority Language as the Language of Instruction*, discusses the minority language teaching in general and the main challenges faced when using Basque as the medium of instruction.

Chapter 4, *Learning through the Minority Language: Linguistic and Academic Outcomes*, looks at the outcomes of maintenance and immersion programs in other contexts and discusses the results in Basque, Spanish and other academic subjects in Basque-medium instruction.

Chapters 5 and 6 focus on the teaching of English as a third language in the BAC. Chapter 5, *Third Language Learning and Instruction through the Third Language*, discusses the increasing role of English in the curriculum in the European context and focuses on English language teaching in Basque schools. It discusses different possibilities having English as a school subject or as additional language of instruction. Chapter 6, *Learning English and Learning through English: Research Outcomes*, focuses on assessment of English proficiency and reports the results of studies on the acquisition of English in the BAC.

Chapter 7, *The Influence of Bilingualism on L3*, analyses the possible effect of bilingualism on the acquisition of additional languages in general first and then in the BAC. This issue has attracted a lot of attention in the BAC where research studies confirm the general trend to associate bilingualism with advantages in third language acquisition.

Chapter 8, *Identities and Attitudes*, relates bilingual and multilingual education in the BAC to its socio-political context and discusses research on language and identity and language attitudes. It reports the differences between the educational models and the students' first language.

Chapter 9, *The Age Factor in Bilingual and Multilingual Education*, focuses on the effect of introducing a second or foreign language at different grades in the school context. It shows comparisons of English language comprehension and production by schoolchildren who have started to learn English at different ages.

Chapter 10, *Bilingual and Multilingual Education at the University*, discusses the challenge of teaching through a minority language at the university and at the same time introducing English as an additional language of instruction. It also looks at adult language learning in the BAC.

In the conclusions the main trends of Basque bilingual and multilingual education are discussed and future lines of research are proposed.

Acknowledgements

Many of the studies reported in this volume have been funded by the Spanish Ministry of Science and Innovation, the Basque Government Research Policy Unit and the European 6th Framework Program.[1] I wish to thank them all for their support. I would like to thank Colin Baker and Nancy Hornberger for their useful comments on the first draft of this volume. I also want to thank the medical profession and particularly my neurosurgeon, Dr Enrique Úrculo for his skillful use of the scalpel, Dr Josep Piera who hit the nail on the head when dealing with a very rare condition and my physician, Dr Isabel Mallaina for her relentless support. Last but not the least, I want to thank my family and friends for taking care of me in difficult times. I cannot possibly express in words how thankful I am to my son and my partner for their daily support and encouragement.

Notes

1. I would like to acknowledge the funding by the Spanish Ministry of Science and Innovation grant *HUM2006-09775-C02-01/FILO and* Basque Government grant IT-202-07 and the European 6th Framework Network of Excellence *Sustainable Development in Diverse World* (sus. div).

Chapter 1
Why Multilingualism?

Introduction

This volume discusses different aspects of bilingual and multilingual education in the Basque Autonomous Community (BAC, henceforth), a specific context with a combination of a minority language (Basque), a majority language (Spanish) and an increasing presence of English as an international language. In this chapter we are going to introduce some of the terminology that will be used in the book and we will discuss the concept of multilingualism and relate it to two different phenomena that are taking place in the world: the spread of English as a language of international communication and the revival of minority languages. The last section of the chapter focuses on languages in the Basque Country and provides the necessary background information about the linguistic, sociolinguistic and socio-political context so as to discuss different aspects of multilingual education in the following chapters.

Multilingualism

Multilingualism and multilingual education are becoming more and more important not only in the Basque context but all over the world. As Edwards (2007: 447) points out '*Multilingualism is a powerful fact of life around the world, a circumstance arising, at the simplest level, from the need to communicate across speech communities*'. Indeed, multilingualism is very common taking into account that there are almost 7000 languages in the world and about 200 independent countries. According to the Ethnologue, the number of speakers of the different languages is unevenly distributed and 40% of the world's population have one of the most common eight languages as a first languages: Mandarin, Hindi, Spanish, English, Bengali, Portuguese, Arabic and Russian (Gordon, 2005). More than 4000 of the world languages are spoken by less than 2% of the world's population and 516 of these languages are nearly extinct. The most multilingual continents are Asia and Africa.

Some researchers have drawn a comparison between linguistic diversity and biodiversity because in both cases some of the species are at risk and need specific protection (Krauss, 1992; Crystal, 2000; Maffi, 2000). Krauss highlights the great loss that the death of a language implies and argues that linguistic diversity is not less important than ecological diversity:

> Surely just as the extinction of any animal species diminishes our world, so does the extinction of any language. Surely we linguists know, and the general public can sense, that any language is a supreme achievement of a uniquely human collective genius, as divine and endless a mystery as a living organism. Should we mourn the loss of Eyak or Ubykh any less than the loss of the panda or California condor? (Krauss, 1992: 8)

The idea of sustainable development as maintaining a balance between economic growth and the maintenance of natural resources and ecosystems has been extended to cultural diversity. For example the European network of excellence *'Sustainable development in a diverse world'* (www.susdiv.org) aims at providing instruments to manage cultural diversity (including linguistic diversity) as a strategy to achieve sustainable development. The idea of linguistic diversity and multilingualism acquires a different dimension in this context. They have an added value and as Cenoz and Gorter (2009) show when discussing the linguistic landscape, an economic valuation model used in the study of biodiversity can be applied to the use of different languages.

Multilingualism is at the same time an individual and a social phenomenon. It can refer to the acquisition, knowledge or use of several languages by individuals or by language communities in a specific geographical area. Multilingualism has been defined as *'the ability of societies, institutions, groups and individuals to engage, on a regular basis, with more than one language in their day-to-day lives'* (European Commission 2007: 6). Multilingualism usually implies more than two languages but individual and social bilingualism can also be considered as part of multilingualism as it is the case in this definition. A broad definition such as this also includes different levels of proficiency in the different languages. Proficiency can range from basic communicative abilities to a very high level in different skills and languages.

Multilingualism is a very complex phenomenon and it can be studied from different perspectives in linguistics, psycholinguistics, anthropology or sociolinguistics. Different aspects of multilingualism receive more or less attention depending on the discipline. For example, a psycholinguist can be interested in the way a multilingual person processes different languages and a sociolinguist in the relative vitality of languages which are in contact. The study of multilingualism in education can bring different perspectives together. It is possible to study language processing, language acquisition and language use by individual learners at school but schools are necessarily linked to the society in which they are located. Schools are not only influenced by society but can also have an important effect on society. Specific studies on multilingualism in education often focus on only one aspect of multilingualism but need to take into account the complexity of the whole phenomenon.

Multilingualism in a specific area can be the result of different factors. One of them is the mobility of the population. Mobility includes immigrants but also refugees, business workers, international agency workers, international students, international aid work (such as NGOs) and soldiers. Languages are also affected by specific historical and political factors such as colonial expansion or the union or separation of different countries.

Definitions and Terminology

In this section a number of terms about multilingualism, multilingual education and the Basque educational system will be defined as used in this volume.

Additive bi/multilingualism: A language is added to the linguistic repertoire of the speaker while the first language continues to be developed.

Basque: Language spoken by 30.1% of the population in the Basque Country. It is a non-Indo-European language of unknown origin.

Basque Autonomous Community (BAC): One of the autonomous regions of Spain. It has three provinces: Araba, Bizkaia and Gipuzkoa.

Basque Country/Euskal Herria: The Basque historical and cultural territory including two autonomous communities in Spain (the BAC and Navarre) and the Northern Basque Country (Iparralde) in France.

Bilingual models: School programs in the Basque Country according to the language of instruction. Model A has Spanish as the language of instruction, model D has Basque and model B has both Basque and Spanish.

Bilingualism: Ability to use two languages in communication.

Bilingual education: The use of two languages in education provided that schools aim at bilingualism and biliteracy.

Castilian: Castilian is the most common word to refer to Spanish in many areas of Spain. In this volume we will use the word Spanish unless we quote other authors.

Common European Framework of Reference for Languages (CEFR): It is a tool developed by the Council of Europe setting standards for different levels of language learning so that there can be mutual recognition of language qualifications. It establishes six stages or levels in language learning: A1, A2, B1, B2, C1 and C2.

Content- and language-integrated learning (CLIL): A context in which an additional language (in many cases a third or fourth language) is used as a medium in the teaching of content. It does not give preference for content or language and it has its roots in Europe.

Ikastola: A Basque medium school that can be either public or private. Ikastolak were the first schools to teach through the medium of Basque and most of them are part of the network Ikastolen Elkartea.

Immersion education: Educational programs using a second language as the language of instruction for all or some subjects.

Immigrant languages: Language spoken by speakers coming from countries where other languages are spoken.

Indigenous language: Language originally spoken in a specific territory. The term autochthonous is also used.

Language of wider communication: The language people commonly use to communicate for many purposes in many parts of the world

Language planning: Plans to influence the acquisition, corpus and use of languages.

Lingua franca: A language systematically used to communicate among people who do not share the same language

Linguistic landscape: Written information available on language signs in public spaces.

Majority language: Dominant language in a community. It is used at the institutional level (education, government, etc ...) and spoken by most inhabitants of a specific area. For example, Spanish is the majority language in the Basque Country.

Minority language: Language spoken by a group numerically inferior to the rest of the population of a State with a more restricted use at the institutional level. For example, Basque is a minority language in the Basque Country.

Multilingual education: The use of two or more languages in education provided that schools aim at multilingualism and multiliteracy.

Normalization: Common term in the Basque Country to refer to the aim of using Basque as the common language in all functions of public and private life.

Plurilingualism: Individual multilingualism.

Subtractive bi-multilingualism: A new language is learned and replaces the first language.

Multilingualism and the Spread of English

Even though multilingualism is more common than monolingualism there are still many countries where the ideal of '*one nation/one language*' is central. In fact, most languages in the world do not have an official status and are not used in education. This means that many children in the world do not have their first language as a school language. The idea of linguistic uniformity is still strong in some parts of the world including European countries but European institutions are clear defendants of multilingualism (see also Baetens Beardsmore, 2008). For example, the European Commission (2005a: 2) states[1]:

> *It is this diversity that makes the European Union what it is: not a 'melting pot' in which differences are rendered down, but a common home in which diversity is celebrated, and where our many mother tongues are a source of wealth and a bridge to greater solidarity and mutual understanding.*

According to the European Commission (2005a: 3), multilingualism has advantages in many different ways. At the individual level, it can improve individual cognitive skills and develop first language skills. Multilingualism can also make European citizens more aware of other cultures, and increase European mobility. The aim of the European Commission (2005a: 4) is that all European citizens have practical skills in three languages: their mother tongue and two more. One of the recent developments to promote multilingualism has been to make multilingualism a separate portfolio for one of the commissioners since January 2007. It is considered that languages have a cultural value and provide a sense of identity. The Council of Europe also fosters multilingualism. It has established the European Centre for Modern Languages (http://www.ecml.at/) and developed some key instruments for language learning such as the European Language Portfolio (ELP) or the Common European Framework of Reference (CEFR). The ELP (http://www.coe.int/portfolio) is a document where personal language learning experience is recorded and the CEFR is a tool for setting standards for different stages of language learning allowing for international comparison in learning and evaluation (Council of Europe, 2002). Both instruments have been developed to promote multilingualism and language learning.

According to a recent survey, 56% of citizens in the European Union are able to have a conversation in a second language (European Commission, 2006). The percentages vary between countries. Ninety-nine percent of the citizens in Luxembourg speak at least one second language, followed by 97% of Slovaks and 95% of Latvians. At the other end, the least multilingual in Europe are the native speakers of English. Sixty-six percent of the citizens of Ireland and 62% of the citizens in the UK only speak one language. In non-English speaking countries, the ones with the highest percentages of monolingual speakers are Italy (59%), Hungary (58%), Portugal (58%) and Spain (56%). English is the most widely spoken language in the European Union and 51% of the European citizens can speak English (13% as a first language and 38% as a second or additional language).

English is the most important language of intra-European communication and it is also the most international language all over the world but English is in contact with other languages even in English speaking countries (Edwards, 2004). Nowadays, English is considered a resource which opens doors for better opportunities and it is associated with social and economic mobility. There have been languages of international communication in the past. For example, Latin or classical Arabic have been used as languages of wider communication but the intensity of the use of English both geographically and affecting different domains is new. This intensity is such that, as Graddol (2006) points out, in some countries (for example, Colombia, Mongolia, Chile or South Korea) the idea is not to learn English as a foreign language but that the country becomes bilingual in English and the national language. Hu (2007) also discusses the spread of English in China and large scale government supported experimentation with Chinese–English bilingual education.

The spread of English is also felt as a threat. For example, Skutnabb-Kangas (2000) considers that English is a killer of languages. Carli and Ammon (2007) focus on the disadvantages that non-native scholars of English have in scientific publications and other aspects of academic life. The spread of English is seen as a reflection of globalization and the loss of cultural identity. On the other hand, the spread of English in the world today is linked to its use along with other languages and can result in the development of multiple identities and in language diversity. Graddol (2006) provides an example of this language diversity in the case of internet. The use of English on the internet is very important in relation to the number of speakers of English as a first language but the relative proportion of English on the internet has gone down in the last years because other languages such as Spanish, French and Arabic are becoming widely used and also lesser-used languages are increasingly used.

The spread of English has resulted in its global use and nowadays the number of non-native speakers of English has outnumbered the number of native speakers (Crystal, 2003). Seidlhofer (2007) points out that the use of English as a lingua franca means that it gets a delimited and distinct status and it is not a threat to other languages. Alcón (2007) supports the use of English as a lingua franca in Europe because of its spread and also because interlocutors use it as a language for communication not as a language for identification. She proposes to accept different types of English that have emerged around the world as well as the need to analyze the discourse constructed by speakers of English from a perspective of intercultural communication.

The Revival of Minority Languages

Minority languages such as Basque are referred to as autochthonous languages but they are also called less widely used languages, indigenous languages, or regional minority languages. Speakers of languages such as Basque are usually fluent in a majority language. In the case of the BAC, this language is Spanish and speakers with Basque as a first language can also communicate in Spanish. In this volume, we will refer to the big effort made in the Basque Country by speakers of Basque and Spanish to use Basque in education. The effort to use a minority language when it seems to be more practical just to use a strong language in education is not very often well understood by speakers of strong languages. Bernardo Atxaga, the most well known Basque writer describes how he tried to explain the use of Basque to an American journalist concerned about his interest in the survival of Basque. His reasoning was the following:

> 'We want our language to last, not because it's pretty or because it's ancient, but for one simple reason, because it's a language we know well and which is useful to us in our daily lives'. I wanted to add: 'Just as English is to you.' But I didn't dare. 'Some people say that Basques could communicate perfectly well with each other in Castilian', she went on, meaning: 'Why insist on continuing to speak a minority language when you could use one spoken by three hundred million people?' I told her that we were bilingual and that, as a writer, I published in both languages, and that since two languages were better than one I could see only advantages in that. 'But advantages apart,' I continued my defence, 'what matters is reality. With some people I speak euskara and with others Castilian. Obviously, I could phone my wife and talk to her in Castilian, but she would find that very odd. We've been speaking to each other in euskara for the last twenty years. (Atxaga, 2007: 23)

Atxaga's words explain how 'small' languages can be important for their speakers. Edwards (2003: 41) considers that the *'importance of being bilingual is, above all, social and psychological rather than linguistic'*. Indeed, small languages can provide a sense of identity and apart from being used for communication can have a symbolic value. This is confirmed by the High Level Group on Multilingualism report which states that regional and minority languages are for many Europeans an important means of communication and part of their identity (European Commission, 2007). According to this report these languages are *'constituent elements of Europe's linguistic and cultural diversity and wealth'* (European Commission, 2007: 18). As we will see in Chapter 8, identity is also closely linked to the use of Basque in the Basque Country.

Some years ago, the Council of Europe (1992) adopted a treaty, the *Charter for Regional or Minority Languages* to protect and promote regional and minority languages. So far 33 countries have signed this treaty and 23 of these have also ratified it. In spite of this protection, most minority languages are not official languages at the European level and are not used by European institutions. Basque, Catalan and Galician achieved a special status in 2006 and can be used to some extent at the European level. Basque was used for the first time by the European Commission in writing in October 2007 to refer to the sea highway between Bilbao and Zeebrugge (Basque News, 2007a) and the first time Basque was used orally at a meeting of the Council of Ministers of the European Union was in November 2007 (Basque News, 2007b).

Minority languages are important in many other areas of the world and some progress has been made in using these languages in education (see Baker & Prys Jones, 1998). An example of this could be the use of Quechua and Aymara and other indigenous languages in Latin America. For example, as Hornberger and López (1998) report, the Puno project started in 1980 and provided education in the students' first language (Aymara or Quechua) and in Spanish as a second language from the early grades in the province of Puno in Peru. Hamel (2007) refers to educational projects to revitalize indigenous languages in Mexico that provide an appropriate development of the first and the second language.

The use of minority languages in education is usually the result of language planning as an effort to protect and develop its acquisition and use (Spolsky, 2004; Paulston & Heidemann, 2006). Bilingual and multilingual education is considered a necessary requirement for the survival and revitalization of minority languages (Baker, 2007a: 142). The UNESCO universal declaration on cultural diversity aims at safeguarding linguistic heritage and at encouraging linguistic diversity at all levels of education respecting the mother tongue (UNESCO, 2002). Bilingual and multilingual education can influence the three levels of language planning identified by Cooper (1989): corpus, status and acquisition. The use of a minority language in education has an influence on status and corpus planning because the minority language is used for new and more prestigious functions. An implication of the use of the minority language for new functions is the adaptation of the corpus of the language which could include graphiza-tion, standardization and the creation of scientific and technological termi-nology. Moreover, it has a direct influence on acquisition planning because the number of speakers can be expanded when the language is learned as a second language and also those who speak the minority language as their first language can acquire literacy skills.

Using a minority language in education (either as a subject or a lan-guage of instruction) implies some important challenges. One of them is the limitations minority languages can have at the corpus level when they are going to be used as the medium of instruction. Major world languages (English, Chinese, Spanish, French, etc.) have been codified for a long time and have a long tradition as written languages and as school languages. In contrast, many minority languages are in the process of codification and do not have a standard. Even if there is a standard, minority languages do not have a strong tradition of being used in all areas. As Idiazabal (1998) points out, in the case of Basque even native speakers do not have exten-sive use of the language in different domains as it is the case with majority languages. Other challenges faced by minority languages which will be discussed in more detail in Chapter 3 are the shortage of teachers who are proficient in the minority language and the development of teaching materials. When a minority language starts to be used as the language of instruction, it is possible that in some cases parents no longer speak the minority language (although grandparents and great grandparents did) and that children acquire it at school. Another fact to take into account is that for minority language speakers learning an international language is in many cases learning at least a third language (see Cenoz & Jessner, 2000). Some cases reporting the use of minority languages in combination with the respective state language and English as a third language can be found in a special issue on trilingual education in Europe in the *International Journal of the Sociology of Language* (Cenoz & Gorter, 2005). Examples of this situation are Swedish in Finland, Basque in the Basque Country, Catalan in Catalonia or Frisian in the Netherlands. Acquiring English as a second or a third language can have some differences because third language learners can develop metalinguistic awareness and language learning strategies when facing the task of learning an additional language (see Chapter 7).

Many of the minority languages in Europe do not have an official status and their use in education is limited. Minority language speakers need to acquire other languages as well and they often do so at school. As Dai and Cheng (2007) point out more and more people in minority nationality regions in China feel an urgent need for bilingualism. Lam (2007) provides some figures and states that the minorities are over 106 million people, which is 8.4% of the population and the number of languages spoken is between 80 to 120. According to Lam (2007) speakers of dialects and minority languages need to be fluent in also Putonghua (standard dialect for oral interaction) and English. Moreover, they also need to be triliterate if their minority language has a written form. Sercombe (2007) refers to the Penan community in the East Malaysian state of Sarawak where speakers learn not only a first language but a neighboring local language before going to school where they learn Malay as a third language and English as a fourth.

Bilingualism and multilingualism can open new possibilities for speakers of minority languages. The development of international communications and international mobility have increased the need that speakers of minority languages have to learn other languages. However, learning second and third languages does not mean that these have to replace the first language. It is possible to make the maintenance and the acquisition of literacy skills in minority languages compatible with the acquisition of other languages. There are many types of multilingual education regarding the role the different languages in the curriculum. In any case, the use of minority languages and languages of wider communication at school both as language of instruction and school subjects needs to be the result of careful language planning. In the following chapters we will see different possibilities in the case of Basque, Spanish and English.

A special case of minority languages is immigrant languages. Extra and Gorter (2001, 2007) point out that regional minority languages and immigrant languages have a lot in common regarding the demography and the vitality of the language. This is true but there are also some important differences between regional minority languages and immigrant languages. Gardner-Chloros (2007) highlights how in the case of regional minority languages the use of the minority language is superfluous to practical requirements because speakers can communicate in a majority language. In contrast, immigrants often have a link to their country of origin and to other immigrants and they need the language for communication. In the European context, autochthonous or regional minority languages receive more support than immigrant languages and are used to a larger extent in education. When making this comparison and the measures taken to support these languages, it is important to consider that some languages such as Breton, Welsh or Basque with fewer than 1 million speakers, are only spoken in one territory along with the majority language and they are languages at risk. In comparison, languages such as Turkish or Bengali are minority languages in some European contexts but are extremely strong languages with many millions of speakers (Gordon, 2005).

The number of migrants is increasing and according to Graddol (2006) migration represents nearly 3% of the world population. Immigration has become a very important phenomenon in Spain in the last years where 11.5% of the population are immigrants. Immigrants are also increasing rapidly in the Basque Country and have reached 5.7% of the population (Instituto Nacional de Estadística, 2007). Almost half of the immigrants who arrived in the BAC in 2006 were from Latin American countries with Spanish as an official language. These immigrants are already speakers of one of the official languages. Other immigrants including schoolchildren have to face more linguistic challenges.

The Role of Education

Education has an important role in the protection and development of minority languages but the use of these languages in education may not be enough for their survival. As Fishman (1991, 2001) points out in his model of 'Reversing Language Shift (RLS)' the nexus between family, neighborhood and community is of central importance for the continued intergenerational transmission of a language. The school is necessary but not enough for the protection and development of minority languages as we will see also in the case of the Basque Country in other chapters of this volume.

Outside the school context, schoolchildren are exposed to languages in the close social networks (parents, siblings, neighbors, friends, etc.) and through music or the media. It is very likely that in most places there will be less general exposure to a minority language than to languages of wider communication but there can also be important differences depending on the sociolinguistic context and the policy followed in different countries. There can be differences in exposure related to the media because countries have different policies regarding the use of subtitles or dubbing for television programs. Listening to programs in one of the languages studied at school could be an opportunity to develop proficiency in that language. Data from the Eurobarometer 237 (European Commission, 2005b) indicate that English is more widely known in countries where subtitles are used on television (Denmark, The Netherlands, Sweden) than in countries where dubbing is used (Germany, France, Spain). Proficiency in a language does not depend on school only and can be related to many factors such as exposure to languages in the media and in society. These factors have to be taken into account along with educational variables when looking at the outcomes of multilingual education.

Schools are part of the society in which they are located and modern society is affected by one of the most important trends regarding languages in the last years, the spread of English. Parents want schools to provide good teaching of English and English has become the most common foreign language in many parts of the world. In the European Union about 90% of secondary school students from non-English-speaking countries are learning English (Eurydice, 2008).

In the European context there have been two main recent trends in the teaching of English: the early introduction of English in primary school or even in pre-primary and the teaching of English through content (see Eurydice, 2008 for data). The early introduction of different languages is also in the action plan for the implementation of the UNESCO universal declaration on cultural diversity (UNESCO, 2002): '*Encouraging linguistic diversity – while respecting the mother tongue – at all levels of education, wherever possible, and fostering the learning of several languages from the youngest age*'.

The teaching of a foreign language from a young age is becoming more common all over the world. Graddol (2006) refers to a survey undertaken by the British Council showing that the teaching of English in primary schools was an innovation in the 1990s in many countries. Indeed, the teaching of English to young children has become very common recently in Asian countries such as China, Japan or Thailand and also in European countries.

The BAC has generalized the early introduction of English from preschool at the age of four. One of the advantages of this early introduction is to provide more time for the instruction of English and to provide a foundation so that students can use English as an additional language of instruction in later grades. As we will see in Chapter 9 of this volume, teaching English to young children has some difficulties regarding the availability of well trained teachers and the high expectation that parents have about young children learning languages very easily.

Another trend that is usually associated with the spread of English is Content and Language Integrated Learning (CLIL) which refers to '*the teaching of subjects in a different language from the mainstream language of instruction*' (Marsh 2007: 233). It is a European approach to bilingual and multilingual education and the focus is both on language and content. CLIL is an umbrella term for different approaches that vary according to the characteristics of the educational setting (see also Chapter 5). The integration of content and language has become very popular in different parts of the world (see for example Met, 1998; De Mejia, 2004; Feng, 2007).

Schooling provides a good opportunity to learn languages and, as Gibbons and Ramirez (2004: 151) point out, a substantial proportion of the language contact takes place at school in childhood and adolescence and this is critical for language development. This opportunity can be used to learn not only English but also other languages including minority languages. Education is a very effective means of developing bilingualism and multilingualism but in some cases the expectations that society has on schools are too high. According to the report by the High Level Group on Multilingualism, a necessary condition to foster multilingualism is that schools help children to develop their awareness of different languages and their motivation for language learning (European Commission, 2007). Language awareness in this context is understood as an awakening to languages and several European projects have aimed at developing abilities for language learning and positive attitudes to other languages and cultures (see for example Bernaus *et al.*, 2007; Candelier, 2007; Hélot, 2007). Outside the European context, some interesting work on language awareness and multilingualism in school contexts has been carried out by Dagenais *et al.* (2007) in Canada. These authors report the way students can carry out activities that develop their awareness of language diversity and how this development based on collaboration between learners with different backgrounds can be beneficial for all children.

Multilingual education can be an opportunity to combine the use of minority languages with the use of languages of wider communication (see also Hélot & De Mejía, 2008). In many cases minority languages are only used as languages of instruction in the first years of school and then a majority language becomes the language of instruction. As Benson (2004) points out in some cases multilingualism in education is only a wish. Benson suggests a possible trilingual schooling model for Guinea-Bissau starting with the L1 indigenous and Kiriol as languages of instruction and adding Portuguese in later grades as an additional language of instruction. This hypothetical model combines the need of minority language speakers to learn other languages with the acquisition of literacy skills in their own indigenous language. In this way, the value and status of the indigenous language increases as a result of its use as a language of instruction in the school context.

The status of the minority language in the Basque Country and its role in education and in society has changed in the last decades and nowadays Basque is the main language of instruction. In the next section we are going to summarize some of the characteristics of the languages spoken and learned in the Basque Country and describe the general sociolinguistic situation. This section will give the background information to understand the need for multilingualism in the Basque Country and the importance of language learning in its educational system.

Basque, Spanish and English in the BAC

This section provides general information about the location and size of the BAC as well as some linguistic information about the Basque language, and the role of Basque, Spanish and English in Basque society.

The Basque Country covers an area of approximately 20,742 square kilometers along the Bay of Biscay, north and south of the Pyrenees in France and Spain. The total population of the Basque Country is almost 3 million. The Basque Country comprises seven provinces, three belong to the French department 'Pyrénées Atlantiques' (Lapurdi, Nafarroa Beherea and Zuberoa), and the other four provinces to two autonomous regions in Spain (the BAC and Navarre).

In this volume we will discuss the educational system and research in education in one of the regions, the BAC, called 'Euskal Autonomia Erkidegoa' in Basque or 'Comunidad Autónoma del País Vasco' in Spanish (see Figure 1.1). Oroz and Sotés (2008) describe the educational system in

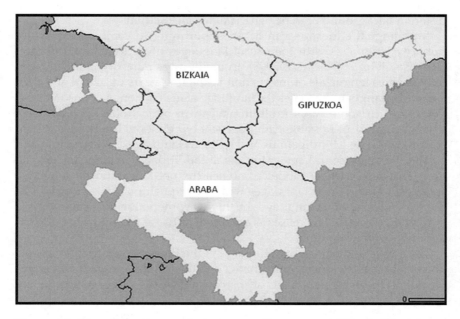

Figure 1.1 Map of the Basque Autonomous Government (Vitoria/Gasteiz: Eusko Jaurlaritza/Gobierno Vasco)

Navarre (see also Gardner, 2000, 2005) and Stuijt and Sanchez (2007) in the French provinces (Iparralde). Multilingualism is increasingly seen as the linguistic aim to be achieved in education in the BAC, combining the development of Basque, Spanish and English.

The BAC is the most populated of the Basque regions with 2,141,116 inhabitants (Instituto Nacional de Estadística, 2007), which is approximately 73% of the total population in the whole of the Basque Country. The BAC has three provinces: Bizkaia with a population of 1,141,072, Gipuzkoa with a population of 694,744 and Araba with a population of 305,300. The main cities in the BAC are the capitals of these provinces: Bilbao-Bilbo, Donostia-San Sebastian and Vitoria-Gasteiz. Bilbao-Bilbo is the biggest city with a population of 354,145 and Vitoria-Gasteiz is the administrative capital.

The official languages of the BAC are Basque and Spanish. The Basque language 'euskara' is the only non-Indo-European language in Western Europe. As it can be seen in Table 1.1, its origin continues to be unknown and it is one of the oldest European languages (see also Hualde et al., 1995).

Unlike other minority languages in Spain (Galician or Catalan), Basque is not a Romance language. This can be seen clearly in its vocabulary, morphology and syntax which are completely different from Spanish (see Laka, 1996; Cenoz, 2008a for a linguistic description). For example when we compare some family terms in Basque and other languages spoken in Spain it is clear that Basque terms are completely different from Catalan, Galician and Spanish (Table 1.2).

Table 1.1 The origin of the Basque language

Where does the Basque language come from?
Just as no one is sure about the origins of the Basques themselves, linguists are not in agreement over the origins of Euskara, the Basque language, either. Although there are theories (none of them proven beyond a doubt) that Basque is related to other languages (such as the Georgian family of languages in the Caucasus, or the Berber language family of Africa, or even the Quechua language of Latin America), so far the only thing most experts agree on is that Euskara is in a language family by itself. That is, it is not related to any other language in the world. It is, therefore, not an Indo-European language (the large group to which English, French, Spanish, and Russian belong).

Source: Center for Basque Studies, University of Nevada-Reno, FAQ http://basque.unr.edu/

Table 1.2 Some examples of family terms in Basque, Catalan, Galician and Spanish

Basque	Catalan	Galician	Spanish	English
aita	pare	pai	padre	*father*
ama	mare	nai	madre	*mother*
semea	fill	fillo	hijo	*son*
alaba	filla	filla	hija	*daughter*
anaia	germà	irmán	hermano	*brother*
arreba/ahizpa	germana	irmá	hermana	*sister*

The following examples in Basque and Spanish also show the differences at the morphological and syntactic level.

Basque: Mary-k bi alaba eta seme bat ditu (*Mary + k two daughters and one son has*)

Spanish: Mary tiene dos hijas y un hijo
Mary has two daughters and one son

Basque: Nire anaia Parisen bizi da (*My brother Paris + n lives*)

Spanish: Mi hermano vive en París
My brother lives in Paris

We can observe that Basque has a different word order as compared to Spanish and English and also that Basque has declensions ('k', 'n'). The linguistic distance between the languages involved in the educational system is a necessary factor to be taken into account when considering the different types of multilingual education as we will see in the '*Continua of Multilingual Education*' in Chapter 2.

Basque is a minority language in the BAC and in the whole of the Basque Country. According to Edwards' (2007) typology of minority languages, the situation of Basque is non-unique, adjoining and cohesive. It is 'non-unique' because it is spread over more than one state, adjoining because of the connection among speakers of Basque in two states and cohesive because there is a high degree of cohesion in the sense of holding together as a group in a given state. This type of typological classification has some problems because reality is more complex than typologies. Is it possible to consider Basque a non-unique minority because it is over two states, France and Spain? For many speakers of Basque, the seven Basque provinces are one nation even though they currently belong to two states;

so Basque would be a unique minority. For others the characterization given by Edwards would be correct.

In any case, Basque is certainly a minority language. According to the most recent sociolinguistic survey conducted by the Basque Government, (Basque Government, 2008), 30.1% of the population in the BAC is bilingual (Basque–Spanish), and 18.3% is passive bilingual. Passive bilinguals can understand Basque but have limited production skills. Monolinguals in Spanish are 51.5% of the population. That means that practically all inhabitants of the BAC are fluent in Spanish with the exception of very young children who have Basque as their first language and learn Spanish in primary school.

The Basque language was widely spoken in most parts of the Basque Country and even in neighboring areas in the Middle Ages, but since then the territory where Basque is spoken has shrunk as the results of contact with Romance languages for many centuries (see Zuazo, 1995). Basque was not used officially or in writing and only isolated sentences and names can be found in documents written in Romance languages. The first whole book in Basque was a collection of poems by the French Basque Bernard Etxepare published in 1545. The intensive contact of Basque with other languages has influenced the phonology and lexis of Basque as well as its use. The Basque language suffered an important retreat in the last three centuries and mainly in the 20th century. There are several factors that have made the Basque language weaker:

- Basque was banned from the public domain and using Basque at school was illegal during Franco's dictatorship (1939–1975). The 'Spanish only' policy during the dictatorship had very negative consequences for Basque.
- Industrialization and the arrival of Spanish-speaking immigrants in the 50s, 60s and 70s. These immigrants, who are about one third of the current population of the BAC, remained in most cases monolingual in Spanish as they did not have problems to communicate with Basque–Spanish bilingual speakers (Azurmendi & Martínez de Luna, 2006a: 15).
- The development of communications and the mass media have increased mobility and have provided more access to information in different modalities but have also increased the role of 'bigger' languages.

The political and social changes that have taken place in the last decades of the 20th century in Spain have favored attempts to maintain and revive the Basque language (Azurmendi *et al.*, 2001). The Basque language is in a process of 'reversing language shift' (Fishman, 1991). Many people consider that the knowledge and use of Basque should be generalized and a collective effort has been made to promote the learning and use of the language.

As we will see in Chapter 3, the revitalization process has been very intense in the educational system and education has contributed significantly to the increase in the number of Bascophones in the last years. Since the Status of Autonomy for the Basque Country was promulgated (1979), one of the priorities of the Basque Government has been the revitalization of the Basque language. Language plans have been developed to promote the use of Basque in different sectors including education (Azurmendi *et al.*, 2001; Cenoz, 2001a; Aldekoa & Gardner, 2002). There are now 138,400 more speakers of Basque than in 1991 and this means that the proportion of people who are proficient in Basque has increased 6% in the BAC, from 24.1% in 1991 to 30.1% in 2006 (Basque Government, 2008). The main increase has taken place in the 16–24 age group, from 25% of Basque speakers in 1991 to 57.5% in 2006. The effect of Basque-medium education is clear here.

Apart from the important changes in education that we will see in the next chapters, there has been significant progress in different areas such as the media, publications or advertising. Nowadays, there is a Basque-medium television channel, several Basque radios and a Basque newspaper. The number of publications in Basque has increased in the last decades and commercials in Basque are common. Language planning has also been applied to the administration of the BAC at different levels: Basque Government, County Halls and Town Halls in different sectors and to a lesser extent to the private industry (see Azurmendi & Martínez de Luna, 2006b).

However, the presence of Basque cannot compete with that of Spanish. Basque speakers use more Basque in the private domain and also with children but they frequently use Spanish when shopping or at work (Basque Government, 1995, 1997, 2003). A study of the linguistic landscape in the city of Donostia-San Sebastian also showed that Spanish was used to a larger extent in street signs than Basque (Cenoz & Gorter, 2006).

According to the 2006 sociolinguistic survey, the most influential factors that determine the use of Basque are: (1) the number of Basque speakers in the subject's social networks and (2) the relative ease with which the subject can use Basque and Spanish (Basque Government, 2008).

In spite of the progress made in the last decades Basque continues to be threatened. Spanish remains the dominant language in most areas of the

BAC. There is no communicative need to use Basque in many situations in the BAC and its acquisition by adults calls for a great effort because Basque is very different from Spanish. Even those who have learned Basque use more Spanish than Basque.

English is becoming increasingly important for Basque citizens as a medium of intra-European and international communication. As in many other areas in Europe, English is considered a third language but in the case of the Basque Country, it is also a foreign language not used in everyday communication. The level of proficiency in English in the Basque Country is much lower than in some other areas of Europe where there is more exposure to English with native and non-native speakers and through the media. Apart from exposure there are other reasons for the low level of English. The phonological system of English is quite different from the Basque and Spanish phonological systems, mainly regarding the vowels and diphthongs and spelling also has difficulties as compared to Basque and Spanish. Many students who have learned English for several years at school lack confidence to use English in oral interaction. French used to be the main foreign language learned at school up to the eighties and many parents do not speak English. However, being proficient in English is seen as necessary by many people in the Basque Country and English has become a lot more important in the school curriculum. English is becoming increasingly seen as necessary by Basque citizens as a medium of communication for wider scientific, academic, commercial and cultural purposes. English is also needed for many jobs nowadays, mainly in the private sector and it is becoming part of the linguistic landscape (see Cenoz & Gorter, 2006). Parents have also lobbied to introduce English at an early age at school and made an effort so that their children can take additional courses in English after school hours or courses in English speaking countries in the summer.

The Basque Country has a tradition of mobility. Basques have emigrated mainly to Latin American countries but also to the USA and other parts of the world (Douglas & Bilbao, 2005). On the other hand, many Spanish workers found jobs in the Basque Country between the 50s and the 70s because of industrialization. In the last years immigrants from other countries are coming to the Basque Country. These immigrants come in many cases from Latin America but also from Africa and European countries (Etxeberria & Elosegi, 2008). As a result, the Basque Country is becoming a more multilingual and multicultural society. As in many other societies in the world, the Basque Country has experienced an important movement of population from rural to urban areas and the effect of globalization can be seen in industry, shops and other services.

Conclusion

This chapter highlights the importance of multilingualism in general and particularly in education and provides some background information about the Basque Country. As Wei *et al.* (2002) state attitudes towards bilingualism and multilingualism are more positive now because experience with two or more cultures makes bilinguals and multilinguals more competitive in international trade. As we have seen in this chapter, the need for multilingualism is obvious and as Baker (2000: 12) lists there are communication, cultural, cognitive, character, curriculum, cash and career advantages associated with bilingualism. The need for bilingualism and multilingualism has been there for speakers of minority languages in the past as well but as Jaffe (2007: 51) points out there is now *'a shift away from bilingualism-as-cultural-deficit towards bilingualism-as-added-value in discourses about what it means to be bilingual in a minority language context'*. This need is also felt in the Basque Country where the effort to maintain and promote the use of its minority language, Basque, is taking place along with the need to learn languages of wider communication (Spanish, French and English) and to integrate speakers of other languages who have recently arrived looking for better economic conditions. The educational system can make an important contribution to the developing of bilingualism and multilingualism as we will see in the rest of the chapters in this book. The possibility of having areas where minority languages are spoken as a referent for the development of multilingualism has been highlighted by European Commission High Level Group on Multilingualism:

> Bilingual communities comprised of speakers of regional or minority languages and of majority languages are good practice laboratories relevant to the EU's aim of promoting multilingualism across the Union. In this context, reference was made to the know-how acquired in bilingual schools in the Basque Country, Galicia, Catalonia and the Valencian Country, where sophisticated methods of language immersion and special teacher training programs had been in place for decades. It was felt, that these methods should be disseminated throughout the Union, as should the promotion of passive bilingualism, the management of linguistic conflicts, and the management of multilingualism in companies and public administration practiced in those territories. The Group came to the conclusion that further research should be conducted into educational and management practices in bilingual communities with a view to assessing their potential for application in other situations. (European Commission, 2007: 18–19)

Key Points

- Multilingualism is a very common phenomenon at the individual and social levels.
- The spread of English as a language of wider communication is such that English is one of the languages in school curricula in most multilingual educational programs in different parts of the world.
- Minority languages such as Basque can provide a sense of identity and are useful in everyday communication.
- Basque is a language of unknown origin unrelated to Spanish.
- Basque speakers in the BAC are 30% of the population and they are bilingual in Basque and Spanish.

Note

1. The European Commission is the executive branch of the European Union (27 member states). The Council of Europe is an organization that aims to develop throughout Europe common and democratic principles and has 47 member states.

Chapter 2
Towards a Typology of Multilingual Education

Introduction

In this chapter we look at different dimensions of multilingual education: linguistic, educational and sociolinguistic. These dimensions which have been identified in different typologies of bilingual education are also going to be crucial to define multilingual education. In this chapter we provide the definition of what we understand by multilingual education as involving at least three languages. Multilingual education is more diverse than bilingual education and the different types of multilingual education can best be described by using a model based on continua. In this chapter '*The Continua of Multilingual Education*' is presented as a tool to identify different types of multilingual schools and programs. The last section of the chapter focuses on different types of education in the Basque Autonomous Community (BAC) and the way '*The Continua of Multilingual Education*' can be applied to this specific context.

Linguistic, Sociolinguistic and Educational Variables

Language acquisition, bilingualism and multilingualism are very complex phenomena related to many variables. In this volume we are focusing on bilingualism and multilingualism in the educational context where languages are learned, maintained and reinforced through education. As Baker (2007a) says, the educational context can provide ample opportunities for the development of bilingualism and biliteracy because children spend a large number of hours at school. Many schools all over the world include more than one language in the curriculum either as school subjects or as languages of instruction.

As it has already been said in Chapter 1, schools are part of society and the relation between schools and the society in which they are located is bidirectional. The beliefs, attitudes and discourses of society are reflected in educational planning and specifically in language planning at school. At the same time, schools have an influence on society and in the case of bilingual and multilingual education the development of multilingualism and multiliteracy can result in increased proficiency in several languages in society. At the same time multilingualism and multiliteracy can also influence the development of individual and social attitudes and identities as we will see in Chapter 8.

Multilingual education can be affected by a large number of individual and contextual variables. Among the individual variables that can affect language acquisition and language use we could include aptitude, attitudinal variables and motivation, gender, anxiety or socioeconomic status (see Robinson, 2002; Dörnyei, 2006, for a review).

When learning two or more languages at school the linguistic characteristics of the languages can also be influential. For example, the typological distance between the languages already known by the speaker (the first language/s or others) and the target language may influence the acquisition process. When languages are closely related to each other they may share aspects of their syntactic structure, phonological system or lexis and this may facilitate the acquisition process. For example, a Spanish speaker may find learning Catalan a lot easier than learning Japanese. Linguistic distance is the basic idea in receptive multilingualism, when interlocutors of related languages use their own first languages in interaction but try to understand the language spoken by their interlocutor (see Ten Thije & Zeevaert, 2007).

The relationship between languages does not have to be always genetic or typological. Some languages that are not typologically related such as Basque and Spanish may have more in common than what is usually thought as the result of centuries of contact. When a Spanish speaker learns Basque, the grammar and vocabulary are completely different but the similarities are very noticeable at the phonological and pragmatic level. Moreover, in spite of the important differences at the lexical level, a Spanish learner of Basque can benefit from the large number of borrowings from Spanish into Basque and from the knowledge of Basque words that are used in everyday conversation in people's names, products or shops.

Examples:

1.   *Zapata berriak erosi ditut* (I have bought new shoes)
2.   *Etxe berria* (new house)

In the first example a borrowing from the Spanish word '*zapatos*' is used instead of the Basque word '*oinetakoak*'. The word '*zapata*' can be easier to remember for a learner with Spanish as a first language. The second example can be easy to remember for learners of Basque living in the Basque Country because '*Etxeberria*' is one of the most common last names.

Apart from linguistic distance, the sociolinguistic environment in which a bilingual and multilingual school is placed is very important. We can look at two different levels, the macro level and the micro level. At the macro level, we can consider the relative vitality of the languages used at school and/or spoken by the students in society at large. One way to look at the different elements associated with vitality is to consider the variables included in Giles, Bourhis and Taylor's (1977) model of ethnolinguistic vitality, which were related to demography, status and institutional support. For example, when French is taught in a Canadian immersion school in an English-speaking city such as Toronto, its vitality is not as high as if the school is located in Montreal where French is the majority language. In the European context, there are important differences between learning German as a second or third language in the European school in Frankfurt (Germany) or in the European school in Alicante (Spain). Learners of German in Alicante will not have many opportunities to use German outside schools or in their close social networks.

At the micro level it is important to take into account the social networks students have. Social networks have been defined as '*the sum of all the interpersonal relations one individual establishes with others over time*' (Hamers & Blanc, 2000: 111). The use of different languages in the family or with friends and neighbors can have an important influence on the development and use of the languages at school. For example, a language that is used to a very limited extent at the macro level can be one of the school languages and can also be used at home. This can be the case of children who have Italian as a first language in the Foyer project (Byram & Leman, 1990). These children use Italian at home and with friends but also at school where they also learn French and Dutch.

In most cases there is a relationship between the macro and the micro contexts and it is more likely that a language is strong in the close social networks if it is also spoken by more people and has a high status and institutional support. For example, when we look at Basque we can see clearly that the macro and micro levels are related to each other. Even though Basque is a co-official language in the whole of the BAC there are important differences regarding its vitality, mainly concerning the demographic variables. In some areas in the South, such as the Rioja area of Araba, most speakers are Spanish-speaking while in many towns and villages in Gipuzkoa most speakers are Basque-speaking. A school can have the same number of hours and identical distribution for different languages but children in Basque speaking areas are more likely to use Basque in everyday life at home and with their friends while children in the Rioja area of Araba are more likely to use Spanish. Of course, other possibilities also exist and a Basque-speaking family may live in a Spanish-speaking area and the other way round. Demography is a very important dimension in the case of Basque because of its weakness but many other minorities have more problems with status and institutional support than with the number of speakers.

Educational variables in multilingual education comprise those related to education in general and those which are specifically linked to the teaching and learning of languages. The specific variables related to languages include the use of the different languages as subjects and languages of instruction, the introduction of languages at different ages, teachers' degree of multilingualism and specific training or use of languages in the school environment.

Strong and Weak Types of Bilingual Education

When trying to identify the different types of multilingual education we can look at typologies of bilingual education as a reference point. Typologies of bilingual education have a long tradition and there are a large number of them. One of the best known is the typology proposed by Mackey (1970). This typology goes into exhaustive detail by considering different possibilities regarding the child's behavior at home, the school's curriculum, the immediate community and the language status. The number of possibilities is at least 250 different types of bilingual education. The strong point of this typology is that it is comprehensive but its weakness is that it is unpractical because of the large number of possibilities.

The problem of typologies is that they have to be comprehensive and at the same time as simple as possible. This is not an easy task taking into account that bilingual education is very diverse and the socio-linguistic context where each bilingual school is located also has specific characteristics.

When referring to a classification of language situations involving minority languages, Edwards (2007) considers that typologies can impose theoretical order and facilitate cross-community comparison but he is aware of their problems: '*Some have criticised typological exercises on the grounds that they embody prevailing assumptions, have limited analytical utility and imply permanence or stasis*' (Edwards, 2007: 459). Edwards adds that in spite of these limitations, typologies can be useful for cross-context comparisons. Baker (2006: 215), who has developed one of the most widely used typologies of bilingual education, is aware of the limitations of typologies because they are reductionist as compared to the complexity of bilingual schools. He also adds that typologies suggest static systems, there are variations within a model and they do not address classroom processes or effectiveness of different models. One of the most important limitations according to Baker (2006: 214) is that many real-life examples of bilingual education do not fit into the typologies. This problem is also highlighted by Martin Jones (2007) who adds that models of bilingual education cannot be readily transplantable from one sociolinguistic context to another.

A starting point to develop, choose or assess a typology is to analyze the definition of bilingual or multilingual education that has been used (see also Baker, 2006, Chapter 10). An important consideration when defining bilingual or multilingual education is whether the school aims at bilingualism or multilingualism or whether the school is called bilingual or multilingual because students speak different home languages (see also Baker, 2007a). European schools have been considered a good example of multilingual education mainly because of the linguistic aims of the schools, the use of the different languages and the processes followed in these schools to promote multilingualism (Baetens Beardsmore, 1993a). On the other hand, sometimes multilingualism in education refers to the linguistic diversity of the students. For example, Aarts, Extra and Yağmur (2004) found that 88 languages other than Dutch were home languages for students in the Dutch city of The Hague but the schools were predominantly monolingual.

The differences related to the linguistic background of the students and the aims of the school are essential in many typologies as it can be seen in the distinction between transitional, maintenance and enrichment programs (see for example De Mejia, 2002; Baker, 2006). Transitional programs aim at language shift from the child's first language to the majority language and imply cultural assimilation. Maintenance programs are typically aimed at speakers of a language minority who acquire the majority language where this second language does not replace their first language. Enrichment programs aim at developing and extending linguistic diversity. The boundaries between maintenance and enrichment programs are not always clear (see also Hornberger, 1991).

Another well known distinction is that between subtractive and additive bilingualism (Lambert, 1974). Additive bilingualism takes place in situations where the second language does not replace the first language and would include both maintenance and enrichment programs. An example of additive bilingualism is immersion programs in Canada, where English-speaking children learn French and have French as one of the languages of instruction and at no cost of their proficiency in English

(Genesee, 1987, 2004). In cases of subtractive bilingualism, the first language is seen as an obstacle for academic development and it is replaced by a second language. This is the case of many immigrant students in Europe and North America (Cummins, 2000).

García (2008a) adds two new models of bilingualism to the additive-subtractive types: recursive and dynamic bilingualism. Recursive bilingualism develops in cases in which the language practices of a community have been suppressed and is reconstituted for new functions. Dynamic bilingualism highlights multiple language practices and multimodality.

Another distinction which overlaps but not completely with additive and subtractive bilingualism is that between elite and folk bilingualism (De Mejía, 2002). Elite or prestigious bilingualism is seen as voluntary or optional and it refers to '*bilinguals who own two high status languages*' (Baker & Prys Jones, 1998: 15). Folk bilingualism is not voluntary because becoming bilingual is a necessity for speakers of autochthonous and immigrant minority languages.

When approaching a complex reality as that of bilingual and multilingual education many other distinctions are possible because the focus can be on different aspects. For example, the distinction between transition, maintenance and enrichment types of bilingual education is mainly on the linguistic aims of the school while the difference between additive and subtractive bilingualism focuses more on the outcomes of education by looking at the consequences of becoming bilingual for the individual. The difference between elite and folk bilingualism looks more at the socioeconomic and linguistic background of the child and his/her family. Other approaches look at the acquisition of literacy skills in the different languages (e.g. Fishman & Lovas, 1972; Hornberger, 1989, 1991, 2003, 2007). Hornberger's 'Continua of Biliteracy' is a framework '*to situate research, teaching, and language planning in multilingual settings*' (Hornberger, 2002: 36). Hornberger provides three continua for each of the four dimensions of biliteracy: contexts, development, content and media. As explained by Hornberger & Skilton-Sylvester (2000) the model can account for real-life situations from different perspectives and for multiple voices instead of adopting a traditional Western perspective.

Focusing on bilingual education, Baker (2006: 215–216) proposes one of the most well-known typologies of bilingual education. This typology distinguishes strong and weak forms of bilingual education according to the language background of the child, the language of the classroom, and the linguistic, societal and educational aims. This typology has some limitations but it is a useful tool to classify a large number of bilingual schools all over the world.

Types of Multilingual Education

In spite of the large number of typologies of bilingual education there are very few attempts to create typologies of multilingual education. Baetens Beardsmore (1993b) looks at different characteristics that can be used to compare different types of programs but he does not focus on the distinction between programs involving the use of two or more languages (see Table 2.1).

As we can see, Baetens Beardsmore considers nine different variables to classify five models of multilingual education. Some variables are educational such as the final exam, the use of the target language as a subject, or the presence of native-speaker teachers while others are sociolinguistic such as the use of the target language in the environment or by peers. This characterization is useful because it compares different types of education but it has the limitations associated with taxonomies in general as it cannot include the complexity of bilingual and multilingual education. For example, in the case of Basque, Baetens Beardsmore considers programs with Basque as a language of instruction with the features given in Table 2.2.

As we will see in this volume, these programs can certainly be considered additive (feature 1) and the languages involved are the home language and other language in most cases. Everybody has access to them (feature 4) and the target language is used as a subject (feature 8). However, there are more complex issues regarding the other features. The outcome of full bilingualism and full biliteracy depends to a large extent on the

Table 2.1 Comparison of some models of multilingual education

Features	*Models*
1. Nature of program	Canadian immersion
2. Languages	Luxembourg
3. Outcome	European schools
4. Population	Foyer project
5. Target language in environment	Catalan/Basque bilingual education
6. Target language used by peers	
7. Final exams in more than one language	
8. Target language as a subject	
9. Native-speaker teachers	

Source: Based on Baetens Beardsmore, 1993b: 205

Table 2.2 Features of Basque-medium programs

1. Nature of program: additive
2. Languages: Home L/Other L
3. Outcome: Full bilingualism + full biliteracy
4. Population: Everyone
5. Target language in environment: Yes
6. Target language used by peers: Yes
7. Final exams in more than one language: ?
8. Target language as a subject: Yes
9. Native-speaker teachers: Most

Source: Based on Baetens Beardsmore, 1993b: 205

environment but also on the type of program. The use of the target language in the environment or by peers depends to a large extent on the area of the Basque Country and the specific social networks of the students. Final examinations in one or the other languages will depend on the language of instruction. Many teachers are not native speakers of the target language and have learned Basque as adults; this feature depends also on the type of school and area of the Basque Country. There is also important variation related to the home language. Some students have Basque as a home language, others Spanish and others both languages as home languages.

Ytsma (2001) proposed a typology of trilingual education consisting of 46 types of trilingual education in primary school based on the linguistic context in which trilingual education takes place, the linguistic distance between the three languages involved and the organizational design of the teaching of the languages at school. The three criteria used correspond to three different types of variables. The linguistic context refers to the sociolinguistic environment, the linguistic distance to the characteristics of the languages involved and the difference between simultaneous or consecutive to the program design, that is, one of the educational variables.

This typology is useful to make some comparisons among different types of multilingual education but has some limitations because it only looks at three aspects of multilingual education. According to this typology, Basque primary education has the characteristics given in Table 2.3.

The features of Basque in this typology are somehow problematic because even though it only looks at three aspects of multilingual education, these aspects are also complex. It is true that in general terms it can

Table 2.3 Features of Basque primary schools (models B and D)

1. Linguistic context: bilingual area
2. Linguistic distance: three non related languages
3. Program design: simultaneous trilingual program

Source: Based on Ytsma, 2001

be said that Basque primary schools are in a bilingual area but it is also true that some Basque schools are in a bilingual area and others in a mainly monolingual area. There are important degrees that go from monolingualism to bilingualism and these differences have implications for multilingual education. Basque, Spanish and English can be regarded as non-related languages because Basque is a non-Indo-European language, Spanish is a Romance Indo-European language and English is a Germanic Indo-European language but genetically English and Spanish are closer to each other than Basque and English or Basque and Spanish. Apart from the origin, the history of the languages is also relevant here. The influence of Latin and French on English as the result of Romanization and the Norman Conquest can be traced in English vocabulary. The contact between Basque and Spanish along the centuries and the dominance of Spanish has also affected the Basque language, mainly at the lexical, pragmatic and phonological levels as we have already seen. The level 'non-related' establishes a boundary that is too hard for languages in contact.

To consider Basque primary education as a case of simultaneous exposure to three languages is not completely accurate in most cases. Some children have their first contact with a second language when they go to day care (zero to two) and others later when they go to pre-primary school (nowadays from the age of two). In most cases children have their first classes of English from the age of four. Over 90% of the children go to day care or pre-primary from the age of two and that means that even if there is a change between the home language and the school languages (usually from Spanish to Basque), classes in English start two years after exposure to the second language. In the case of Basque speakers, English is chronologically the second language at school and it is introduced at the age of four and Spanish some years later in primary school. In sum, Ytsma's (2001) proposal is an interesting tool for cross-context comparison but when applying it to a specific case of trilingual primary schools we can see that reality is a lot more complex than the possibilities accounted for.

In spite of their limitations typologies are interesting because they provide a tool to look at different aspects of bilingual and multilingual education and to compare different situations.

The '*Continua of Multilingual Education*'

Before discussing other possibilities and different tools to analyze multilingual education, it is important to define multilingual education. This is not an easy task. A recent definition of bi/multilingual education is provided by Skutnabb-Kangas and McCarty (2007: 4) who consider it as the '*use of two or more languages as media of instruction*'. This definition is based on the use of the languages as languages of instruction and not just as subjects. A similar definition is given by Cummins (2007: xiii) '*The term bilingual education refers to the use of two (or more) languages of instruction at some point in a student's school career. The languages are used to teach subject matter content rather than just the language itself*'. Baker (2007a: 131) also considers that bilingual education is '*ideally reserved for those schools and classrooms that teach some, most or all subject content through two languages*'. Also May (2007: 20) considers that the key to define a bilingual program is that both languages are used as media of instruction.

These definitions are mainly referring to bilingual rather than multilingual education and they try to exclude schools that have bilingual children but do not aim at bilingualism and biliteracy. For example, many schools have children who speak one language at home which is different from the school language. Children in this situation can be regarded to a certain extent as bilingual although in many cases they do not have the opportunity to develop literacy skills in their home language. However, the type of education they receive at school is not bilingual. This was the situation of native speakers of Basque in the Basque Country for many years when the only language of instruction at school was Spanish and Basque was not even studied as a school subject. When more than two languages are involved, it is more difficult to use all the languages as languages of instruction even if the school aims at developing multilingualism and multiliteracy. Examples of trilingual and multilingual education such as the European schools or the Foyer project do not use three languages as languages of instruction and use some of them just as a subject (Byram & Leman, 1990). Many other examples of trilingual primary education given by Ytsma (2001) do not include the use of three languages as languages of instruction either. This is the case of the Basque educational system which aims at multilingualism and multiliteracy but the models that are generally considered bilingual (and in some cases multilingual) have either Basque and Spanish or Basque as the languages of instruction and in some cases English as an additional language of instruction. The weak position of Basque in society, the study of Spanish as a subject, and the aim of acquiring full proficiency in both languages are strong reasons to consider that even when Basque is the only language of instruction Basque-medium education can be regarded as bilingual education. When English is added as an additional language of instruction we can refer to multilingual education.

Table 2.4 is an example of the distribution of teaching hours in a European school and a Basque school where Basque is the medium of instruction at the age of 12. In both cases languages have an important weight in the curriculum: 32.6% in the European Schools and between 36.6% and 43.3% in the Basque school where the L4 is an optional subject. In both cases there is a main language of instruction at this level (the L1 in the case of the European school and the L1 or L2 in the Basque school). Another language can become the language of instruction in later grades. Both schools aim at multilingualism but do not use all the languages as languages of instruction (Table 2.4).

These timetables show that a Basque-medium instruction is even more multilingual than a European school regarding the number of hours devoted to teaching different languages and through different languages.

The definition of multilingual education that we adopt here focuses on the aims of this type of education and is the following:

Multilingual education implies teaching more than two languages provided that schools aim at multilingualism and multiliteracy.

Table 2.4 Hours devoted to languages and other school subjects in secondary school (age 12) in a European school and a Basque-medium school

	European school	*Basque school*	
		Basque L1	*Spanish L1*
L1	3.45	4	3
L2	3	3	4
L3	1.15	4	4
L4 (optional)		2	2
Other subjects	16.30 (through L1)	17 (through L1)	17 (through L2)
Total	24.30	30	30

Source: Based on distribution of hours in 2nd class of the secondary section, European schools brochure (http://www.eursc.eu/index.php?id=134) and timetable of 1st year of secondary in Santo Tomas Lizeoa (http://www.santotomaslizeoa.net).

In many cases some or all the languages will be used as languages of instruction. In other cases, it may not be necessary to use all the languages as languages of instruction because there is enough exposure to them outside the school and they are taught as school subjects. At the curriculum level it means that at least three languages have to be taught in the school curriculum but it does not mean that the three languages are necessarily languages of instruction. There are many more schools that aim at multilingualism and multiliteracy and call themselves 'trilingual' than schools that use three or more languages as languages of instruction. In fact, it is difficult to establish hard boundaries between bilingual schools where a third or fourth language is taught and schools that call themselves trilingual or multilingual. Strictly speaking bilingual schools can also be considered a type of multilingual school because the term 'multilingual' refers to multiple languages and this can be understood as two or more languages. In this volume we adopt a definition of multilingual education so as to focus on schools and programs that aim at achieving communicative competence and literacy skills in more than two languages.

As we have already seen, one of the main problems of typologies of bilingual education is that they cannot fit all the specific cases. This problem becomes more acute in the case of multilingual education because of the diversity of languages involved, program designs and sociolinguistic variables.

Taking into account that it is difficult to establish dichotomic or trichotomic differences when analyzing the features of multilingual education, it can be more appropriate to look at these features as continua. As it has already been mentioned, Hornberger (2003, 2007) has applied the idea of continua to biliteracy by characterizing contexts for biliteracy (micro-macro; oral-literate; bi(multi)lingual-monolingual), the development of individual biliteracy (reception-production; oral-written; L1-L2), the content of biliteracy (minority-majority; vernacular-literary; contextualized-decontextualized) and the media of biliteracy (simultaneous-successive exposure; dissimilar-similar structures; divergent-convergent scripts). Hornberger represents the continua as nested and intersecting. In the case of multilingual education we adopt her idea that continua represented as two-way arrows '*represent the infinity and fluidity of movement along each of the continua*' (Hornberger, 2007: 277). We also think that continua are more appropriate to represent the different variables than polar opposites also in the case of characterizing different types of multilingual education and Hornberger's idea of continua has been adopted in the '*Continua of Multilingual Education*'.

Instead of a typology based on polar opposites, the features of multilingual education can be represented in a model based on continua (see Figure 2.1). This model includes specific educational variables inside a triangle and also linguistic variables and sociolinguistic variables both at the macro and micro levels. May (2007: 25) also uses a triangle to refer to different types of bilingual programs but his purpose is to highlight the difference between additive and subtractive programs. In the '*Continua of Multilingual Education*' the idea is to provide a tool that can describe as many situations of multilingual education as possible (Figure 2.1). The result of using the different continua for this description will provide types of education that can be considered more additive or more subtractive.

The educational variables are four continua: subject, language of instruction, teacher and school context. Each of these variables can be represented as a continuum that goes from '*less multilingual*' to '*more multilingual*' (Table 2.5).

'*Subject*' refers to the use of different languages as schools subjects in the curriculum and each school can be on a specific point on the continuum depending on three features: (1) the use of more languages as school subjects (language arts); (2) the integration of the different language subjects in syllabus design and lesson planning and (3) the intensity of instruction and age of introduction. The importance of teaching languages as subjects has been highlighted by Baetens Beardsmore (1993b). He points out the more frequent use of target languages as school subjects in the European schools and Luxembourg as compared to Canadian immersion where French is used mainly as a language of instruction (see also Baetens Beardsmore & Swain, 1985). The importance of designing a syllabus that integrates the different languages when they are used either as subjects or languages of instruction is highlighted by Elorza & Muñoa (2008). A school where several languages are taught as subjects in an

Table 2.5 Educational variables

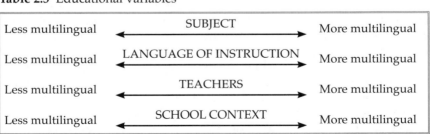

Less multilingual	SUBJECT →	More multilingual
Less multilingual	LANGUAGE OF INSTRUCTION →	More multilingual
Less multilingual	TEACHERS →	More multilingual
Less multilingual	SCHOOL CONTEXT →	More multilingual

Source: Based on Baetens Beardsmore, 1993b: 205

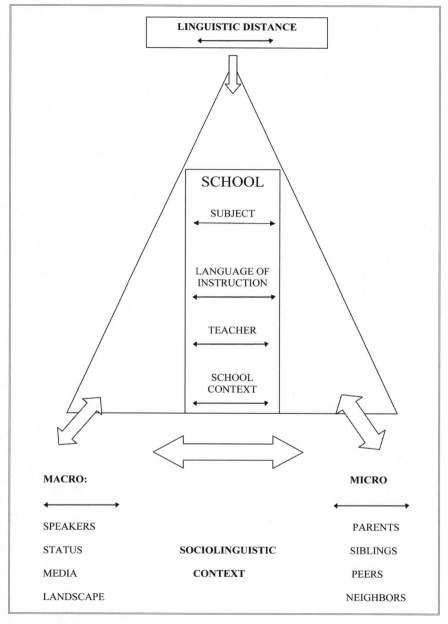

Figure 2.1 Continua of multilingual education

integrated curriculum can be considered more multilingual in the '*Continua of Multilingual Education*'.

'*Language of instruction*' refers to two features: (1) the use of different languages as languages of instruction (one, two, three languages as languages of instruction) and (2) their integration in syllabus design and language planning (coordination between teachers and syllabuses of different languages). A school with several languages of instruction will be more towards the 'more multilingual' end of the continuum particularly if the school uses integrated syllabuses.

'*Teachers*' refers to two features related to teacher education: (1) language proficiency in different languages and (2) specific training for multilingual education. If most teachers in a school are multilingual and they have also been trained for multilingual education including teaching content through a second or additional language then the school or the model of multilingual education will be 'more multilingual'.

'*School context*' refers to the use of languages inside the school for communication between teachers, supporting staff, students and parents including informal conversations, meetings and written information. The linguistic landscape inside the classrooms and in the school in general also belongs to the school context. If more than two languages are used for these functions the school or program of education would be more towards the more multilingual end of the continuum.

The linguistic variable considered in this model is linguistic distance and it refers to degree of variation between the languages involved in multilingual education. Linguistic distance not only refers to the origin of the languages (Germanic, Romance, etc) but also to the distance between the languages as related to their historical contact. The languages involved in multilingual education may be relatively more or less distant (see Table 2.6).

Learning a language that belongs to the same family and has been in contact with the first language is generally easier than learning a completely different language (see for example Bild & Swain, 1989). For example, when children who have Luxembourgish as a first language learn German they can find it easier than when Basque L1 children learn English. Luxembourgish

Table 2.6 Linguistic distance

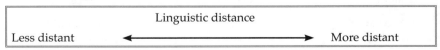

is a Germanic language closely related to Low German and the two languages have been historically in contact. Basque and English are not genetically related and with the few exceptions such as that of Basque immigrants in the USA (Douglas & Bilbao, 2005), they have not been in contact. When comparing multilingual education in Luxembourg (Luxemburgish, German, French) and the Basque Country (Basque, Spanish, English) on the linguistic distance dimension, Basque schools could be placed towards the 'more distant' end of the continuum as compared to schools in Luxembourg. Other schools also use languages that belong to different families and could be placed at the 'more distant' end of the continuum such as schools with the combination Arabic, Hebrew and English in some Israeli schools or Sinhalese, Tamil and English in Sri Lanka.

Linguistic distance has an influence on multilingual education because it can influence the design of the different programs and the need to devote more or fewer hours to the different languages either as subjects or languages of instruction. It can also have some influence on the degree of multilingualism of the teachers. The distance between languages and varieties can best be placed on a continuum because there are no absolute categories and the distance can also be relative when comparing different combinations of languages. Contact between languages also has to be considered when looking at linguistic distance because languages can have a different origin and still be influenced in the most permeable levels such as the lexicon and the phonological levels. Linguistic distance can affect different aspects of multilingual education but multilingual education cannot have a direct effect on linguistic distance.

Schools are part of society and the sociolinguistic features are also part of this model. The model makes a distinction between the macro and the micro levels (see Table 2.7).

The macro level refers to the general vitality of the languages involved in multilingual education and it looks at variables such as the number of speakers of the different languages, their status nationally and internationally, their use in the media or in the linguistic landscape. The more the different languages are used in these contexts the 'more multilingual' the

Table 2.7 Sociolinguistic variables

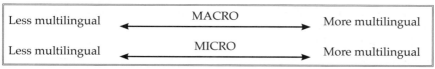

| Less multilingual | MACRO | More multilingual |
| Less multilingual | MICRO | More multilingual |

macro level will be. Nowadays it is difficult to think of countries and cities which are completely monolingual and to classify them according to close categories such as 'multilingual' or 'monolingual'. However, it is possible to place at different points on the continuum a more multilingual country such as South Africa with 11 official languages and a less multilingual country such as Iceland.

The micro level focuses on the student and refers to his/her close social networks including the languages used at home with the parents, siblings or the extended family, the languages used among peers or in the community. The more languages used in these contexts the 'more multilingual' the sociolinguistic context at the micro level will be. A school with students who are towards the more multilingual end of the continuum at the micro level can be multilingual regarding the characteristics of the students but not necessarily according to our definition if the school does not aim at multilingualism.

The difference between the macro and the micro levels is considered important when analyzing multilingual education because there are many cases in which they do not coincide. For example, in the case of international schools and European schools the home language can be different from the school languages. This is also the case with many immigrant students. In many cases, the macro and the micro levels are closely related and they do have an influence on each other. There is also interaction between both levels and the school variables. If a language has a high level of vitality in the sociolinguistic context it may be possible to develop it without devoting so many hours of the school curriculum as it is the case with Spanish in the Basque Country. The home language of the students will be a very important factor to be taken into consideration in multilingual education.

The '*Continua of Multilingual Education*' highlights the interaction of linguistic, sociolinguistic and educational variables because multilingual education is the result of the interaction of the school with the sociolinguistic context in which it is located. As many typologies of bilingual education, the '*Continua of Multilingual Education*' considers the complexity of education by including different types of variables but by using continua it also highlights the dynamics of education at the same time. The possibility of selecting different points on the different continua allows for the complexity of multilingual education and makes it possible to accommodate different specific situations.

The '*Continua of Multilingual Education*' can be used as a tool to describe different types of multilingual education and make international comparisons and it can be used by schools to analyze their own situation as compared to other schools in the same country. In the last section of this chapter we will see how the '*Continua of Multilingal Education*' can be applied to the models of bilingual and multilingual education in the BAC. The use of these continua not only allows for different types of multilingual education to be included but also gives a dynamic character to different situations allowing for changes along the different continua. The interaction between the different types of variables (linguistic, educational and sociolinguistic) allows for many types of multilingual education.

Applying the '*Continua of Multilingual Education*' to Different Contexts

The '*Continua of Multilingual Education*' can accommodate some of the most typical cases of multilingual education that cannot easily find a place in other taxonomies. In this section we look at different examples of multilingual schools around the world so as to see the complexity of the different models and the possibility of using the '*Continua of Multilingual Education*' as a tool to see the different degrees of multilingualism. We are going to distinguish between multilingual schools aimed at the whole population and those aimed at specific groups (see also Hélot & De Mejía, 2008). In general terms, schools aimed at the whole population of a specific area, region or country are either the only type of school for the whole population or an option for all those parents who would like their children attend this type of school. These schools typically include indigenous and minority languages, national and international languages in the curriculum. Multilingual schools aimed at specific groups are in some cases restricted to the children of employees of some institutions and companies and others are only affordable by some sectors of society. These schools typically include languages of wider communication such as English, French and German.

Multilingual schools aimed at the whole population

The important trend to use minority and indigenous languages as the languages of instruction in many parts of the world on the one hand and the need to acquire fluency in languages of wider communication and particularly in English has reinforced the trend towards multilingual education in many parts of the world.

Mohanty (2007) discusses the situation of multilingual education in India. The three language formula established in 1957 has had modifications and there have been different interpretations and applications. The three language formula generally has three languages as school subjects:

(1) the mother tongue or regional language taught for five years; (2) Hindi in non-Hindi areas and another Indian language in Hindi areas for three years; (3) English from the year three onwards. The three language formula was changed in 1964 and Hindi is no longer compulsory. As Khubchandani (2007) says, the three language formula has been interpreted in different ways by different states. Mohanty (2007) explains that there is a variety of programs including transitional programs for language minorities but that it is not very common to have three languages as languages of instruction. The *'Continua of Multilingual Education'* can accommodate these different types of programs because it does not establish hard boundaries between bilingual and multilingual education. For example, the programs (see Table 2.8) with multiple languages as medium of instruction are more towards the multilingual end of the continuum on the educational variables than the multilingual education programs with a single medium of instruction.

The *'Continua of Multilingual Education'* could also be applied to other contexts in different parts of the world. Bahry, Niyozov and Shamatov (2007) give an example of a trilingual school in Tajikistan where English, Tajik and Russian are taught. These authors also mention the bilingual Turkish programs in Turkmenistan and Kyrgyzstan. In these programs, English, Turkish and Turkmen or Kyrgyz are used as languages of instruction. Another country where the *'Continua of Multilingual Education'* can be applied is China. Apart from the development of Chinese-English bilingual education, Dai and Cheng (2007) refer to programs aiming at trilingualism and triliteracy in primary schools in the Qinghai Henan Mongolia Autonomous County in China. The languages are Tibetan, Mongolian and Mandarin Chinese. Other programs aim mainly at bilingualism and biliteracy but most of these are including English as a foreign language. Cobbey (2007) also refers to schools using Dong, Mandarin Chinese and

Table 2.8 Multilingual education programs in India

Population	States with a high percentage of tribal language children (Andhra Pradesh, Orissa, Chhattisgarh, Jharkhand)
Aim	High levels of multilingual and multiliteracy skills
Languages	Mother tongue, regional majority language, English
Curriculum	Consecutive introduction of L1, L2 and L3. Consecutive acquisition of literacy skills.

Source: Based on Mohanty, 2007: 173

intensive English in the province of Guizhou. Jiang *et al.* (2007) refer to multilingual education for ethnic minorities in the Gansu Province in Northwest China where there are 54 ethnic nationalities. In this context, English is learned as a third language.

An interesting project is also the *School of Tomorrow* in Paraguay (http://www.schooloftomorrow.org.py/). This network of 14 schools (mainly public) has included English as the language of instruction along with Spanish but in some schools Guaraní is also used. In these cases the linguistic aim is to acquire competence in three languages (Mercosur Educacional, 2007). Guaraní is a language spoken in Paraguay by almost 90% of the population where it is the home language for 59.6% of the population (Melià, 2004). Guaraní is in contact with Spanish which is the most prestigious language but other indigenous languages are also spoken in Paraguay. The spread of English in Latin America reinforces the trend towards multilingual education in the cases in which schools aim at developing literacy skills in indigenous languages and Spanish (see for example Hornberger & López, 1998). For example, as the result of the 1994 Education Reform indigenous languages such as Quechua, Aymara and Guaraní are more commonly used in education in Bolivia. The proposal for the new law of education in Bolivia, Ley Avelino Siñani and Elizardo Pérez Law (http://www.constituyentesoberana.org/info/?q=nueva-ley-educacion-avelino-perez) goes beyond bilingualism and aims at promoting communicative ability in the first language, Spanish and English. There is also a strong emphasis on intercultural and intracultural education. Other countries with multilingual education aimed at the whole population are Eritrea and Morocco (see Dutcher, 1998; Ennaji, 2005). All these situations with different types of curricula and in different sociolinguistic contexts can fit into the '*Continua of Multilingual Education*'.

Within the European context, Luxembourg is usually considered a good case of multilingual education that scores towards the 'more multilingual' end of the '*Continua of Multilingual Education*' on most variables. Luxembourg schools are for the whole population living in the country. All students start with Luxembourgish as the language of instruction and then German is introduced in primary school, first as a subject and then as a language of instruction. French is introduced in primary school as a subject and it is used as an additional language of instruction in secondary school (see Baetens Beardsmore & Lebrun, 1991; Hoffmann, 1998, for a description). Luxembourgish is replaced by German and French as school languages but it remains very active at the oral level. Baetens Beardsmore (1993b) considers that the outcomes of this program are trilingualism and biliteracy. According to Baetens Beardsmore and Lebrun (1991: 120):

'*The Luxembourg case is also significant in that it forces one to rethink about bilingualism in a way which breaks away from dichotomous oppositions*'. The '*Continua of Multilingual Education*' proposed in this chapter could be used for Luxembourg and even include other aspects of multilingual education in that country such as the teaching of English and other languages as school subjects (see Kirsch, 2006). The '*Continua of Multilingual Education*' could also account for the increasing number of students who are speakers of languages other than Luxembourgish when they go to school (micro-level). The use of French and German by parents and in society in general is an important feature of Luxembourg which to a certain extent can account for the good results in French (Baetens Beardsmore & Lebrun, 1991). This situation would be explained as the result of the interaction between the school and the macro and micro levels in the '*Continua of Multilingual Education*'.

There are several other cases of multilingual education in Europe which involve regional minority languages, national languages and a foreign language (see for example Cenoz & Gorter, 2005, 2008a). English is the most popular language in non-English speaking countries and French or German in the UK. Although in most cases these languages are taught as a subject and not as an additional language of instruction exposure to English is increasing inside and outside the school. In some cases English is also an additional medium of instruction as we will see in the Basque Country.

The '*Continua of Multilingual Education*' can also accommodate another type of multilingual school which is not usually given as a typical example, the Gymnasium. The Gymnasium is a type of secondary school common in many European countries which prepares students for the university. Some of the options imply a strong presence of modern languages (and also the classical languages Latin and Greek) in the curriculum. Languages are taught as subjects and are not languages of instruction and this type of program is usually considered as foreign language acquisition rather than multilingual education. However, it is difficult to draw a clear boundary between the two, at least in some specific situations. In some contexts, the use of the target languages in the sociolinguistic context and the relative proximity of the languages can favor the acquisition of languages at school and the outcomes of the language teaching in schools that are not usually considered multilingual can possibly be comparable to the outcomes of other types of multilingual education. Although the data are not on the outcomes of the Gymnasium but on the population in general, the Eurobarometer 237 (European Commission, 2005b) shows that there are very high percentages of speakers of other languages in countries such as the Netherlands or Denmark. These countries are relatively small and languages other than Dutch or Danish are used in the media. In the *'Continua of Multilingual Education'*, these situations would be 'less multilingual' in languages of instruction, and probably in 'school context' or in the use of several languages in the close social networks but they would be placed towards the 'more multilingual' end of the continuum in studying languages as subjects, the level of multilingualism of the teachers, the number of speakers of other languages, or the use of other languages in the media. The fact that some of the languages involved are Germanic (Dutch, German, Danish, English) can also contribute to the development of multilingual competence. An additional reason not to draw hard boundaries between different situations is that even in cases where languages are only taught as a subject a content-based approach such as CLIL may be used (see Marsh, 2007). García (2008b: 6) considers that depending on the type of program *'it may be difficult to differentiate between bilingual education and second or foreign language teaching programs'* but she considers that bilingual education has broader goals than foreign language teaching regarding tolerance and the appreciation of diversity.

Multilingual education aimed at specific groups

A well known example of multilingual education which does not fit neatly into existing typologies is that of the European schools (Baetens Beardsmore, 1993b). Nowadays, this is a network of 14 schools attended mainly by European civil servants in seven countries (Belgium, Germany, Italy, Luxembourg, The Netherlands, Spain and United Kingdom). The European Schools are controlled by the governments of the European Union states and altogether had 21,021 students in 2007 (Schola Europea, 2008). Most pupils (68.9% in 2007) are the children of civil servants working in the European Union institutions and this explains that the biggest schools are in Brussels and Luxembourg. Some children attend the schools as the result of agreements between the schools and some companies and organizations (5.3% of the total) and others (21.13% in 2007) do not belong to the previous categories and parents have to pay a fee.

In these schools, most students have their first language as the language of instruction in the primary level and a foreign language (language 2) is introduced as a subject in the first year of primary school. This language 2, which is English, German or French, is used as the language of instruction in the last years of primary and more increasingly in secondary. Most children who do not have English as their first language choose English as a second language. Then, a third language is introduced as a subject and in some cases as a language of instruction. The most popular third language is Spanish except for children who have not had English as a first or second language (Schola Europea, 2008). The total number of languages offered in the European schools goes from four to twelve. The schools which offer more languages are those located in Brussels and Luxembourg. Students usually have the first or second language as the languages of instruction but in some cases, particularly in secondary schools when there are more optional subjects they also have a third or even a fourth language as the language of instruction. The teachers are native speakers of the languages they teach as subjects or use as medium of instruction.

Apart from the development of personal, social and academic skills the European schools have specific aims regarding multilingualism and European citizenship as it can be seen in Table 2.9.

As European schools aim at multilingualism and multiculturalism, there are some specific activities to foster intercultural contact such as the 'European Hours' for groups speaking different first languages (see Baetens Beardsmore, 1993a; Hoffmann, 1998; De Mejía, 2002 for a more detailed description). The *'Continua of Multilingual Education'* proposed here can account for this model and the interaction between the sociolinguistic context and the schools. In many cases, students in these schools come from families with a high level of mobility and their use of the languages at the macro and micro levels can interact with the school variables.

Other schools that are considered multilingual although they do not usually have more than two languages as languages of instruction are international schools (Carder, 2007). Many of these schools have English as the main language of instruction and in some cases they also teach other languages but mainly as subjects. The idea of these schools is to be bilingual in the language of the country where they are located and in English or another widely spread European language. In some cases these schools are located in countries where other languages are also important and have been added to

Table 2.9 Linguistic and cultural aims of the European schools

> - To develop high standards in the mother tongue and in foreign languages.
> - To encourage a European and global perspective overall and particularly in the study of human sciences.
> - To give pupils confidence in their own cultural identity – the bedrock for their development as European citizens.

Source: The European Schools (http://www.eursc.eu/)

the curriculum. In the case of international schools with German, French or Italian as the medium of instruction, English is often taught as a third language. Some international schools with English as the main language of instruction aim at multilingualism in English and two other languages. They are in most cases private and many of them can be considered elitist (see De Mejía, 2002). Many international schools were originally aimed at children of European and American employees working abroad but in many cases some local children also attend these schools. There are different types of international schools and some are funded by government agencies. For example, the German Central Agency for Schools Abroad supports 117 schools abroad with 70,000 pupils who can obtain German certificates of education as well as the certificate of the country where the school is located. These schools are originally aimed at German children who are living abroad temporarily but nowadays they also attract children who speak other languages (see Zentralstelle für das Auslandsschulwesen www.auslandsschulwesen.de for additional information).

Some international schools that are 'German' schools can be considered multilingual because of the importance of English in the curriculum. Some examples of these multilingual schools are shown in Table 2.10:

These schools are German schools and as such they aim at teaching the German language and culture but they also include the national language of the country in which they are located and have added English. French schools in different parts of the world are often trilingual because of the teaching of English as a second or third language. Some examples can be

Table 2.10 Examples of 'German' multilingual schools

School	Country	Languages
Deutsche Int. Schule Jakarta	Indonesia	German, Indonesian and English
Hölters Schule	Argentina	German, Spanish and English
Deutsche Schule Tripolis	Libia	German, Arabic, English
Deutsche Schule La Paz	Bolivia	German, Spanish, English
Deutsche Schule Seoul	Korea	German, Korean, English, Spanish
Deutsche Int. Schule Jeddah	Saudi Arabia	German, Arabic, French
Deutsche Schule Kapstadt	South Africa	German, English, French (Afrikaans, Sotho, Xhosa)

Source: www.auslandsschulwesen.de

Table 2.11 Examples of 'French' multilingual schools

School	Country	Languages
École Française Harare	Zimbabwe	French, English, Spanish
École Française S.Petersbourg	Russia	French, Russian and English
École Française Shangai	China	French, Chinese, English
Lycée Jean Mermoz	Argentina	French, Spanish, English
Lycée Stendhal Milan	Italy	French, Italian, French
École Française Kyoto	Japan	French, Japanese, English
Lycée Pasteur Sao Paulo	Brazil	French, Portuguese, English, Spanish or German

Source: http://www.aefe.diplomatie.fr

seen in Table 2.11. This type of school, which is generally private, is funded in many cases by governmental institutions.

Apart from German or French, international schools can also have other languages. For example, there are international schools in Argentina with Italian as the main language of instruction where Spanish and English are taught as additional languages (see Banfi & Day, 2004; Banfi & Rettaroli, 2008). One example of these is the Scuola Italiana Cristoforo Colombo (http://www.cristoforocolombo.org.ar). Most international schools have English as the main language of instruction but in many cases only English and a local language are part of the curriculum. An example of trilingual education in an international school with English as the main language of instruction is the George Washington Academy in Morocco (http://www.gwa.ac.ma/). This is an American school and English is the language of instruction in the first year of kindergarten but French is introduced as a language of instruction in the second year. Arabic is introduced as a subject in the first year of primary and from the 5th to the 12th year (ages 10–18) the three languages are languages of instruction. English is taught for approximately 45% of the time, French for 33% and Arabic for 22% (see (http://www.gwa.ac.ma/). Another trilingual school with English as the main language of instruction where Arabic and French are also taught is Adma International School in Lebanon (www.admais.edu.lb).

A specific type of trilingual schools are Hebrew schools in some countries. These schools are aimed at Jewish children and provide religious education through the medium of Hebrew. Hebrew schools located in non-English speaking countries usually include English in the curriculum as well. For example, the so called 'double immersion' schools in Canada have Hebrew, French and English as languages of instruction (Genesee, 1998). There are different types of double immersion schools and Hebrew is usually taught as a language and as the medium of instruction for Jewish studies. For example, the Akiva School in Montreal has French, English and Hebrew from kindergarten onwards (http://64.34.149.23/BJEC_Akiva//). Other schools, such as the Hebrew Foundation School in Montreal, start with French and Hebrew and then add English in Grade 4 (http://www.hfs.qc.ca/). Outside Canada an example of a trilingual school is the Maguen David Hebrew School with Hebrew, Spanish and English (http://www.maguen-david.net/). The '*Continua of Multilingual Education*' can include all these schools in spite of their diversity regarding the curriculum and the sociolinguistic context.

In sum, the '*Continua of Multilingual Education*' is conceived as a comprehensive tool to include the complex reality of multilingual education by looking at different possibilities that go from 'less multilingual' to 'more multilingual' and by looking at multilingual education resulting from the interaction of linguistic, sociolinguistic and educational variables. It can be useful to describe and compare different types of multilingual schools. There are many other factors that can influence the success of multilingual education. For example, individual variables (IQ, language aptitude, motivation, anxiety) can influence the outcomes of multilingual education but the '*Continua of Multilingual Education*' is a tool to define different types of schools and multilingual programs and not a model to predict the outcomes of multilingual education.

The '*Continua of Multilingual Education*' and the Basque Educational system

In this section the '*Continua of Multilingual Education*' will be applied to the different types of multilingual education in the BAC. Before discussing the different types of education we are going to describe some of the general characteristics of the Basque educational system and introduce the different types of bilingual and multilingual education in the BAC. We are going to refer to general education excluding the teaching of Basque or other languages to adults (see Chapter 10 about university and adults).

Compulsory education in the BAC includes six years of primary (6 to 12 year-old children) and four years of secondary school (12 to 16 year-old children). The different levels of education can be seen in Table 2.12.

Apart from being bilingual or multilingual the educational system in the BAC has the following characteristics:

Table 2.12 Educational levels in the BAC

Age	Level
2 to 6	Pre-primary: 4 grades
6 to 12	Primary: 6 grades
12 to 16	Compulsory secondary: 4 grades
16 to 18	Higher secondary: academically oriented or vocational training: 2–3 grades
18 onwards	Vocational training or university: 1–6 grades

- Basque children go to school at a very early age. School starts at the age of two for most children and depending on the school, children can stay in the same school until 18 or change to another school for secondary. Before the age of two, children either stay at home or go to day-care centers. When children go to school at two, the activities are very similar to those of day-care centers but these groups are already part of the educational system and they go to school five days a week. Although compulsory education does not start until the age of six, it is exceptional not to go to school before that age.
- Compulsory education up to the age of 16 is the same for all children. Children are mixed in the same class and there are no different groups for more or less talented children. Most children with learning difficulties and children who are physically or mentally challenged are integrated in ordinary classes. They can have special materials and special support but are mixed with other children. At the beginning of non-compulsory secondary education, at the age of 16, students can either go to academically oriented higher secondary education so as to go to the university, to vocational training or they can leave school. Once they finish higher secondary school students can go to higher vocational training or to the university. The general characteristics of compulsory education are the same all over Spain but there are differences regarding the languages of instruction and the subjects in the curriculum.
- As compared to many other countries the number of private schools is very high. Approximately 50% of the total students attend private schools in the BAC. Some of these schools are Catholic and others are non-religious schools and involve different ideological and pedagogical orientations. Private schools are partly or fully funded by the

Basque Government Department of Education but parents have to pay a fee. Public schools belong to the government and are fully funded. The differences in socioeconomic status are linked to the type of school but multilingual education in the Basque Country can be considered as aimed at the whole population because it is spread to all schools.

The best known feature of the educational system in the BAC is its bilingualism and multilingualism. The legal support for this came after many years of banning Basque from education. In 1978, the Spanish Constitution declared Spanish the state official language and guaranteed the rights of Spanish speakers to use their language but also raised the possibility of recognizing other languages as co-official in their own territories. One year later, the Statute of Autonomy of the BAC (Article 6) declared Basque official along with Spanish (Ley Orgánica 3/1979; BOE 22-12-1979):

> 1. *Euskara (Basque), the Basque Country's own language, will have the status of official language of Euskadi -alongside Spanish- and all the country's inhabitants have the right to know and use both languages.*

In 1982, the Law for the Normalization of Basque (Ley 10/1982, BOPV 16-12-1982) acknowledged the right of every student to receive his/her education either in Basque or Spanish and the parents' right to choose the medium of instruction. The law also makes it compulsory for primary and secondary students to study as a subject the official language that has not been chosen as the language of instruction. The development of the Law for the Normalization of Basque included the design of the bilingual teaching models of the BAC and many other measures such as the policy regarding teachers' language competence, the organization of in-service training or the production of teaching materials. The expression 'normalization of Basque' used in the title of this law is very common in the Basque Country. It reflects the idea of promoting the language until its normal use is achieved, that is, until it recovers its prestige and it can be used for all functions in society.

At the European level, as we have already seen in Chapter 1, the Council of Europe (1992) proposed the Charter for Regional or Minority Languages so as *'to protect and promote regional and minority languages as a threatened aspect of Europe's cultural heritage and on the other hand to enable speakers of a regional or minority language to use it in private and public life'*. The Charter contains objectives, principles and concrete measures to protect and promote regional and minority languages. The Charter was adopted as a convention by the Committee of Ministers of the Council of Europe in 1992. Spain signed the Charter in 1992 and ratified it in 2001.

The Spanish Ministry of Education has a number of powers in education and these include the general design of the educational system (different levels, compulsory education, etc), the qualifications needed for teachers at different levels and the part of the curriculum which has to be common all over Spain. The LOE (Ley Orgánica de Educación 2/2006 BOE 4-5-2006) passed in 2006 establishes that 55% of the school time is devoted to the common Spanish curriculum in regions with a co-official language such as the BAC and 65% in other regions.

The Basque Government has financial control (public school salaries, funding of private schools, buildings) and the control of the organization of the educational system (control of materials, control of schools, in-service training, language policy, etc). The Basque Government cannot go against the regulations of the Spanish general educational laws but has substantial autonomy to run the educational system in the BAC.

Basque was used in education before the Law of the Normalization of Basque was passed in 1982 as we will see in Chapter 3 but it is this law that defines the bilingual models in the BAC. Basque and Spanish became compulsory subjects in all schools in the BAC, and the Decree of Bilingualism 138/1983 (BOPV 108/19-7-1983) established three models of language schooling: models A, B and D (there is no letter 'C' in Basque). These models differ with respect to the language or languages of instruction used, their linguistic aims, and their intended student population.

Model A is intended for native speakers of Spanish who choose to be instructed in Spanish. Basque is taught as a school subject (between three and five hours a week) which accounts for about 15% of the classroom time. According to the Decree it would be possible to use Basque as the language of instruction for some lessons.

Model B is intended for native speakers of Spanish who want to be bilingual in Basque and Spanish. Both Basque and Spanish are used as languages of instruction for approximately 50% of school time. Both languages are also taught as school subjects. According to the Decree, mathematics and literacy skills could be taught in Spanish but there is considerable variation in the distribution of the subjects from school to school (Arzamendi & Genesee, 1997). Originally model B was only for primary school and it was expected that by the end of primary school students could change to model D. Nowadays, model B has been extended to secondary school.

Model D was originally created as a language maintenance program for native speakers of Basque and has Basque as the language of instruction and Spanish is taught as a subject. Basque is used in this model approximately 75% of the time. The other 25% of the time is for Spanish and a foreign language, generally English. As we will see in Chapter 3, model D currently includes a large number of students with Spanish as their first language.

Some of the characteristics of the educational models are the following:

- Model A is not usually considered a bilingual model because students who are speakers of the majority language (Spanish) only learn Basque as a subject.
- Model D is usually considered a bilingual model because even though Spanish is not a language of instruction, it is studied as a subject and students usually become balanced bilinguals.
- Speakers of Spanish as a first language are mixed with speakers of Basque as a first language in the D model. This is a clear difference between the D model and the Canadian models of total immersion. Another difference is that in the D model Spanish is not used as a language of instruction while in Canadian immersion English is used as a language of instruction. The relative number of speakers of Basque and Spanish inside D model classes is highly dependent on the area where each school is located.
- There are schools with one model but in other cases two or more models can coexist in the same school in separate streams.
- With very few exceptions students do not change models from primary to secondary school.

The three models of bilingual education are in a process of discussion and there are different positions about their future (see Zalbide & Cenoz, 2008). These positions are related to the fact that A model children have very poor results in Basque but are linked to different ideologies and attitudes towards the use of the Basque language in education (see Chapter 8). Apart from the three models there are some international schools with other languages (German, English, French) as the main language of instruction. These schools have one of these languages as the main language of instruction but also teach Spanish and Basque as school subjects and in some cases as languages of instruction for some subjects.

Apart from the increasing use of Basque as the main language of instruction, English has acquired a more important role in Basque education as it can be seen in its use as an additional language of instruction in some schools (see Chapter 5) and the early introduction of English (see also Chapter 9). This has created a great diversity in the curriculum in Basque schools. Basque, Spanish and the first foreign language (English in most

Table 2.13 Languages of instruction in BAC schools

Official models	A: Spanish B: Basque and Spanish D: Basque
New types	A+: A model with extra Basque or Basque as the language of instruction for one subject A + English: Spanish as the main language of instruction and English as an additional language of instruction for some subjects B: This model has always had a great diversity regarding the distribution of the languages B + English: Basque, Spanish and English as languages of instruction D + English: Basque as the main language of instruction and English as an additional language of instruction for some subjects Foreign: English, German or French as the main language of instruction and Spanish (and Basque in some cases) as an additional language of instruction

cases) are compulsory subjects. A second foreign language is an optional subject in secondary school. The different possibilities regarding the languages of instruction can be seen in Table 2.13.

The combination of the three models, the diversity of model B with more or less use of Basque and Spanish and the increasing use of English as an additional language of instruction make it impossible for the Basque educational system to fit as a single type in a typology. This diversity is increased when other educational factors are taken into account: age of introduction of the languages, teaching methodology, etc. Moreover, according to the *Continua of Multilingual Education* the languages used at the micro and macro levels have to be considered. Proficiency in Basque cannot be the same when comparing Basque L1 and L2 speakers or speakers who use Basque in everyday communication outside school and those who use Spanish. In fact we could distinguish even more types of bilingual and multilingual education in the BAC. Basque schools in the last decades have aimed at enrichment and additive bilingualism and biliteracy without replacing the first language (Basque or Spanish) by another language. With the exception of model A which can be defined as a weak form of bilingual education (Baker, 2006: 215), Basque schools provide strong forms of bilingual education. In the last years the aims are even more ambitious because multilingualism and multiliteracy in Basque, Spanish and English have become the aim and at the same time the recent immigration of speakers of other languages to the Basque Country creates new challenges.

Different types of schools according to 'The Continua of Multilingual Education'

The different types of bilingual and multilingual education in the BAC can fit into the *'Continua of Multilingual Education'*. The use of Basque, Spanish and English (or other languages), both as subjects and languages of instruction, and the interaction of other school and context-related variables result in different possible programs of bilingual and multilingual education. We can look at the different continua in *'The Continua of Multilingual Education'* so as to discuss the different types of Basque schools.

Educational variables

As we have already seen earlier in this chapter the dimensions to be considered are subject, language of instruction, teacher and school context.

- *Subject*. In the case of the BAC all languages in the curriculum are school subjects (Basque, Spanish, English and in some cases French and German) so the position would be the same for the different models but there could be a difference between schools that have three languages as school subjects and others that have more than three languages as school subjects. There could be differences in the positions along this continuum when looking at the integration of different subjects. Some Basque schools plan the syllabuses for the three (or more) languages in an integrated way so that the language teachers work together and develop the aims and activities for the different languages in an integrated way. In other schools there is no special coordination between the language teachers and the syllabuses are not developed in an integrated way. The integrated approach is a more multilingual approach (Elorza & Muñoa, 2008). Nowadays there are not so many differences in Basque schools regarding the other features that define this continuum: age of introduction of the different languages or the number of hours devoted to the different languages as school subjects. Taken into account the different features of this continuum, the position of all Basque schools is towards the multilingual end because there are at least three languages, the three are school subjects in primary and secondary school and at least two languages are taught from kindergarten onwards.

The main differences between schools are related to the integration of the syllabuses of the different languages.

- *Languages of instruction*. Basque schools have different positions on the continuum 'languages of instruction'. Some schools have three languages of instruction (usually Basque, Spanish and English but in a few cases German of French), other two languages of instruction: Basque and English, Basque and Spanish, Spanish and English and others only one language: Basque or Spanish. The more languages of instruction a school has the more multilingual its position is along the continuum. The language of instruction continuum also refers to the integration of the different languages in syllabus design and language planning when they are used as languages of instruction and, as we have also seen when referring to languages as school subjects, there are important differences when schools are compared.

- *Teachers*. Basque schools also differ along the 'teachers' continuum regarding the language proficiency of the teachers in different languages and their specific training. Teachers who teach through the medium of Basque are at least bilingual in Basque and Spanish while teachers who teach through the medium of Spanish can have different levels of proficiency in Basque. Teachers have different levels of proficiency in English and other languages but there is no specific association of level of proficiency with specific types of schools. The same can be said about specific training for multilingual education. This training was not common in the past but now there is more attention to multilingualism at the universities and there are also specific courses. However, there are not important differences regarding this specific training associated with different models or schools.

- *School context*. There are differences among schools when looking at the languages used in the 'school context', the fourth educational continuum. Schools where Basque is the main language of instruction have mainly Basque as the language in the linguistic landscape inside the school and the main language of communication is also Basque. Written documents for external communication in these schools are usually in Basque and Spanish. Other schools are more 'Spanish speaking'. In some schools some English can be seen in some posters but its use is very limited. Therefore, Basque schools are not at the most multilingual end of the continuum regarding the school context because only one or two languages are used in most cases outside the classrooms.

Linguistic Distance

Regarding the linguistic distance continuum there are not important differences when comparing different schools in the BAC because the combination of languages in the Basque Country always includes Basque, Spanish and English and in some cases French and German.

Sociolinguistic variables

As we have already seen we can distinguish the macro and the micro levels. There are some general aspects that are common for the whole of the BAC at the macro level such as the general status of Basque, Spanish and English or the use of different languages in the media. These aspects are quite similar all over the BAC. Basque and Spanish are official languages but Basque is used to a lesser extent than Spanish. The status of Basque and Spanish in the BAC is high but internationally Spanish has a much higher status than Basque. English has a very high status internationally but its use is very limited in the BAC. Spanish is the main language of the media. The relationship between the sociolinguistic variables at the macro level and the types of schools can best be seen when looking at the number and distribution of Basque speakers. Some schools are located in a more bilingual context than others in the cases in which Basque and Spanish are used in everyday life. In other cases, schools are placed in a more monolingual context when only one language, generally Spanish and Basque in a few cases, is used in everyday life. This situation also influences the micro level and the use of one or more languages in the social networks in the family or with friends and neighbors (Basque Government, 2008). The number of languages in the micro context can also be increased as the result of immigration. Schools located in areas where more languages are used in the macro and micro context will be placed towards the more multilingual end of the continua. It is not the same for a multilingual school (Basque, Spanish, English) to be located in an area where most of the population are proficient in Basque and Spanish and both languages are used in everyday life or in an area where only Spanish is used. It is also different for that school to have speakers of different languages (Romanian, Berber, Ukranian) at home or speakers of one of the school languages.

Conclusion

When compared to bilingual education, multilingual education can present more diversity and '*can present additional challenges because it is more ambitious*' (Cenoz & Genesee, 1998: vii). In this chapter we have defined multilingual education as '*teaching more than two languages provided that schools aim at multilingualism and multiliteracy'*. This definition is goal-oriented in the sense that multilingualism and multiliteracy are the aims to be achieved. It also goes beyond bilingual education focusing on three or more languages.

When using a model to describe and compare different types of multilingual education it is necessary to account for the different possibilities and for different sociolinguistic and educational contexts. The *'Continua of Multilingual Education'* offers the possibility of looking at different linguistic, sociolinguistic and educational aspects of multilingual education without establishing closed categories and hard boundaries. This model can be used to compare different types of multilingual education in an international context but also to compare different types of schools in the same country or area.

The Basque educational system, with three official models but many other possibilities in educational practice, is an example of the complexity of bilingual and multilingual education that can fit into the *'Continua of Multilingual Education'*. In the case of Basque education, the main differences between the different models are in educational variables and in the use of Basque or Spanish in the sociolinguistic context.

Key Points

- Multilingual education implies teaching more than two languages provided that schools aim at multilingualism and multiliteracy.
- The *'Continua of Multilingual Education'* is a model to analyze different types of multilingual schools. It is an alternative to typologies.
- The different types of multilingual education in the Basque Country and in many other contexts can be defined on the *'Continua of Multilingual Education'*.
- The different types of multilingual education are linked to educational, sociolinguistic and linguistic factors.
- Schools in the BAC vary regarding the languages of instruction, SES and the sociolinguistic context in which they are located.

Chapter 3

Using the Minority Language as the Language of Instruction

Introduction

As we have seen in Chapter 1, there are approximately 7000 languages in the world and there are important differences in the number of speakers between strong languages and languages at risk (Gordon, 2005). In this chapter we focus on the use of a minority language, Basque, as a language of instruction. This situation shares many characteristics with other minority languages. The Charter for Regional or Minority Languages defines these languages as *'languages that are traditionally used within a given territory of a state by nationals of that state who form a group numerically smaller than the rest of the state's population and [are] different from the official language(s) of that state'* (Council of Europe, 1992). Minority languages are often 'small languages' such as Basque or Navajo but they can also have millions of speakers such as Catalan or Quechua.

Maintenance and Immersion Programs

Many languages are not officially used at school and it is common for many children not to be educated through their first language, particularly in the cases in which the first language is a minority. This was the case for most schoolchildren with Basque as a first language for many years. Basque-speaking children spoke Basque at home and only had Spanish or French as the language of instruction. In the last years, there has been an increasing use of Basque but also of other regional minority languages in many areas of Europe such as Wales (Williams, 2001; Lewis, 2008), Scotland (Robertson, 2001; Johnstone, 2007), Catalonia (Vila, 2008) or Norway (Hirvonen, 2008).

Outside the European context, there are many examples of successful teaching through indigenous minority languages in different parts of the world. Some examples have been reported from North America by McCarty (2007, see also McCarty *et al.*, 2006). The use of native American languages such as Hawaiian or Navajo in bilingual programs helps to develop these languages and their cultures and at the same time, students in these programs also make more progress in English. The use of Māori as the language of instruction has increased in New Zealand (May, 2004; May & Hill, 2005). The development of Intercultural Bilingual Education, based on the use of different native languages as the medium of instruction in most Latin American countries, with a longer tradition in Mexico, Peru, Guatemala, Bolivia and Ecuador, is also based on the use of minority languages (see Hornberger & López, 1998; López & Sichra, 2007; Hamel, 2007).

Other programs using the minority language as the language of instruction along with English are developmental bilingual programs and two-way immersion programs in the USA (see Baker, 2006, Chapter 11; Genesee & Lindholm-Leary, 2007). Minority languages are also used as languages of instruction in other parts of the world. For example Khubchandani (2007) reports that many minority languages are used in education as languages of instruction in India in the first grades and original materials in these languages have been produced. However, these languages are replaced by English and Hindi as languages of instruction in later years.

Even though bilingual education is not a recent phenomenon, a particular type of bilingual education known as 'immersion' is associated with Canadian schools and it is relatively recent (Johnstone, 2006). Canadian immersion started in the 60s in Quebec as a result of the pressure from some English-speaking parents who wanted their children to learn more French at school. French started to be used as a school language and different types of programs emerged depending on the year of introduction of French and the intensity of its use (Genesee, 1987; Swain & Lapkin, 1982; Genesee, 2004). Originally, immersion started in the French-speaking province of Quebec where English speakers are a minority in a country where English speakers are a majority. Canadian immersion spread all over Canada and in most cases it is immersion in French, a prestigious international language:

> For the most part, French immersion in Canada has served the political, economic and social aims of the middle- and upper-middle class or the English-speaking majority. (Swain & Johnson, 1997: 4)

The model of Canadian immersion also spread to many other countries in the world. Nowadays Canadian immersion is one of the most important references in bilingual education and one of the main reasons for this is the important research tradition that has informed the international research community about many aspects of immersion education (Swain & Johnson, 1997; Genesee, 2004; Lyster, 2007). The term 'immersion education' is sometimes used as a synonym of bilingual education but immersion is a specific type of bilingual education as it can be seen in the list of core features of a prototypical immersion program given by Swain and Johnson (1997: 6–8):

(1) The L2 is a medium of instruction.
(2) The immersion curriculum parallels the local L1 curriculum.
(3) Overt support exists for the L1.
(4) The program aims for additive bilingualism.
(5) Exposure to the L2 is largely confined to the classroom.
(6) Students enter with similar (and limited) levels of L2 proficiency.
(7) The teachers are bilingual.
(8) The classroom culture is that of the local L1 community.

There are different models of Canadian immersion and their application to different contexts results in further diversification because of the differences regarding linguistic distance, the sociolinguistic context and school variables as described in the '*Continua of Multilingual Education*' in Chapter 2 (see also Swain & Johnson, 1997; Johnstone, 2006).

Immersion can also take place when a minority language is the language of instruction but in this case it will be immersion only for students who are not speakers of the minority language and learn it as a second language. For example, bilingual education in the Basque Country can be considered immersion when Basque is used as a language of instruction for speakers who have Spanish as a first language. In other cases instruction through Basque is mother tongue education in the minority language. When Basque is the language of instruction (D model) it is very common in the BAC to have in the same class children who have Basque as the L1 and children who have Spanish as the L1 and children who have both Basque and Spanish as their first languages. This combination of immersion in a second language and mother tongue education is also common in other European contexts such as Catalonia, Wales, Ireland or Friesland (see Gardner *et al.*, 2000; Cenoz & Gorter, 2008a). Outside Europe, Baker (2007a) reports the case of Navajo speakers in the USA who can be mixed with a small proportion of language majority children in Navajo-medium classes. Other cases are Māori-medium schools (see May & Hill, 2005) or dual education in the USA (Genesee & Lindholm-Leary, 2007)

Teaching through the Minority Language in the Basque Educational System

In this section we will look at the origin of Basque-medium education and the distribution of students in the different educational models in the Basque Country.

The Ikastolak

Some isolated bilingual or even trilingual (in Basque, Spanish and French) schools existed in the BAC at the end of the 19th century and the first decades of the 20th century but the situation for the use of Basque at school got worse after the Spanish Civil War (1936–39). Basque was banned from education during the Franco regime (1939–75) and Spanish was the only language of instruction in most schools. Despite legal strictures, Basque was used in education in three different ways (see also Dávila, 1995):

- Extra-curricular classes to teach Basque literacy skills to children who had Spanish as the language of instruction at school.
- A few home schools for children up to the age of nine when children went to other schools. These schools were organized by teachers in their own houses and used more modern pedagogical approaches than traditional schools.
- In the 1960s, groups of enthusiastic parents and teachers in the BAC fought for and succeeded in establishing or re-opening a number of private Basque-medium schools called '*ikastolak*'. This was a non-official parallel educational system. The first '*ikastolak*' were very modest but they received widespread popular support and their number grew rapidly. The '*ikastolak*' were not officially recognized in the beginning, the Spanish government was eventually forced to accept them or at least to tolerate them because they had attracted so many students that they could not be ignored. The '*ikastolak*' have the following characteristics:

    (1) The Basque language is the main language of instruction both for learners with Basque as the first language and for second language learners.
    (2) Motivation and solidarity have traditionally been considered very important values for teachers and parents.
    (3) Parents' participation is more important than in some other schools.
    (4) From an educational perspective the '*ikastolak*' have been more innovative regarding teaching methods, teacher training and

extra-curricular activities. These schools had to create their own material in Basque and were more ready for innovation.

(5) The '*ikastolak*' are independent from each other but they have a coordinating body 'Ikastolen Elkartea' so as to provide teacher training, to develop materials and also to organize extra-curricular activities and deal with financial and legal problems.

The '*ikastolak*' became legal in the late 70s and they got financial support from the Basque Government. There have been changes in the '*ikastolak*' along the years but the most important one took place in 1993 when each '*ikastola*' had to decide whether to join the public or the private network. Over half of the existing '*ikastolak*' remained private. In fact, the Basque educational system has a bit over half of the students in the private sector. Private schools including '*ikastolak*' receive funding from the Basque Government. Both public and private '*ikastolak*' have a coordinating body so as to develop educational projects and to share teacher training and materials (www. ikastola.net). The '*ikastolak*' also organize festivals to promote the use of Basque and collect funds for new buildings. For example, '*Kilometroak*' was the festival organized in Gipuzkoa in 2008 and approximately 100,000 people joined and donated money to build a new '*ikastola*' in Irura (Noticias de Gipuzkoa, 6 October 2008). Four more similar festivals take place every year in other provinces. The slogans in Figure 3.1 are from Gipuzkoa ('*Kilometroak*') and Bizkaia ('*Ibialdia*'). The one in Gipuzkoa says '*eraikitzen*' ('building') both for the idea of building a Basque-speaking society together and the idea of a new school building. The one from Bizkaia '*amore bi eta*' (two loves) refers to the two loves parents who send their children to '*ikastolak*' have, the love for their children and their love for the Basque language (Figure 3.1).

Nowadays, the '*ikastolak*' are in general more 'Basque' than other D model schools but the motivation and volunteering of parents and teachers is not as strong as in the beginning. As it is the case with other model D schools, Basque is not the L1 for many children. At the same time, different strategies have been used to prepare Spanish-speaking children to have Basque as the language of instruction including starting school at a very early age or to allocate Spanish and Basque speaking children to different classes. The '*ikastolak*' using this allocation according to the L1 have the possibility of working more intensively on language skills before mixing students in the same class but this strategy is not used in all the '*ikastolak*'.

Distribution of the models

As we have seen in the previous chapter there were important legal changes both in Spain and the BAC in the late 70s and early 80s. Basque,

Figure 3.1 Slogans of ikastolak festivals

along with Spanish, became an official language, and the bilingual models were established in 1983 (Decree 138/1983, BOPV 19 July, 1983). At that time, approximately 12% of students attended Basque-medium schools which were '*ikastolak*'. The three models, which have already been introduced in Chapter 2, have different objectives regarding language proficiency:

Model A. Spanish-medium instruction with Basque and Spanish as subjects. The aims of this model are the following:

- To acquire good comprehension skills in Basque.
- To be prepared to discuss everyday matters in Basque.
- To develop positive attitudes towards Basque.
- To prepare students to take part in Basque environments.

Model B. Basque and Spanish as subjects and languages of instruction. The aims of this model are:

- To acquire a high level of comprehension in Basque and the appropriate level of production to work in Basque.
- To prepare students to carry out further studies through the medium of Basque.

Model D. Basque-medium instruction and Basque and Spanish as subjects. The aims of this model are:

- To strengthen competence in Basque and to enrich language skills so that Basque becomes the language of conversation and teaching.
- To strengthen the Basque speaking community of students so that the school becomes a driving force in the Basquization of the BAC.
- To achieve a satisfactory knowledge of Spanish.

The use of Basque as the medium of instruction has increased steadily over the years and at present, 96.63% of kindergarten schoolchildren, 90.43% of primary schoolchildren and 80.14% of compulsory secondary schoolchildren have Basque as a language of instruction of some or all the school subjects (B and D models). Figure 3.2 shows this change in the language of instruction and that the X model with no Basque has practically disappeared in primary and secondary school.

The figures corresponding to the distribution in the three models in the academic year 2008–09 can be seen in Table 3.1.

The data indicate that the use of Basque as the language of instruction has attracted an increasing number of students with the exception of vocational training. Model D with Basque as the language of instruction is the most popular at all the levels followed by model B. This means that there

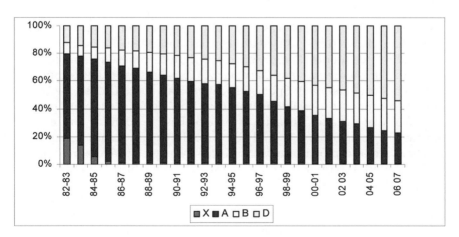

Figure 3.2 Primary and secondary school student percentages by model in each school year, 1982–2007

Source: Zalbide and Cenoz, 2008: 10

Table 3.1 Bilingual models in kindergarten, primary and compulsory secondary school in 2008–09 (%)

	A *Spanish*	*B Basque* *and* *Spanish*	*D* *Basque*	*No* *Basque*
Pre-primary (2–6)	4.80	24.47	70.21	0.51
Primary (6–12)	8.80	29.96	60.47	0.75
Compulsory secondary (12–16)	19.08	27.54	52.64	0.72
Secondary, Higher (16–18)	47.75	1.50	50,12	0.65
Secondary Vocational (16–18)	75.93	2.36	21.68	0

Source: Basque Government: Department of Education (www.hezkuntza.net)

has been a real language shift in the educational system of the BAC. This shift has many implications for the educational system as we will see in the next section.

Taking into account that the total number of Basque speakers in the BAC is 30.1% of the population and 18.3% is passive bilingual (Basque Government, 2008), the data indicate that many Spanish speaking families choose not only the B model with Basque and Spanish as the languages of instruction but the D model with only Basque as the language of instruction. The D model was originally designed for Basque speaking children and practically all children from Basque speaking homes are enrolled in this model. Parents have the right to choose the model they want for the children and as Gardner (2000: 54) says it is not completely clear what triggers many Spanish speaking parents to choose the D and not the B model. A possible reason could be ideological; many parents may feel that speaking Basque is part of Basque identity and even if Basque has been lost in the family they would like their children to speak it. There are also practical reasons because Basque speakers may find it easier to find a job but there is no research to confirm the influence of these or other factors.

The data also indicate that Basque is more commonly used as the language of instruction in the lower levels of education. That means that the use of Basque as the language of instruction in primary and secondary school is likely to increase in the future when these children get older. The trend to use Basque as a language of instruction is not strong in vocational training where the main language of instruction is Spanish.

Spanish as the language of instruction has undergone a significant decline all over the BAC. The distribution is not the same in different areas of the BAC but the trend to use more Basque as the language of instruction has taken place in all three provinces of the BAC (Araba, Bizkaia and Gipuzkoa).

Before the establishment of the bilingual models in 1983, teaching through the medium of Basque took place mainly at the 'ikastolak' which were private schools. Nowadays the use of Basque is more common in the public network which includes some of the 'ikastolak' that became public in 1993. The total percentages corresponding to the distribution of the three models in public and private schools can be seen in Table 3.2.

The data indicate that there are important differences between public and private schools regarding the distribution of the models, particularly between models B and D. Teaching through the medium of Basque either in model B or D is the most common option in both the public and the private network but the percentage of students in model D is much higher in the public than in the private schools. Both private and public schools include 'ikastolak' but other types of private schools have started to teach some or all subjects through Basque later.

As we have already seen in Chapter 2, in practice, there are more models than the A, B and D models. When the models were established there was also a model without any Basque (model X) with less than 1% of the students now which is not included in Table 3.2. This model is for the few students who do not learn Basque because they live only temporarily in the BAC. Other possibilities that can develop into 'new models' involve the use of a foreign language as an additional language of instruction as we will see in Chapter 5. Another source of variation is model B. Both Basque and Spanish are used as the languages of instruction in this model but it varies from a very intensive use of Basque, which is very close to model D, in some schools to the teaching of just one or two 'less important' subjects in Basque (Arzamendi & Genesee, 1997). The acquisition of

Table 3.2 Bilingual models in kindergarten, primary school and compulsory secondary education in public and private schools in 2008–09 (%)

	A Spanish	*B Basque and Spanish*	*D Basque*
Public schools	6.2	13.3	80.4
Private schools	14.0	41.50	44.4

Source: Basque Government: Department of Education (www.hezkuntza.net)

literacy skills takes place first in Spanish in most model B schools but not in all cases. The decision about the subjects to be taught in each language in the B model can also depend on the number of bilingual teachers in the school. The B model is exceptional in post-compulsory secondary school when students are supposed to be ready to go to model D although in practice most students go to model A.

An important characteristic of the educational models is that schools can offer different models so that there are schools with only one model and others with combinations. Instructional methods for the teaching of Basque vary from school to school depending on whether Basque is used as a medium of instruction or is taught as a school subject. In models B and D, where Basque is used as the language of instruction, the methodological approach is 'content-based' and children learn different subjects (mathematics, science, music, sports, etc.) through the medium of Basque. Basque is also taught as a subject in models B and D and, in these classes, instruction focuses on Basque grammar, discourse, language use and literature. Basque is a school subject in model A and is taught as a second language. Most teachers in model A schools adopt traditional second language instructional approaches with relatively structural syllabuses. Spanish is taught as a subject in model D due to the extended use of Spanish in society it is not taught as a second language.

Another fact to take into account when looking at the distribution of the models and its implications is that there has been a dramatic drop of the birth rate in the BAC and consequently of the number of children in the Basque educational system. The birth rate has dropped from 19.1 per 1000 inhabitants in 1975 to 9.5 per 1000 inhabitants in 2006 (Eustat, 2008). This figure is below the European Union and the Spanish averages (Eustat, 2008). As a consequence of the drop of births the number of students in pre-primary, primary and secondary education has fallen dramatically. This fall has implied that very few new teachers have entered the educational system and competition between schools to attract more children. Because of this competition, schools try to offer more services such as the possibility of enrolling children from a very early age or the very early introduction of English. The number of students is increasing in the BAC in the last years because of a slight increase in the birth rate and because of immigration, a recent phenomenon which implies new challenges.

The use of Basque as the language of instruction in schools in the BAC has been evaluated in different research studies focusing on Basque, Spanish and English proficiency and also in academic development. The results of these studies will be discussed in Chapter 4.

Main Challenges Using the Minority Language as the Medium of Instruction

The development and maintenance of bilingual education in the Basque Country has required an enormous effort on the part of the Basque Government Department of Education, individual schools, and teachers. The shift from Spanish into Basque as the main language of instruction has had important consequences. In this section we will discuss the four main challenges that the Basque educational system has faced over the last years: teacher education, the development of teaching materials, the use of Basque and the integration of immigrants.

Teacher education

Primary school teachers need a certificate of education from a teachers' college and secondary school teachers need a university degree and special pre-service courses in education. When the Law of Normalization of Basque (1982) was passed, very few teachers in public schools (about 20%) could speak Basque and many of them were not proficient in its use in written form or for academic purposes. Teachers who teach Basque or through the medium of Basque need a certificate of proficiency. Nowadays 80% of public school teachers are proficient in Basque and have obtained the certificate required to teach through the medium of Basque. Approximately 63% of the teachers in the private network also have the qualifications to teach through Basque.

These figures are quite impressive and match the preference for Basque-medium models. Who are these Basque-speaking teachers? Some of them are new teachers who had Basque or Spanish as their first language and have been trained through the medium of Basque at the teacher training colleges and the universities. New teachers are usually proficient in Basque. However, there have not been many new teachers recently in Basque schools because of the dramatic drop in birth rate and consequently in the number of students at school. As most public school teachers are civil servants, who have tenured jobs, the main way to get enough Basque speaking teachers has been in-service training.

The Basque Government Department of Education offers extension courses and leaves of absence for teachers who want or need to learn Basque (see also Zalbide & Cenoz, 2008). There are classes organized for teachers with a leave of absence and they receive their full salary for a period of up to three years. So far there have been almost 23,000 positions available for full-time Basque learning in the last 25 years. Teachers who complete these courses are required to take examinations to certify that they have attained sufficient proficiency to teach in Basque. For many years, teachers needed to reach an intermediate level of Basque by taking courses outside their working hours so as to be able to get into a full-time Basque language course but more recently more teachers are allowed to start from lower levels. Teachers in the private sector are increasingly getting full-time release on full pay to learn Basque. In these cases the Basque Government Department of Education also pays for the teacher's tuition and the replacement teacher's salary. There are also full and part time courses for teachers who already teach through the medium of Basque and have the required qualifications so as to refresh their knowledge and to get to know recent advances in the standardization and terminology of the language. Some years ago it was very common to organize courses for teachers who had Basque as a first language and were fluent in Basque but had had Spanish as the medium of instruction at school and at the university. These teachers had to acquire literacy skills in Basque and enrich their grammar and vocabulary. The extended use of Basque in education means that Basque is used in fields where it had not been used before even by those teachers who had a good command of the language.

Even though the conditions for teachers in the BAC to learn Basque are objectively very good some teachers are facing difficulties. There is a lot of pressure resulting from the increasing need to use Basque as the language of instruction because of parents' preference for the B and D models. Teachers in public schools are tenured but in some cases they have to go to a different school so as to go on teaching through the medium of Spanish. Some teachers who are over 45 can have an exemption to learn Basque because they consider themselves unable to learn the language. In some situations, mainly in the past, the requirements to teach through the medium of Basque have been lowered in order to face the shortage of teachers who were proficient in Basque.

As the result of in-service training, nowadays most teachers in the BAC are bilingual. However, many teachers are second language speakers of Basque and find it difficult to teach through the medium of Basque even after obtaining the Basque language certificate which is required for this purpose. This situation, which involves second language speaking teachers teaching through Basque to L1 and L2 students, could potentially have some influence on academic achievement as we will discuss in the next chapter.

All school teachers can get advice from specialists in the special centers for educational advice. There are 18 of these centers which are supported by the Basque Government Department of Education and are distributed all over the BAC. All the advisory centers, *Berritzeguneak*, have a coordinator for language planning. According to the Basque Government Department of Education (Decree 15/ 2001, BOPV 16-2-2001) the aims of these centres are: to give advice to teachers on general didactics, specific programs, materials, in-service teacher education and to conduct experiments and research in language learning.

Apart from Basque language planning, the advisory centers have specialists in new technologies, English, special needs for students, diversity and in specific school levels. The '*ikastolak*' and some private schools have their own consultants and specific networks for counseling. Teaching in a bilingual or multilingual program requires specialist training in immersion pedagogy, curriculum, materials and resources and L2 or target language assessment (May & Hill, 2005). In the BAC, there are over 200 courses organized by the Basque Government as in-service training courses in different areas per year. Some examples of these courses are given in Table 3.3.

Teachers in bilingual and multilingual education have some special challenges. In the Basque Country, they have to teach mixed groups with various levels of proficiency in Basque. As Arzamendi and Genesee (1997) point out, preparing teachers for diversity can be difficult but at the same time a desirable goal. Teachers in the Basque Country also face some challenges associated with the minority status of Basque. Many teachers are not native speakers of Basque and even some teachers who are native speakers have limited literacy skills as the result of the short history of using Basque for academic purposes.

Table 3.3 Examples of in-service courses for teachers in 2008–09

Kindergarten	Cooperative games Theatre as a tool Oral communication in kindergarten
Primary	Learning to learn and learning to think Text comprehension and production Classroom observation
Secondary	Competence in linguistic communication Blogs as a didactic tool in language teaching The new language curriculum
General	Digital boards GPS as a didactic tool New technologies at school

On the other hand, as Ellis (2004) points out, teachers who have gone through the process of learning a language can understand their students better than monolingual teachers because they have developed a higher level of language awareness. Teacher language awareness as a crucial need in bilingual and multilingual education is also highlighted by Hélot (2007) and García (2007).

The development of teaching materials

Another challenge faced by the Basque educational system has traditionally been the shortage of teaching materials in Basque. A lot of progress has been made in this area and nowadays teachers and schools have a choice of different materials in Basque, except in the case of some subjects in vocational training. The development of new materials is an ongoing process as materials change to adapt to developments in society and also to new Spanish and Basque legal regulations. The materials used to teach Spanish and through the medium of Spanish are in many cases the same as those used in Spanish schools outside the BAC. Materials to teach Basque and through the medium of Basque include books, workbooks, guidebooks for teachers, and reference materials (dictionaries, encyclopaedias, maps, tests, etc). Some examples of books can be seen in Figure 3.3.

Materials are not only printed and they include audiovisual material, multimedia and internet-based products. They have been especially developed in the Basque Country and in many cases are not translated from other languages. Some examples can be seen in Figure 3.4.

Other more general tools available in Basque are Microsoft and Open Office systems http://www.euskara.euskadi.net/ and Wikipedia as can be seen in Figure 3.5.

Figure 3.3 Examples of textbooks in Basque published by Elkar (http://www.elkar.com), and Anaya-Haritza (http://www.haritza.es)

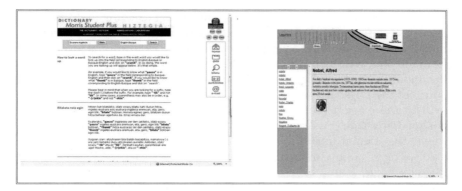

Figure 3.4 Examples of English-Basque online dictionary and an on-line encyclopaedia

Source: http://www1.euskadi.net/morris/ and http://www.donostia.org/euskara/entziklopedia.nsf

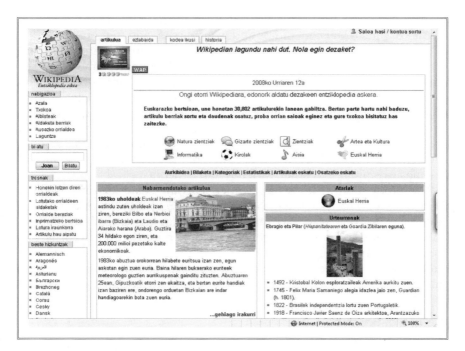

Figure 3.5 Wikipedia in Basque

Source: http://eu.wikipedia.org/

One of the main decisions to be made regarding teaching materials concerns the variety of Basque to be used at school. Basque has traditionally been used orally and had a very limited use at the institutional level. Apart from the poor writing tradition and the low social prestige of the language, the mountainous terrain of the Basque Country spreading North and South of the Pyrenees and the administrative division of the country can explain the existence of different Basque dialects. The Academy of the Basque Language (Euskaltzaindia), founded in 1918, has played a crucial role in the standardization of the Basque language at the oral and written levels. The Academy defined a unified standard variety of Basque called 'Euskara Batua' (unified Basque) in the 60s. This variety is based on the central dialects of Lapurdi and Gipuzkoa and includes standard orthography, morphology and forms for place names. The Basque Academy and other institutions have also published grammar books and dictionaries. Other varieties are used mainly for oral communication and there are important differences in pronunciation mainly between the Northern and the Southern provinces. 'Euskara Batua' is nowadays the most widespread variety of Basque and is generally used in official documents, the mass media (Basque television, radios and newspapers) and in literature.

'Euskara Batua' is also the variety used at school, in educational materials and in the teaching of Basque as a second language. Some years ago there were some reactions against standard Basque mainly in the case of speakers of varieties which were not very close to 'Euskara Batua' and as Idiazabal (1998) points out, some mistakes were made banning other varieties of Basque. Nowadays, many teachers use other varieties orally but textbooks are usually in 'Batua'. The dispute about the variety to be used in education is not at the forefront because of the extended use of standard Basque as compared to other varieties in the media.

The production of books and other teaching materials in Basque is funded by a grant system which started in 1996 so that the price of these materials is not higher for parents than that of similar materials in Spanish. The approximate number of school materials published per year is 400, including printed materials, audiovisual materials and software. These materials also include important aspects of Basque culture as part of the curriculum, particularly in areas such as geography and history.

The use of Basque

Another challenge for the survival of Basque is the actual use of Basque. The success promoting the minority language in formal situations in the school context is not reflected in language use in informal contexts at school and in society at large. It can be said that the Basque language is still a language 'at risk'. Proficiency in the language has increased but many Basque speakers have Spanish as their first language and they feel more comfortable using Spanish than Basque. This is also the case of schoolchildren. Their communicative need to use Basque outside the classroom is low because Basque speakers are also proficient in Spanish. There are important geographical differences in the use of Basque and Basque is the dominant language inside and outside the school in some towns and villages (mainly in Gipuzkoa) but Spanish is dominant in the majority of the cities and towns of the Basque Country. It is common for schoolchildren instructed through the medium of Basque to use Spanish with their classmates or in sport and leisure activities.

The Basque Government Department of Education has special programs to promote the use of Basque in the school context. The activities funded include school drama, traditional sung verse, school choirs, story telling, school radio, short-stays in a Basque speaking atmosphere, visits to schools by Basque authors, prize contests to improve elocution and writing skills, etc. Individual schools apply for funding for specific activities. Approximately 2500 activities are funded every year.

A related program to promote language use which benefits from the funding for specific activities is the Ulibarri project. The idea is that each school participating in this project develops a language policy plan to improve the use of Basque in their own school. The goal of this program is to increase the quality and use of Basque in the school context. As Aldekoa and Gardner (2002) explain, the first step for schools is to conduct a diagnosis of the knowledge and use of Basque. The diagnosis is based on the general information about the oral and written use of Basque in the school in general and on the responses to questionnaires completed by students on the use of Basque in specific situations. Then a language normalization plan including a long term five year reference point and short term objectives is elaborated and the tasks to be carried out are described. Once the plan is approved, it is implemented and different activities are carried out. At the end of the academic year, the language policy plan is assessed by the different parties involved. The evaluations indicate that there has been an improvement in the use of Basque in the schools where the Ulibarri projects have been implemented. The Ulibarri projects vary from school to school because they are designed by the schools themselves in coordination with the language plans in the municipality. This bottom-up approach makes the plans more specific for each school and develops a sense of ownership which is not achieved with top-down plans that are designed by the Government and just implemented in the schools. The organization of school-based projects is more complex than when the same project is implemented in different schools and its assessment is also more context-related but school directors and teachers' degree of involvement can produce better results. Over 150,000 students and 16,000 teachers have taken part in this program up to now (www.ulibarri.info). In spite of these efforts it is very difficult to reverse the habits acquired over the years to use one language. As Aldekoa and Gardner (2002) point out, when a minority language such as Basque is in contact with a strong language spoken by everybody it is to be expected that there will be a gap between language knowledge and language use.

Martínez de Luna and Suberbiola (2008) conducted a research study so as to identify the variables that could predict the use of Basque at school. Participants were 1325 students in the sixth year of primary school from 50 schools in different areas of the BAC. Apart from completing tests and questionnaires, the students were observed both inside the classroom and in the playground. The research study was conducted mainly with model D students and the results indicate 68% of the sample used Basque in the playground. When looking at the predictors of language use the variables related to the student's network of close relations were the most influential. Variables such as the use of Basque with friends or at home were significant predictors but other variables such as the relative ease to speak Basque or the use of Basque in the hometown were also significant.

Torres-Guzman and Etxeberria (2005) reported that B model students use Basque approximately 50% of the time at school with their classmates. However this study was based on self-assessment of the use of Basque and the percentage may be much lower because students may report what they think they should do rather than what they do in actual practice. Another study on the use of Basque at school both in class and in the playground is reported by Martínez de Luna (2006). Participants were 1415 schoolchildren in the 6th year of primary (11–12 years old) in 42 different schools. The percentages of use of Basque can be seen in Table 3.4.

Table 3.4 Use of Basque in class and the playground in 42 Basque schools (%)

	In class	*In the playground*
A model	35	0
B model	66	11
D model	83	67

The data indicate that there are not only very important differences between the models but also between the class and the playground particularly in models A and B where it is exceptional to have children with Basque as their first language. Martínez de Luna and Suberbiola (2008) analyzed the influence of different factors on the use of Basque in the playground and found that the use of Basque by other members of the group was the most important predictor followed by the use of Basque in the student's hometown and student's relative ease with Basque. This study confirms the strong links between use of Basque and the social networks.

Apart from the specific focus on schools, there are campaigns to promote the use of Basque in society in general. The most recent one was *'Pixka bat es mucho'* which is a mixed Basque-Spanish sentence that can be translated as *'A little is a lot'*. It also uses the virus *'ukan'*, a good virus that you get when you speak Basque (see Figure 3.6). This campaign had a very catchy song and tried to encourage the use of Basque among speakers who are not fully proficient. According to the Basque Government

Figure 3.6 The virus *'ukan'* and the logo *'Pixka bat es mucho'*

Language Policy Department, it has been the first campaign with a massive response and had 100,000 hits on internet, 2000 DVDs and 2000 CDs (http://www.ejgv.euskadi.net/). Obviously, it is difficult to estimate the impact of this campaign on the actual use of Basque.

Apart from the amount of Basque students use, there is also a strong concern regarding the quality of the Basque language used by non-native speakers of Basque and the important influence of Spanish on Basque mainly in the lexicon and grammar (Larringan & Idiazabal, 2005). Some teachers and parents are concerned about the low quality of Basque even in the case of students with Basque as a first language. This is a concern also in monolingual situations but in the case of minority languages the problem can have implications for the future survival of the language because it is related to its limited use in everyday life. This concern has also been reported by Hickey (2007) in the Irish context. Hickey discusses the possibility of separating students according to the L1 rather than just dispersing speakers of Irish among the speakers of English without a specific language plan. In the Basque Country, the policy of separating native and non-native speakers of Basque is somewhat controversial but has been adopted in the early grades by some schools (see Cenoz, 1998). The advantage of this policy is that it creates a critical mass that can better withstand the dominating influence of Spanish and that it can provide the opportunity to develop literacy skills of speakers of Basque as a first language to a higher level. On the other hand, this policy has the problem of being considered as less egalitarian.

Another concern some people have is codemixing and codeswitching. These phenomena are common in bilingual and multilingual contexts but there is usually more influence from the majority language to the minority than the other way round (see for example Boix & Sanz, 2008). Apart from the minority situation of Basque, there are two other facts that explain this hybridity: the increasing number of speakers of Basque who have Spanish as their first language and the fact that everybody in the BAC understands Spanish. The term '*euskañol*' (euskara + español, Basque + Spanish) is sometimes used to refer to this codemixing and codeswitching in a similar way as 'Spanglish' in the USA. Boundaries between languages are softer in daily communication than in textbooks and classes. New technologies are contributing to softening boundaries between languages and between oral and written language. This hybridity is multimodal with symbols and visuals combined with language (see Jewitt & Kress 2003; Magnan, 2008). These uses of different resources in communication are also affecting Basque. For example the logo '*Pixka bat es mucho*' in Figure 3.6 combines Basque and Spanish and it is multimodal combining words and

Table 3.5 Examples of texting dictionary in Basque

}i{	tximeleta	butterfly
BIN	Berandu iritsiko naiz	I will be late
2ar	bihar	tomorrow
HNDN	Hitz egin nahi duzu nirekin?	Do you want to talk to me?

Source: Based on http://www.argia.com/cgi-bin/mantxut/sms.cgi

visual elements and even a song. New ways of using Basque in texting have also been developed as in the examples in Table 3.5.

There are no studies about the actual use of Basque for new types of communication (texting, chatting, emailing, etc) but both the amount of Basque and the way Basque is used could be worth analyzing. Schools can teach Basque and through Basque but the time spent by a child in class is limited and the use of Basque is closely linked to its development in society at large.

Immigrant students

An additional challenge for the Basque educational system is to adapt the educational system so as to integrate the increasing number of immigrant children who live in the BAC. The Basque Country received important waves of immigrants from the fifties to the seventies due to industrialization. In contrast to that earlier immigration these new immigrants do not come from Spain but from other countries. Spanish immigrant students in the past had the same language of instruction, Spanish, in almost all schools in the Basque Country. Nowadays the situation is different because many immigrants also come from countries where Spanish is not spoken and because Basque has become the main language of instruction.

The number of immigrants is not as high as in many other parts of Western Europe but it has increased substantially in the last years. The BAC had 121,776 immigrants in 2007 and this was 5.7% of its populations. The number of immigrants in Spain in the same year was 5,214,390, which is 11.56% of the total Spanish population. The percentage in the Basque Country has increased from 0.72% in the year 1998 to 5.7% in 2007. Immigrants in the BAC live in the three provinces but the percentage of immigrants is higher in Araba. According to 2007 data, most immigrants come from Latin America (Ikuspegi, 2007). The countries most immigrants living in the BAC come from are Colombia, Bolivia, Romania, Morocco, Portugal and Ecuador.

The educational data indicate that the number of immigrant students in schools in the BAC was approximately 0.6% in the academic year 1999–2000 but in the year 2008–09 there were 21,000 immigrant students in the BAC and that accounts for 6.58% of the total number of students in primary and secondary school. Most immigrants attend public schools (66.5%) and only 33.5% attend private schools (www.hezkuntza.net). The Basque Government has established 30% as the maximum number of immigrants in each school so that immigrants mix with the local population. As a result of the low birth rate in the BAC in the last decades Basque schools have enough space and enough teachers to cope with immigrant students, at least for the time being. More than half of the immigrant children attending schools in the BAC (59%) come from Latin America and already speak Spanish. The rest of the immigrant students come from Africa (20%), Europe (17.4%) and Asia (3.2%) (Etxeberria & Elosegi, 2008).

The percentage of immigrants who have Basque as the language of instruction is much lower than for the total number of students in the BAC. Approximately 50% of the immigrant students are enrolled in model A, approximately 27% in model B and 23% in model D. The distribution of the total number of students in the three models is different with a much higher percentage of students learning through the medium of Basque. Therefore, half of the immigrant students do not study through the medium of Basque and only have the minimum compulsory number of hours of Basque. This creates a concentration of immigrant students in some schools, mainly in public schools in the A model. The reasons for immigrant students not to have Basque as the language of instruction can be several. In many cases, the children are speakers of a language other than Spanish and depending on their age, they may have problems to get used to a different system in a different language. In other cases the parents may think that it is not interesting to learn a minority language and that perhaps in the future they may live in another place or go back to their home country. Some parents are not aware of the different possibilities and do not realize that speaking Basque could have advantages for their children if they lived in the BAC.

Manzanos and Ruiz Pinedo (2005) asked immigrant parents to complete a questionnaire about different aspects of education including the languages at school. The results indicate that 64.8% of the parents would like their children to learn through the languages of the Basque Country and also to promote the knowledge of their own language. Some parents (21.5%) would like their children to learn through their L1 but also to learn the languages of the Basque Country. Some other parents (12.3%) thought that it was better that they just learned the languages of the Basque

Country. These data indicate that parents realize that children have to learn the languages of the host country but many of them would also like their children to speak their first language and to use it at school to a certain extent.

The integration of immigrants in Basque schools and in Basque society is complex as it is the case in other schools and societies in other countries. Some of the main worries are the following:

- There could be a process of *'ghettoisation'* with high concentrations of immigrant children in A model schools in some areas.
- The effort made to teach and use Basque in the educational system could be threatened by the integration of more non-Basque speakers.

The Observatory for Immigration, a Basque Government agency, explored these concerns in a study conducted in 2004 (Ikuspegi, 2004). Participants were 1787 subjects who had been living in the BAC for at least five years. The data were elicited by means of an interview about different aspects of immigration including questions related to schooling. The majority of the participants (77%) considered that having immigrant children in Basque schools can be a positive and enriching experience but that the number of immigrants is an important factor. When asked if the quality of the schools with a large number of immigrants was lower, 25% of the participants agreed but 58% did not agree. The study does not include any questions about the bilingual models but when asked about the possible influence that the arrival of foreign people could have on the development of Basque, most participants (71.4%) said that they did not think it was a problem but 17.8% were concerned about this issue.

The Basque Government Department of Education (2003) elaborated guidelines for programs aimed at the schooling of immigrants in the BAC (http://www.hezkuntza.net). The aim of these programs should be that immigrant students learn the official languages of the BAC and that they have the same curriculum as Basque children. In order to achieve these aims the first step is to make a diagnosis of the educational and linguistic needs of immigrant children and to attend to those needs by reinforcing the teaching of some areas and adapting the curriculum. Another important point is to teach Basque children to accept immigrant children as their equals and to promote the knowledge and integration of different cultures.

The specific actions that are being carried out include the publication of a multilingual guide explaining the main characteristics of the Basque educational system in nine languages: Basque, Spanish, English, French, Portuguese, Russian, Romanian, Arabic and Chinese (www.hezkuntza.

net). Other actions include specific guidelines for the schools to deal with new immigrant students, the development of specific materials, teacher education in interculturalism, additional teachers for classes with immigrants and support for programs to teach the immigrants' mother tongue and culture. Some direct economic measures are grants for immigrant children and additional funding for schools with a high percentage of immigrant children. These actions have not been spread to all schools with immigrants to the same extent and teachers consider that they need more support to deal with this new situation mainly regarding specific materials and teacher training. The Department of Education also encourages parents to enroll their children in models B and D and there is a trend to do this in the cases of very young children but not so much when immigrant students arrive to the Basque Country at a later age.

The arrival of immigrant students has affected the general organization of many schools as well as their teaching methodology. Some schools have developed their own projects so as to highlight interculturalism and multilingualism. The idea is that when immigrant students feel that their own language and culture is valued they will integrate better and will also obtain higher proficiency in different languages.

There are also some specific programs to develop the first language and its culture. The most important ones are for Portuguese and Arabic (see Etxeberria & Elosegi, 2008). As Etxeberria and Elosegi state the Portuguese Language and Culture Program, which has been running in the Basque Country for 13 years, is truly intercultural and has more Spanish than Portuguese students enrolled in it. This program is part of the school curriculum. The Arab Language and Moroccan Culture program has two models with classes taught either within the school timetable or as an additional subject not included in the curriculum. The case of Arabic is complex because the language taught is official classical Arabic and most children have either colloquial Arabic or Berber as their first language. In contrast with the Portuguese program there are very few non-immigrant students in the Arab language program.

Research on immigration is still extremely limited in the BAC. There are some studies that have collected some data from questionnaires and interviews about different aspects of the degree of integration of immigrants as it can be seen in Table 3.6.

The first two studies in this table were carried out in Araba and the third one in Gipuzkoa. They look at different aspects of integration and the study by Etxeberria and Elosegi also looks at achievement.

Septien (2006) reported that most immigrant students enjoyed going to school in their countries of origin except for some Moroccan and Romanian

Table 3.6 Studies with immigrant students

	Sample	Models	Questionnaires
Septien 2006	103 secondary school students 120 teachers	A	Students' background, educational situation in country of origin and host country, SES, family relations, social relations. Teachers' questionnaire School directors' questionnaire
Ibarrarán et al. 2007	71 secondary school students 9 teachers	A	Students' background questionnaire and attitudes towards Basque, Spanish, English, other L1 Teachers: focused discussion
Etxeberria and Elosegi 2008	160 primary school students (2nd and 6th years)	D	Tests of Basque: reading, writing, listening, speaking Questionnaires: self-esteem and expectations, levels of satisfaction, motivation about Basque

who complained about the schools in their own countries. Immigrant students are generally happy in schools in the BAC. Most students (62%) think that the relationship with their teachers is good or very good and 31% that it is just average. Latin American students reported that their relationship with teachers was closer in their country but students from other countries say that teachers are closer to students in the BAC. When asked about the relationship with their classmates 66% think it is good or very good and 29% think that it is just average. The study also gives interesting information about school subjects. Spanish is considered a difficult subject for those immigrant students who do not have Spanish as a first language. Spanish speaking immigrants find mathematics the most difficult subject. The participants in this study are in secondary schools and most of them (74%) do not study Basque at all.

Septien also got information from teachers and school directors. Teachers think that the number of immigrants can have some influence on achievement and that the age of arrival is strongly related to achievement. Younger immigrants obtain better grades and integrate better than older immigrants. Even though there is some specific teacher training for teachers working with immigrants, teachers and school directors highlight the need for more specific training programs.

Ibarraran, Lasagabaster and Sierra (2007) focused on attitudes towards Basque, Spanish, English and the immigrants' first language. All the participants were in model A and their questionnaires were compared to those of 53 non-immigrant students in model A. The results indicate that there were no differences in attitudes towards Basque when immigrants and autochthonous students were compared and that the attitudes towards Basque were quite negative or neutral for both groups. The attitudes towards Spanish were more positive and there were no differences between immigrant and non-immigrant students either. Immigrant students had more positive attitudes towards English than local students and in general, attitudes towards English were more positive than attitudes towards Basque. Those students who did not have Spanish as a first language were also asked about their attitudes towards their own first language and these were in general very positive. Even though the sample in this study is very small, it is interesting to see the differences between the attitudes towards the different languages. The fact that attitudes towards Spanish are more positive than attitudes towards Basque both for immigrant and non-immigrant students could be related to the characteristics of the sample with a majority of students with Spanish as the first language. It is interesting to observe that there are differences in the attitudes towards English and it is difficult to explain the specific reasons for this but one possibility is that immigrant students are more aware of the importance of English internationally. This is just a possibility that needs to be confirmed in future studies.

Etxeberria and Elosegi (2008) conducted their study in primary school in the D model. They reported that immigrant schoolchildren who attended school from a very early age (2–3 year old) had achieved the same level of oral skills in Basque as the rest of their classmates by the second year of primary. Children, who had arrived to the Basque Country when they were about 9 or 10 years old, had lower scores than Basque children when they were evaluated at the end of primary school (11–12 years old). Immigrant children obtained lower results in the different skills in the Basque language test and in the levels of self-esteem and motivation to learn Basque. They scored similarly to Basque children in the level of expectations and the degree of satisfaction with the school. As Etxeberria and Elosegi (2008) say, these results are quite worrying because the level of competence in Basque can affect immigrant students' progress in other areas of the curriculum and their low level of self-esteem can also make their integration more difficult.

It is important that immigrant children are provided with the same educational tools as the rest of children. These tools include the knowledge of the official languages of the BAC. As Sainz and Ruiz Bikandi (2006) point out, one of the objectives of school is socialization, and the tool for socialization is language. Immigrant children usually need special linguistic and non-linguistic support in the first years so as to be able to follow the same curriculum as other children. It is difficult to predict what the impact of immigration will be on the survival of the Basque language. This impact is probably linked to the development of language awareness and interculturalism so that both immigrant and non-immigrant students value and get interested in others' languages and cultures (see Kenner, 2004; Candelier, 2007; Hélot, 2007).

Conclusion

This chapter discusses the use of the minority language as the language of instruction. In the case of Basque, the minority language has become the main language of instruction in the BAC. This shift from majority-medium to minority-medium instruction has faced many challenges which are also shared in bilingual and multilingual education in other contexts. The information in this chapter shows that schools and the society in which they are located are dynamic and the needs and challenges that Basque in education faced some decades ago are different today. Nowadays, Basque bilingual education has solved some problems but faces new challenges. One of the main challenges is the need to move from bilingualism to multilingualism and from a relatively homogeneous society to a multicultural society. In order to do this, the Basque educational system needs to combine its own experience in bilingual education with the experience of other countries with a longer tradition in multilingual and multicultural classrooms.

Key Points

- Basque, a minority language, which was not taught in most schools until 1982, is the main medium of instruction in the Basque Autonomous Community.
- Teaching through a minority language faces pedagogical challenges: the development of teaching materials, the use of a standard variety or the need for qualified teachers.
- Education is dynamic and Basque and other minority languages face new challenges nowadays: the need to acquire English as an additional language, the use of new technologies or the arrival of immigrant speakers of other languages.
- Language use in everyday communication is a major challenge in the case of Basque and other minority languages.

Chapter 4

Learning through the Minority Language: Linguistic and Academic Outcomes

Introduction

Assessment is an integral part of the educational process. It is necessary so as to check academic progress and to guide and improve instruction. As Zalbide (2000) points out, there are different aspects of education through the medium of Basque that can be assessed. First, we can consider whether Basque-medium instruction has been successful in attracting students. Second, we can also examine whether appropriate learning has taken place and third, we can see whether instruction through the minority language has had an impact on the degree of use of the language and the vitality of the language. Regarding the first point, the Basque educational system has been very successful in attracting a large number of students as it can be shown in the increasing number of students in the B and D models. The percentages of students using Basque as the language of instruction given in Chapter 3 are quite impressive as compared to those of other contexts such as Ireland (Ó Riagáin, 2007) or Friesland (Riemersma & De Jong, 2007). The third aspect of assessment looks at the effect of education on the general revitalization of the language. In this case it can be said that bilingual education has contributed to develop proficient speakers of Basque but the impact of the Basque-medium education on language use seems to be more limited. According to studies on language use based on observation, the use of Basque is the BAC is increasing but in a limited way (see Altuna, 2007).

The second point, the question of appropriate learning, is extremely important not only for students and their families but also for society at large. Assessment is considered an integral part of the learning process. Apart from traditional tests, many other tools can also be used for assessing students' progress: observational checklists, journals, portfolios including work samples, anecdotal records, collective group work, day-to-day activities, interviews, etc. The information obtained from these sources can provide feedback to students and teachers. Teachers have to evaluate also their own teaching process and practice as related to students' achievement. Apart from continuous assessment, external evaluations are also needed to have a global perspective of achievement in bilingual programs. The results of these external evaluations will be discussed in this chapter.

Linguistic and Academic Outcomes in Mother Tongue Education and Immersion

Research on bilingual education has shown that the use of the minority language at school can have positive consequences. Cummins (2003: 61–62) highlights that bilingualism can have positive effects on children's linguistic and educational development because the level of development of the L1 is a strong predictor of development in the L2. It is also interesting to look at the results of meta-analyses of research studies on minority language children in the USA reported by Genesee and Riches (2006). These analyses show that learners who receive some reading instruction in the L1 in the primary grades achieve, at least, the same level of performance and in some cases even a higher level of performance in L2 reading than learners of similar linguistic and cultural backgrounds who have only received initial literacy and instruction in English.

López (2006) reports the successful transfer of key competences from indigenous first to the second language in Guatemala and Bolivia when first languages are used as languages of instruction. According to López and Sichra (2007: 300) the benefits are not only limited to L1 and L2 development but extend to *'academic achievement, active participation in learning and development of positive self image, self-esteem and respect'*. Additional evidence to prove the advantages of using the first language as the language of instruction can be found in the large scale studies conducted in the USA by Thomas and Collier (1997, 2002) who reported faster development of the second language and better academic performance. Mohanty (2006) also points out that there are social psychological and educational benefits when the first language is maintained along with other languages in India. McCarty (2007: 242) explains that students who 'experience sustained initial literacy instruction' in the minority language, e.g. Navajo in the USA, obtain better scores in the majority language, English.

In general terms, research in immersion education for language-majority students has also shown that students learn another language and acquire literacy skills at no cost to their overall academic achievement or their first language skills (Genesee, 1987, 2004; Swain & Lapkin, 1982; Johnson & Swain, 1997). These results work for early total immersion but also for dual language programs or two-way immersion programs, where students from language minority and majority backgrounds are in the same class and both languages are used as languages of instruction (Genesee & Riches, 2006). These results indicate that language-majority students who use the L1 on a daily basis outside school can have an L2 as a language of instruction at no cost for their L1 or for achievement in academic domains such as science, mathematics and social studies. Proficiency in the L2 in immersion programs is higher in receptive skills than in productive skills. Students in total immersion generally achieve higher levels of proficiency in the L2 than those in partial immersion but intensity seems to be also an important factor. In general terms, these results originally reported for Canadian immersion have been confirmed in other contexts (Johnson & Swain, 1997; Genesee, 2004).

Immersion has some limitations because students do not have many opportunities to practice the second language particularly in contexts where the second language is not used outside the classroom (see Swain, 1995; Baetens Beardsmore & Swain, 1985). Lyster (2007) highlights the need to provide 'counterbalanced instruction' in immersion classes so that students pay attention to language form in a meaning-oriented context.

The use of Basque as the language of instruction in the BAC combines teaching through the L1 to language-minority students with immersion in the L2 for language-majority students. According to international research both situations could be beneficial for language majority and minority children. However, bilingual and multilingual education is linked to the sociolinguistic and educational context in which it takes place and specific evaluations are necessary to confirm these outcomes.

In this chapter we look at different types of external evaluations of bilingual education regarding proficiency in Basque and Spanish and academic achievement. The results focusing on the influence of bilingual education on the acquisition of additional languages will be discussed in Chapter 7.

Basque Achievement in International Perspective

One of the main points to consider when examining bilingual education is the overall level achieved by children in different subjects in the curriculum. The ideas of the very early studies on bilingualism suggesting that bilingualism could be a handicap for normal cognitive development are no longer accepted. In contrast, bilingualism and multilingualism have been associated with a higher level of metalinguistic awareness and other aspects of cognitive development (Bialystok, 2003; Baker, 2007b). We also know that bilingualism is not always associated with advantages. Following Lambert's (1974) distinction between additive and subtractive bilingualism, we can also find cases of subtractive bilingualism mainly associated with weaker social and economic backgrounds. For example, many immigrant students in Western Europe and North America, who speak a home language which is different from the school language, have more problems at school than non-immigrant children. In these cases the first language does not develop fully because it is limited to the home context and it is replaced by the language of the host country. Basque-speaking children also had their first language replaced by Spanish in the past but nowadays they have Basque as the main language of instruction and also study Spanish and English at school.

In this section we will look at the results obtained by Basque children, who are in a bilingual educational system and we will compare them with the results of children in other contexts. In order to do so we are going to focus on the results of two international evaluations: the PISA (Programme for International Student Assessment) evaluation conducted by the Organization for Economic Cooperation and Development (OECD[1]) and the TIMSS evaluation conducted by the International Evaluation Association (IEA[2]). The results of these evaluations can give us information about the general level of achievement of the Basque educational system as compared to the average results in Spain and other countries.

The PISA evaluation

The PISA assessments (http://www.pisa.oecd.org) started in 2000 and are carried out every three years. There are specific data for the BAC for the years 2003 and 2006 (ISEI-IVEI, 2004a, 2008). The main focus of the test in 2003 was on mathematics and in 2006 on science. The aim of the PISA assessment is to evaluate how well prepared students are for life and to provide comparative data for educational authorities:

> to develop indicators to the extent of which the educational systems in participating countries have prepared 15-year-olds to play constructive roles as citizens in society. (PISA Assessment Framework, OECD 2003: 24)

The tests are pencil-and-paper and students also complete a questionnaire for background information including motivation and learning strategies. Tests items include multiple-choice questions and open questions and students are tested when they are 15–16 years old. School directors fill in a questionnaire to provide background information about the school and the students.

The 2006 PISA assessment was signed by 57 countries including Spain and measured mathematics, reading literacy and science. The tests try to measure the students' capacities to use knowledge in real life situations. The tests are based on curricular subjects but the idea is to measure how the knowledge of these subjects is applied to solving problems in everyday life. The 2006 PISA results include 57 countries, 30 belonging to the OECD and 27 non-OECD countries. Apart from these countries, several regions such as the Basque Country have taken part in the evaluation. The ISEI-IVEI institute (Basque Institute for Research and Evaluation in Education) is the Basque Government agency responsible for the PISA evaluations in the BAC.

The PISA assessment identifies different levels of performance and students are placed in a performance level according to their responses to the items. Table 4.1 includes the countries with the best five scores for the three tests in 2006:

The results obtained in the Basque Country are not among the highest for any of the tests. The following table includes the results for the BAC, Spain and the OECD average (see Table 4.2).

The BAC achieved significantly higher results than the Spanish average in Mathematics and Reading Literacy. Reading literacy in the BAC was measured in only one language, the student's first language. There were no significant differences between the results of the BAC and the OECD average in any of the three tests. There were no significant differences

Table 4.1 PISA 2006: Countries with the highest scores

Science		Mathematics		Reading literacy	
Finland	563	Taipei	549	Korea	556
Hong Kong	542	Finland	548	Finland	547
Canada	534	Hong Kong	547	Hong Kong	536
Taipei	532	Korea	547	Canada	527
Estonia	531	Netherlands	531	New Zealand	521
Japan	531				
OECD average	500		498		492

Source: OECD, 2007

Table 4.2 PISA 2006: Results for the BAC, Spain and OECD

	BAC	*Spain*	*OECD average*
Science	495	488	500
Mathematics	501	480	498
Reading literacy	487	461	492

Source: ISEI-IVEI, 2008

between the BAC and Spain in Science but the Basque curriculum for these participants had fewer hours of science than the Spanish curriculum. Even though these results cannot be regarded as excellent and there is a lot of space for improvement, they indicate that Basque students are doing better that many students who are not in bilingual education in other areas of Spain. The comparison of the results for the BAC between 2003 and 2006 indicates that this trend is quite stable with a significant improvement in science and no significant differences from the average of the OECD in any of the three areas. The results in reading literacy are worse in 2006 than in the previous evaluation for the Basque Country but this is also the case for the average of the OECD. The results of the students in the BAC are relatively homogeneous and there are few students with very high or very low scores.

The TIMSS assessment

TIMSS, the 'Trends in International Mathematics and Science Study', undertaken by the 'International Association for Evaluation of Educational Achievement' (IEA) is another test which is carried out every four years (http://isc.bc.edu/). The Basque Country took part in the 2003 and 2007 evaluations but other areas of Spain did not take part (ISEI-IVEI, 2005abc, 2009). The TIMSS evaluation is carried out in the fourth and eight years which in the Basque system correspond to the fourth year of primary and the second year of secondary. In this case, the grade is taken into account and not the students' age as it is the case with the PISA assessment. Approximately 50 countries take part in each of the evaluations. As compared to the PISA assessment, TIMSS measures more traditional classroom content. For example, in the case of mathematics there are cognitive domains (knowing facts and procedures, using concepts, solving routine problems and reasoning) and contents domains (numbers, algebra, measurement, geometry and data). The TIMSS assessment provides information about different countries and information about performance over time. It also includes questionnaires to be filled in by students, directors, teachers and national coordinators. These questionnaires contain questions about many different factors related to the school such as the use of computers, teacher education, attitudes, evaluation or the curriculum (http://isc.bc.edu/). Table 4.3 includes the countries with the best five scores for Science and Mathematics in 2007. As it can be seen, some of them were also among the first in the PISA evaluation.

The ISEI-IVEI organized the 2007 assessment in the Basque Country. This assessment was carried out only in the eighth grade which is the second year of secondary. A sample of 2296 students from 120 schools enrolled in the three linguistic models took the test. The results are shown in Table 4.4.

The results of the TIMSS corresponding to the Basque Country are very close to the average results for the countries participating in the TIMSS evaluation both in Mathematics and Science. The results in mathematics were better than the average results in numbers, but not in algebra, measurement and data and geometry. In science, the results were significantly better in Life Science, but worse in Chemistry and there were no significant differences in Physics and Biology.

Another index to see the results of Basque education in international perspective is to look at the percentage of students who finish post-compulsory

Table 4.3 TIMSS 2007: Countries with the highest scores

Science		_Mathematics_	
Singapore	567	Taipei	598
Taipei	561	Korea	597
Massachusetts	556	Singapore	593
Japan	554	Hong Kong	572
Korea	553	Japan	570
TIMSS average	500		500

Source: ISEI-IVEI, 2009

Table 4.4 TIMSS 2007: Data from the Basque Country

	Basque Country	_TIMSS_
Science	498	500
Mathematics	499	500

Source: ISEI-IVEI, 2009

secondary education. A recent comparison made by the OECD shows that the percentage of Spanish students has reached 64% but it is still far from the OECD average of 77%, and the European Union 79% (Ministerio de Educación y Ciencia, 2007: 14). This percentage in the Basque Autonomous Community is 81% which is slightly higher than the European Union percentage and 17% higher than the Spanish percentage.

These results along with those of the PISA assessment indicate that the scores of the BAC can be placed within the average or higher than average in international evaluations. The results also indicate that the Basque Country is above the Spanish average scores in the PISA evaluation. These evaluations include students in all the models and the A model cannot be regarded in a strict sense as a bilingual model but they indicate that bilingual education is not preventing the Basque Country from getting competitive scores. This does not mean that bilingualism is a causal factor and there are other factors such as socioeconomic status or the amount of money invested in education which can be explain the results. This type of evaluation has its limitations and can only be considered as a reference but it shows that bilingual education is compatible with academic achievement. Obviously, the scores also indicate that there is room for improvement as compared to highest scores in Tables 4.1 and 4.3.

Achievements in the Different Models

Another important issue to consider is the differences between the linguistic models, taking into account that many students with Spanish as their L1 have Basque as the language of instruction. There has been a lot of interest over the last decades to see whether teaching through Basque has an effect on linguistic and academic achievement. In this section we will consider early research and more recent evaluations.

Early research

Several evaluations of the Basque bilingual programs were carried out between 1974 and 2000, with approximately 26,000 students having taken part in these evaluations (see Etxeberria, 1999). Some of these evaluations are research studies conducted at the university and others have been carried out by different institutions. In many cases the aim was not to get results which were representative of the BAC but to analyze a specific school or a specific area. The evaluations have focused on several areas: proficiency in Basque and Spanish, academic development, and foreign language acquisition. In some cases they also looked at the influence of different factors on language acquisition and language use. In this chapter we will discuss results of early and more recent research on these areas with the exception of the effect of bilingual education on the acquisition of a foreign language which will be discussed in Chapter 6.

   Basque. The results of the Basque language evaluations indicate that there are significant differences in Basque proficiency when the three models are compared (Gabiña *et al.*, 1986; Sierra & Olaziregi, 1989, 1991a; Sierra 1996; see also Cenoz, 1998 and Etxeberria, 1999 for a review). Students in model D are more proficient in Basque than students in model B who, in turn, are more proficient than students in model A. Some studies have reported differences in model D according to the home language. Students who speak Basque at home obtained higher scores but not in all cases.

   Spanish. Results from most evaluations of the students' proficiency in Spanish indicate that there are no significant differences among the models (see Cenoz, 1998; Etxeberria, 1999 for a review). Even model D students, who study Spanish for only 4–5 hours a week and are in many cases native speakers of Basque, achieve very high levels of proficiency in Spanish. Some research studies indicate that the level of Spanish is slightly higher when Spanish is used as the home language (Urrutia *et al.*, 1998).

   Academic Development. Evaluations of achievement in mathematics and science indicate that there are no significant differences between students in different models (Aierbe *et al.*, 1974, 1989; Sierra, 1996). Some studies have also looked at the influence of the language of testing. For example, Lukas (1994) analyzed results in mathematics in the B model when the test was in Basque and in Spanish. He found that B model students did better than A model students when tested in Spanish but worse than D model students when the language used was Basque and they had studied mathematics through the medium of Spanish. Lukas (1994) also reported differences between the scores obtained in public and private schools when the language of testing was Basque. The private B model schools did better than the public B model schools. Good results for private A and B model schools were reported by Urrutia *et al.* (1998) in a study conducted in 1992–93. In this study it was also found that students in model A, which was the one with most students at the time, obtained better results than students in models B and D in some subject areas.

   In sum, the results of the early comparisons of the models regarding academic development are quite mixed. One of the possible explanations for this can be related to the language of testing and the tests used to measure subjects such as social science which to a certain extent have a different curriculum in the materials used for the different models. For example, geography or history can focus mainly on Spain in some A model schools and mainly on the Basque Country in some D model schools. This problem has been taken into consideration in more recent evaluations.

More recent evaluations

The establishment of the Basque Institute for Evaluation and Research in Education (ISEI-IVEI) in 2001 has been crucial for the evaluation of different aspects of Basque education. Apart from taking part in international evaluations, ISEI-IVEI has carried out many other evaluations in recent years. As compared to the early evaluations reported above, the evaluations carried out by ISEI–IVEI try to be representative of the BAC and include large samples of students from the three Basque provinces enrolled in public and private schools in the three linguistic models. In this section we will look at evaluations of primary and secondary schools. In the case of primary school, the evaluation was carried out in 2004 and includes different areas of the curriculum (ISEI-IVEI, 2006). In the case of secondary school we will look at four different evaluations so as to cover the different areas: the PISA assessment, the TIMSS assessment, secondary school evaluation 2000 and Basque language B2.

The characteristics of the samples participating in these evaluations are given in Table 4.5.

The primary school evaluation 2004 (ISEI-IVEI, 2006) was carried out in the 6th level of primary school, that is, in the last year of primary school when children are 11–12 years old. A similar evaluation but including fewer areas was conducted in 1999 and is not included in this table (see ISEI-IVEI, 2002). The PISA and the TIMSS assessments are the ones we have already reported but in this section specific information about the models will be given. The secondary education evaluation was carried out in 2000 and the B2 Basque language evaluation in 2004–05. All the evaluations have been carried out by the ISEI-IVEI (ISEI-IVEI, 2002, 2004a, 2005abcd, 2006, 2008). All these evaluations include public and private schools and students enrolled in the different models. It can be observed that the higher number of students in the B and D models in the primary school evaluation corresponds to the increasing number of students in the Basque-medium models which is more noticeable in primary school than in secondary school. The B2 Basque language evaluation did not include students in the A model because the pilot study showed that students in this model did not have enough proficiency to take this test. Table 4.6 shows the different areas measured in these evaluations.

Table 4.5 Samples in more recent evaluations

	Sample	*Grade*	*Models*
Primary school evaluation 2004	N 2053	Primary 6	A 472 B 562 D 1019
PISA 2006	N 3929	Secondary (age 15)	A 1075 B 851 D 2003
TIMSS 2007	N 2296	Secondary 2	A 549 B 557 D 1190
Secondary school evaluation 2000	N 2154	Secondary 4	A 926 B 455 D 773
Basque language B2	N 1191	Secondary 4	B 447 D744

Table 4.6 Tests included in the evaluations

	Primary school evaluation 2004	*Secondary school evaluations*
Basque proficiency	Listening, reading, writing, dictation, grammar and lexis	Secondary 2000: Listening, reading, writing, grammar and lexis B2: Listening, reading, writing, grammar and lexis, oral interaction PISA: Reading literacy
Spanish proficiency	Listening, reading, writing	2000: Reading, listening, writing, grammar and lexis, literature PISA: Reading literacy
Mathematics	Geometry, measurement, numbers, organization of the information	PISA tests TIMSS tests
Science	Different areas of science including social science Basque curriculum: specific on science and social science related to the Basque Country	PISA tests TIMSS tests

The different evaluations measure the most important areas of the curriculum. Some of the evaluations also included questionnaires for students, parents, directors, teachers and coordinators. In general, the tests were taken in Spanish when students had Spanish as the home language and in Basque when they had Basque as the home language and were enrolled in model D.

The results corresponding to the scores obtained in each of the tests by primary school students are given in Figures 4.1 to 4.4. The results indicate that private schools obtain higher scores than public schools in all the tests and models. This is going to be the common pattern that we are going to find in the Basque educational system, with the exception of the B2 evaluation in secondary school. The socioeconomic and socioeducational factors play an important role here. The comparison of the different models is the following:

Basque language proficiency. The results reflect the amount of Basque language in the curriculum. The best results correspond to the D model in which Basque is the language of instruction, followed by the B model with Basque and Spanish as the languages of instruction and the A model (Figure 4.1).

Spanish. The results do not show a clear pattern related to the models. The highest scored is the A model in the private system but the lowest results is the A model in the public system (Figure 4.2). Therefore the use of the majority language, Spanish, as the language of instruction does not seem to be as important as in the case of Basque.

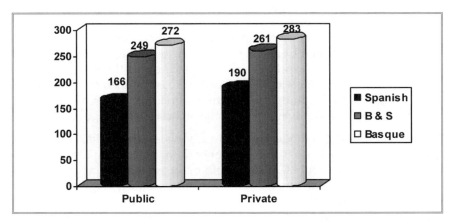

Figure 4.1 Basque proficiency in the 6th year of primary education (ISEI-IVEI, 2006)

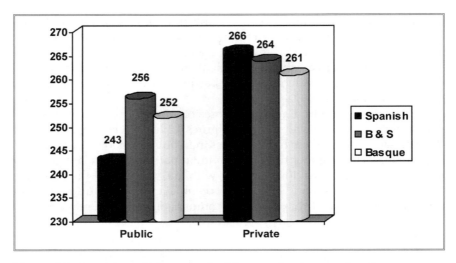

Figure 4.2 Spanish proficiency in the 6th year of primary education (ISEI-IVEI, 2006)

Mathematics. The highest score corresponds to the D model in private schools but there is no clear pattern regarding the models; private schools do better than public schools regardless of the model (Figure 4.3).

Science. There have been two different tests of science (including social science): one on the general aspects of the curriculum (Science G) and another on the specific aspects related to the Basque Country, Science B (knowledge of the environment, Basque institutions, Basque history, etc). In the case of the general curriculum, the highest score is achieved by the A model in private schools. Once again there is no pattern regarding the models and the lowest score is obtained by the A model in public schools. In the case of the Basque curriculum, the D model (both public and private) obtains the highest scores (Figure 4.4).

The results of the D model in private schools are the highest in Basque, Mathematics and Science B and are higher than the mean in the other two tests (Spanish and Science G.). The results of the A model in private schools are the highest in Spanish and Science G and are over the mean in two other tests (Mathematics and Science B.) but are relatively low in Basque. The B model in private schools also achieves relatively good results. The A model in the public system obtains the lowest results in all the tests and the results in the areas related to the Basque curriculum (Basque language

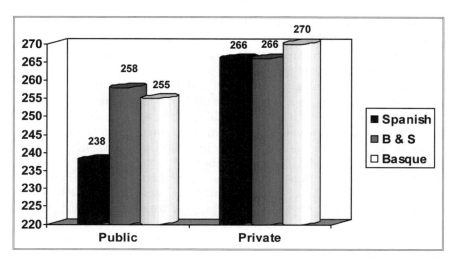

Figure 4.3 Mathematics in the 6th year of primary education (ISEI-IVEI, 2006)

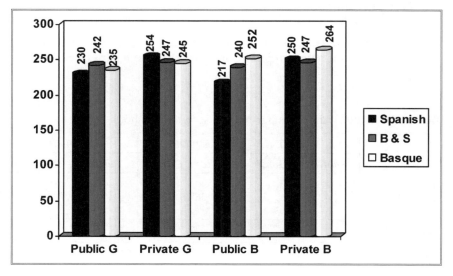

Figure 4.4 Science (General and Basque Curriculum) in the 6th year of primary education (ISEI-IVEI, 2006)

and Science B) are extremely poor. These results could be associated with a lower socioeconomic background of the students.

The ISEI-IVEI also compared the results of the 2004 evaluation to a previous evaluation conducted five years earlier in 1999 (ISEI-IVEI, 2002). In 1999 only three of the five areas were included: Spanish, Mathematics and Science G. The model that has improved most is the D model in private schools.

The results of the Primary 6 evaluation indicate that the differences between public and private schools are more important than the differences between the models. They also indicate that the best results are obtained by the D model in private schools.

The results of the different evaluations carried out in secondary schools are given in Table 4.7 and Figures 4.5 and 4.6. The evaluations include two different tests of Mathematics, two tests of Science, one of Spanish, two of Basque and the PISA reading literacy test which is for some students in Basque and for others in Spanish according to their first language. The reason for discussing different tests is that the tests have different aims and their items are also different. Comparing different tests to measure the same area of the curriculum can be interesting so as to see if the trends observed can be confirmed or not.

When we compare the different models in the different language tests in secondary school the findings indicate the following:

Basque. We have two measurements for Basque language and there is no distinction between public and private schools. In the Secondary

Table 4.7 Results of the language tests in secondary school

	A MODEL		B MODEL		D MODEL	
	Public	*Private*	*Public*	*Private*	*Public*	*Private*
Basque Secondary 2000	212.4		265.6		286.9	
Basque B2			27.5%		57.2%	
Spanish (Secondary 2000)	259.9		250.9		240.6	
Reading Literacy PISA 2006	423	507	468	506	479	490

2000 evaluation, which measures Basque language and literature, the highest results correspond to the D model and the lowest to the A model. The mean is 250 and the D model scores are significantly higher than the mean and the A model scores are significantly lower than the mean. These results go in the same direction as those of Basque in the Primary education evaluation (see ISEI-IVEI, 2004a).

The B2 evaluation is a pass/fail test of the Common European Framework B2 level (Council of Europe, 2002). The B2 level is described as the Vantage Independent Level:

> *Can understand the main ideas of complex text on both concrete and abstract topics, including technical discussions in his/her field of specialisation. Can interact with a degree of fluency and spontaneity that makes regular interaction with native speakers quite possible without strain for either party. Can produce clear, detailed texts on a wide range of subjects and explain a viewpoint on a topical issue giving the advantages and disadvantages of various options.* (Council of Europe, 2002: 24)

The results indicate that over 50% of the students in the D model have achieved the B2 level but only 27.5% of the students in the B model. The measures included listening comprehension, reading, writing, grammar and lexis. There were 1191 participants and a sub-sample of 243 students undertook an oral test. The results for this group including the oral test were a bit higher: 32.8% of the students in model B and 68% in model D passed the test. The results were higher among those who use Basque in their daily life and 72.6% achieved the B2 level. The results of this evaluation have been discussed in the press and have been quite controversial. There are different interpretations of the results but in general they are considered too low (see Chapter 8).

Spanish. The best results in the Secondary 2000 evaluation correspond to the A model and the lowest to the D model. This evaluation does not make a distinction between public and private schools. These results are different from those of Spanish in the Primary Education evaluation where there were no differences associated with the models. The differences in Spanish proficiency between the models have also been reported by Santiago *et al.* (2008). This study reports the results of a longitudinal study ranging from the last year of primary (age 12) to the last year of compulsory secondary education (age 16). It was expected that there would be differences between students in the A and B models and students in the D model at the end of primary school but that these differences would disappear by the end of compulsory secondary school. Participants were 2166 students in the last year of primary and the sample was 1384 four years later. The study focused on reading comprehension skills in Spanish by using different types of texts and looking at different aspects of comprehension, linguistic, sociolinguistic and literary knowledge. The results indicated that the scores for Spanish in the D model were lower not only in the first measurement but also four years later. These findings mean that D model students did not catch up in their Spanish scores as it was expected. The authors highlight the need to work more specifically with the learning of Spanish in the Spanish language classes and the need to consider the limited use of Spanish in some sociolinguistic contexts in future research.

Reading literacy. This test, which is part of the PISA evaluation, was completed in Basque by students who have Basque as their home language and in Spanish by students who have Spanish or Basque and Spanish as their home language. Therefore it was completed in one language or the other according to the home language and not the language of instruction. The results indicate that students in private schools obtain the best results. The best results correspond to the A and B models in private schools and the lowest to the A model in public schools.

Mathematics. The results of the PISA and TIMSS evaluations can be seen in Figure 4.5.

The results of the PISA assessment indicate that the private schools obtain higher scores than the public schools. The highest scores correspond to the A and D models in private schools and the lowest to the A model in public schools. The differences in socioeconomic status seem to be more important than the linguistic model. The TIMSS results in Mathematics confirm the PISA assessment. Once again the private schools obtain better results than the public schools. In this case, the A and D model private schools obtain the highest scores and the A model public schools the lowest.

Science. The results of the PISA and TIMSS evaluations can be seen in Figure 4.6.

The PISA and the TIMSS results in Science go in the same direction as the results in mathematics and private schools obtain once again the best results. In the PISA evaluation the best results are obtained by the A model private schools and the lowest by the A model public schools. In the TIMSS

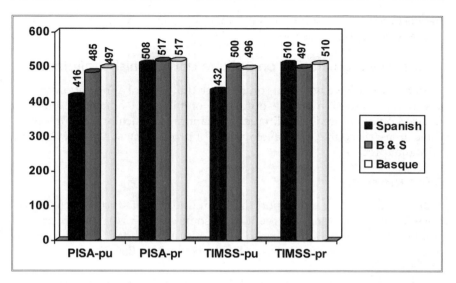

Figure 4.5 Mathematics (PISA and TIMSS) in secondary education (ISEI-IVEI, 2008, 2009)

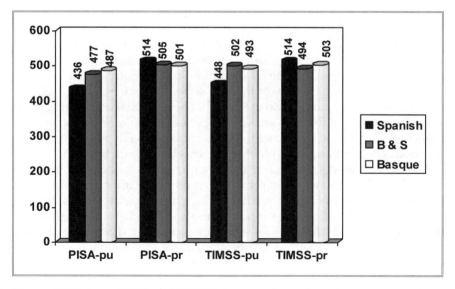

Figure 4.6 Science (PISA and TIMSS) in secondary education (ISEI-IVEI, 2008, 2009)

the best results correspond to the A model private schools and the lowest to the A model public schools.

Other Research Studies on Basque and Spanish Proficiency

In this section we will focus on research that has not aimed at providing a general evaluation of the outcomes of bilingual education but has focused on other areas of bilingual education. Specifically we will look at three areas: discourse, the development of proficiency at an early age and bilingual proficiency.

Discourse studies

In this section we will report the main findings of studies focusing on the effect of educational intervention in some specific aspects of discourse competence. These studies try to test if a specific didactic sequence can improve some aspects of discourse competence in Basque or in Basque and Spanish.

Idiazabal and Larringan (1997, 1999) report a study with 40 students in the first year of secondary school in the D model. Half of the students were assigned to the experimental group and the other half to the control group and they all took pre-tests and post-tests in Basque and Spanish. Only the experimental group had a specific didactic sequence to work on argumentative texts in Basque. The sequence included the teaching of general characteristics of argumentative texts, polite expressions, specific morphosyntactic structures and negotiating strategies. The texts produced by the experimental group scored better than those of the control group on most indexes (tokens, the structure of the text, cohesion devices, modalizations, etc) not only in Basque but also in Spanish. These results indicate that there is positive transfer from Basque into Spanish because teaching specific aspects of discourse competence in Basque not only has a positive effect on the production of Basque argumentative texts but also on Spanish.

Sainz (2001) used a similar research design to analyze the effect of teaching a didactic sequence to improve the production of an encyclopaedic text in the 6th year of primary school. The main focus of Sainz's study is lexical and grammatical cohesion but she also looked at the length of the texts, the topic included and the structure of the text. The study focused only on Basque and the results indicate that the experimental group did better in the post-test in some of the measures such as lexical and grammatical cohesion.

García Azkoaga and Idiazabal (2003) reported a study with 40 secondary school students (aged 14 to 16) in the D model. The texts analyzed were in Basque and Spanish and they did not find important differences related to age. They reported that the ability of the students to achieve nominal cohesion was very similar in Basque and Spanish even though students were in the D model. They also found that there was a clear separation of the languages and that students were able to use different linguistic resources to achieve nominal cohesion in Basque and Spanish.

Sagasta and Etxeberria (2006) conducted a study using a research design similar to the others with 16 students in the 6th year of primary. The didactic sequence was taught only in Basque. The data from the post-tests indicate that the length and quality of the texts had improved after the intervention both in Basque and Spanish. The implication of this study is that there is transfer of discourse competence from Basque into Spanish.

In contrast to the evaluation studies discussed in the previous section, these studies have very limited samples and their results cannot be generalized. However, they show the positive effect of teaching different aspects of discourse competence and the possibility of transferring competence between languages. The teaching of discourse and textual competence also has the advantage of focusing on form and providing a context at the same time. Sainz (2006) has also reported that students at a teacher training college have a very positive attitude towards the use of didactic sequences and like working at the textual level.

The development of proficiency at an early age

Some studies have focused on the early development of competence in the school context. The first study to focus on an early age was an ethnographic study of Spanish speaking children in the D model in Navarre (Sotés, 1996). Sotés analyzed the interaction between the teacher and five children by looking at communicative strategies and the negotiation of meaning. He also observed that there were important individual differences in the interaction and development of Basque proficiency (Sotés & Arnau, 1996).

A more recent study conducted in kindergarten is Luque (2003, see also Azurmendi & Luque, 2006). This study analyzed general psychological development and the development of the Basque language in the D model when children had either Basque or Spanish as a first language. The sample included 38 children who had started going to school either at the age of two or at the age of three.

In this research, the data were collected by video recordings in individual and group situations and a vocabulary test and tests to measure general development were also used. They also got information about contextual and educational variables by using questionnaires filled in by teachers and parents. The results indicate that Spanish speaking children who go to kindergarten from the age of two have a psychological and linguistic development which is close to that of native speakers of Basque in the same model. Their proficiency in Basque and use of Basque is also higher than in the case of children who go to kindergarten at the age of three. This research study showed that all the children developed their proficiency in Basque and that the mixing of languages was minimal. However, some differences were found when the L1 was compared and children with Basque as the L1 used more Basque than children with Spanish as the L1.

Beloki *et al.* (2005) conducted a study in kindergarten with children in the D model in two different sociolinguistic contexts. All the children were in their final year of kindergarten (age 5–6) in the D model and had been at school since the age of two. Twenty-four children spoke Basque at home and lived in a Basque speaking environment and 37 spoke Spanish at home and lived in a Spanish speaking environment. The task to be completed was to tell a story to another child by looking at some drawings. The measures that were analyzed were the length of the text, the structure of the text, the number of verbs and the density of verbs. The results indicate that both groups were able to structure their stories in a similar way and that they followed identical strategies.

Conducting research on language development at an early age has methodological difficulties mainly in the case of external evaluations. The use of more ethnographic approaches including longitudinal studies is really important in kindergarten in order to get valid and reliable data.

Bilingual proficiency

Some studies have aimed at looking at bilingual proficiency by comparing proficiency in both Basque and Spanish and identifying the factors that can be influential. For example Gorostiaga and Balluerka (2002, see also Balluerka & Gorostiaga, 2005) analyzed the influence of social use and the history of acquisition of Basque on the comprehension and recall of scientific texts in Basque and Spanish. Their hypothesis was that if participants used Basque to a greater extent and they had learned the language in wider and more varied contexts they would score better on an inferential task and a recall task based in Basque but not in Spanish. Participants were 104 secondary school and university students who were proficient in Basque and Spanish. The results confirmed that '*the wider and more varied the contexts in which participants had learned Euskera and the more developmental stages in which this learning had taken place, the higher their comprehension level of the text in Euskera*' (Gorostiaga & Balluerka, 2002: 509).

The results also indicated that the social use of Basque and a 'rich' history in the acquisition of Basque had a negative effect on the comprehension of Spanish texts. The fact that the hypothesis was not confirmed for the recall task shows the complexity of language proficiency.

Erriondo *et al.* (1998) conducted a comparison of lexical production in Basque and Spanish so as to get specific information about how balanced Basque-Spanish students are. They conducted a study with 3059 students in the last three years of primary school and the first two years of secondary school (ages 9 to 14). The participants were divided into two groups. The Basque group (n = 1288) were in the D model and came from an area where the percentage of Basque speakers is approximately 90%. The Spanish group (n = 1771) were in the A model and came from areas where the percentage of Basque speakers was lower than 9%. The selection of these groups corresponds to the extremes of a continuum so as to have clear differences between the Basque and the Spanish groups.

All participants took a bilinguality test in Basque and Spanish (Erriondo *et al.*, 1993). They had to react in writing to linguistic stimuli in Basque and Spanish. The stimuli belonged to five semantic fields: family, body, animals, clothes, nature (see Table 4.8). Participants were given three minutes to write as many words as possible in response to each of the stimuli so that the total number of minutes for the five stimuli in each language was 15.

Table 4.8 Stimuli for lexical production

Stimuli in Spanish to produce words in Basque:
hermano (brother)
nariz (nose)
caballo (horse)
pantalón (trousers)
sol (sun)
Stimuli in Basque to produce words in Spanish:
aita (father)
begia (eye)
txakurra (dog)
alkandora (shirt)
mendia (mountain)

Source: Erriondo *et al.*, 1993

Table 4.9 Number of words produced in Basque and Spanish by both groups

	Basque group	*Spanish group*	*Total*
Basque words	76,987	62,812	139,799
Spanish words	81,353	140,298	221,651
Total	158,340	203,110	361,450

Source: Erriondo *et al.*, 1998: 162

When analyzing the results, only the words that were included in the Elhuyar Basque Dictionary (Elhuyar Kultur Elkartea, 1993) and Espasa Calpe Spanish Dictionary (Espasa Calpe, 1994) were accepted but spelling errors were not taken into account. Table 4.9 shows the number of words (tokens) produced by the Basque and the Spanish groups.

This table only reflects the number of words produced in each of the languages but the results are very interesting and to a certain extent unexpected taking into account that Basque is supposed to be the dominant language for one group and Spanish for the other. There are no surprises regarding the Spanish group. This group produces a lot more Spanish than Basque words (77,486 more words in Spanish). They produce more Spanish words and fewer Basque words than the Basque group. These results reflect that their languages are very unbalanced because of their limited knowledge of Basque. The most interesting results are those of the Basque group. The difference between the production in Basque and Spanish for this group is not as big (4366 words). This could be explained because the students in the Basque group are more balanced bilinguals than students in the Spanish group. However there are two other questions regarding the results of the Basque group: Why did this group produce fewer words in Basque than in Spanish? Why is their total repertoire much smaller than that of the Spanish group? A further analysis of the data is presented in Table 4.10. The number of words (tokens) and number of different words (types) produced by both groups have been divided into three categories: those produced by both groups, those produced by the Basque group only and those produced by the Spanish group only.

The results indicate that most words are produced by both groups both in Basque and Spanish but some trends can be observed in the tokens and types produced by each of the groups only. The Basque group produces a lot more tokens and types in Basque which are not shared with the Spanish

Table 4.10 Types and tokens in Basque and Spanish

	Basque group only	*Spanish group only*	*Produced by both groups*	*Total*
Basque tokens	11,275	1153	127,371	139,799
Spanish tokens	2057	5416	214,170	221,651
Basque types	2220	401	1082	3703
Spanish types	1024	2403	2970	6397

Source: Erriondo *et al.*, 1998: 167–169

group and also a lot more tokens and types in Basque than in Spanish. The Spanish group produces a lot more tokens and types not shared by the Basque group in Spanish and also more tokens and types in Spanish than in Basque. By looking only at the specific tokens and types not shared by both groups we can see that Basque seems to be the dominant language for the Basque group and Spanish is the dominant language for the Spanish group. On the other hand, if we look at the total number of types produced by the Basque group including those shared with the Spanish group we can see that it is 3302 in Basque and 3994 in Spanish. This would indicate that the lexicon of the Basque group is richer in Spanish than in Basque. As it can be expected this is also the case of the Spanish group. According to Erriondo *et al.* (1998), these results show the differences in status between the two languages and their speakers and it is an example of linguistic asymmetry. It shows that both groups have developed their lexis in Spanish to a larger extent. There are also a lot more attempts to invent words in Basque by adding a Basque suffix to a Spanish word but students do not add Spanish endings to Basque words when they have to produce words in Spanish. The minority status of Basque is also reflected in spelling mistakes. Erriondo *et al.* (1998) give some interesting examples. They found 57 ways to write the word 'lehengusua' (*'cousin'*) in Basque when only four ways can be accepted (including morpheme variation). The variation even went further for the Basque word referring to male underwear *'slip'*. This word is a loan from Spanish 'calzoncillos' and the accepted word in Basque is 'galtzontzilo' along with the word plus the article 'galtzontziloa' and the plural 'galtzontziloak'. It is not a very easy word in any of the two languages but participants wrote this word in 133 different ways in Basque and 24 different ways in Spanish.

This study focuses on a very limited area of proficiency, the lexicon and uses a very specific methodology to measure lexical production. In spite of these limitations, it raises interesting questions regarding the effect of the minority status of Basque on bilingual proficiency both for the Basque and the Spanish groups. This status could be also related to the total number of words in the lexicon of each of the languages. A strong point in this study is that it looks at both languages at the same time.

Conclusion

The evaluations of teaching through the minority language in the BAC confirm some of the trends observed in other contexts. International evaluations indicate that the results of the BAC, where the minority language is the most common language of instruction, are at least the same and even higher than in similar education contexts which are monolingual. As it has already been pointed out this does not imply a cause-effect relationship but it shows that bilingual education is compatible with successful academic development. Regarding the specific comparisons between the educational models the results of the evaluations clearly indicate that students with more exposure to Basque obtain the best results in Basque and that the proficiency in Basque achieved by students who only have Basque as a subject is extremely limited. This finding confirms similar results on studying the minority language only as a subject in other contexts (O'Laoire, 2005). As Murtagh (2007: 450) points out when referring to secondary Irish schools, subject-only instruction in the minority language is not enough for learners to get access to the social networks and therefore to use the language. The results also indicate that although there are some differences in some cases in the majority language, students taught through Basque achieve in general a good command of Spanish and in many cases Spanish remains their dominant language. The relative proficiency in Basque and Spanish is not only dependent on the language of instruction and it is also closely related to the interaction of the specific sociolinguistic context at the macro and micro levels as illustrated in the '*Continua of Multilingual Education*'. The results related to other areas of the curriculum indicate students with Basque as the language of instruction can achieve, at least, similar scores to those of students with Spanish as the language of instruction and that other factors such as socioeconomic status can be more important than the language of instruction.

Key Points

- The use of Basque as the language of instruction has an important influence on Basque proficiency.
- The use of the minority language as the language of instruction results in more balanced bilingualism.
- The socioeconomic background has a more important effect on academic achievement than the language of instruction.
- The sociolinguistic context can have an important effect on language proficiency.

Notes

1. The OECD has 30 members including most EU countries, Australia, Canada, Iceland, Japan, Korea, Mexico, New Zealand, Norway, Switzerland, Turkey and the USA and has exchanges with many other countries (www.oecd.org).
2. The International Association for the Evaluation of Educational Achievement (IEA) is an independent, international cooperative of national research institutions and governmental research agencies (www.iea.nl).

Chapter 5
Third Language Learning and Instruction through the Third Language

Introduction

Learning foreign languages, and particularly English, has become very important all over the world. In bilingual education, this means adding a third language to the curriculum and this language can be either a subject or a language of instruction.

English is the most important language of international communication and also of intra-European communication and it is the first foreign language learned in European schools. There are many situations in which English becomes the third language at school and these include the situations where there is a minority language, a national language and English as a language of international communication (see Cenoz & Jessner, 2000). In Europe, apart from the Basque Country, Switzerland, Friesland and Catalonia are examples of this situation (see also Cenoz & Gorter, 2005). English is also a third language in many other parts of the world and we have already seen some examples in Chapter 2. One of the countries with a very important development in the teaching of English is China. Yang (2005) and Jiang *et al.* (2007) refer to bilingual programs in a minority language and Mandarin Chinese in China where English is learned as a third language. India became independent in 1947 but as Khubchandani (2007) points out the position of English in education is much stronger now than under British domination. Taking into account the great language diversity of India, in many cases English is a third language. In this chapter the focus is on the teaching and learning of English as a third language in the BAC.

Third Language Learning in School Contexts

The European Commission has seen the need to be proficient at least in three European languages as it is said in the White paper '*Teaching and*

Learning: Towards a Learning Society' (European Commission, 1995). The idea is that the knowledge of languages will facilitate mobility, and build up a feeling of being European. Although the aim was to be proficient in three national languages later it has been changed to proficiency in any three languages and that could include a language of wider communication, the national language and another language.

The Eurobarometer 243 (European Commission, 2006) reports the results of a survey on language skills conducted with a sample of 28,694 subjects in the 27 EU countries, Croatia and Turkey. As we have already seen in the first chapter of this book, 56% of the sample can have a conversation in one or more languages other than their first language. The results of this survey also indicate that English is the most common second or foreign language used and that 77% of EU citizens consider that children should learn English as their first foreign language at school. There is no specific data about the Basque Country but the ability to participate in a conversation in another language is relatively poor in Spain in general. According to Eurobarometer 237 (European Commission, 2005b), only 36% of the sample has skills in a second language and only 20% of these in English. This is a clear contrast as compared to countries such as the Netherlands, Sweden or Denmark where more than 80% of the population can hold a conversation in English.

The role of English in the curriculum is becoming more important because English is seen as necessary for wider communication and there are different approaches to teach English and other foreign languages at school. One of the most important developments in foreign language teaching is CLIL (Content and Language Integrated Learning) as we have already mentioned in Chapter 1. CLIL developed in Europe in the nineties and has been influenced by socio-constructivist ideas (Coyle, 2000), the 'focus on form' approach (Doughty & Williams, 1998) and the language awareness movement (Cots, 2007).

CLIL includes a wide range of teaching practices but the idea is to take content from other subjects and academic disciplines so that students pay attention to the content and to the language at the same time (see also Marsh, 2007; Dalton-Puffer, 2007; Ruiz de Zarobe & Jiménez Catalán, 2009). CLIL methodology focuses on the acquisition of concepts and skills as well as language. Both language and content are equally important; CLIL is contextually bound and can develop in different ways (Coyle, 2007). CLIL is used mainly in foreign language teaching in Europe and the idea is to learn an additional language at the same time as content. CLIL has received strong support from European institutions such as the European Union:

It can provide effective opportunities for pupils to use their new language skills now, rather than learn them now for use later. It opens doors on languages for a broader range of learners, nurturing self-confidence in young learners and those who have not responded well to formal language instruction in general education. It provides exposure to the language without requiring extra time in the curriculum, which can be of particular interest in vocational settings. (European Union Education and Training, http://ec.europa.eu/education/)

It is difficult to establish clear boundaries between CLIL and other content-based approaches developed outside Europe (see Met, 1998; Carrasquillo & Rodriguez, 2002). One of the characteristics of CLIL is its origin in foreign language teaching and not in bilingual education. CLIL and other content-based approaches are generic terms that include a great range of different teaching practices but they share the basic idea of combining language and content. All these content-based approaches are not that far from immersion because in all cases a language other than the first is used as the medium of instruction. Seikkula-Leiono (2007) discusses the differences between immersion and CLIL and points out that reading and writing are taught in the second language in immersion and in the first language in CLIL. Apart from this clear difference, the other points of comparison she lists are not always in practice so different because there are many types of immersion and many types of CLIL. In both cases there can be previous knowledge of the L2, teachers can be bilingual and there can be more or less exposure to the target language in the school curriculum. Another point that makes hard boundaries difficult is that bilingual and multilingual education and foreign language teaching are dynamic and immersion programs are nowadays different from immersion programs 40 years ago. There has also been a shift from '*focus on content*' to '*focus on form and content*' in many immersion programs (Lyster, 2007). As we have already seen in Chapter 2, the '*Continua of Multilingual Education*' can accommodate these different possibilities along a continuum without establishing hard boundaries. Following the trend of other European areas (Eurydice, 2008), CLIL has had a very important influence on the teaching of English as a foreign language in the BAC and English is also increasingly used as a language of instruction.

Legal Framework for the Teaching of Foreign Languages in the Basque Country

The new Spanish Organic Law of Education (2/2006; BOE 4-5-2006) approved in 2006 aims at improving the quality of education including foreign language teaching. Two decrees (1513/2006-BOE 8-12-2003 and 1631/2006-BOE 5-1-2007) establish the minimum curriculum of primary and compulsory secondary education. These decrees have produced some controversy in some autonomous communities about the competences in education because it could mean a higher number of Spanish language lessons. The minimum competencies in education are regulated according to laws and decrees and the additional legislation from the autonomous communities.

The Spanish decree for pre-primary (Decree 1630/2006-4-1-2007) states that a first contact with a foreign language should be encouraged so as to develop positive attitudes towards foreign languages, by using the foreign language orally for communication in the classroom. The decree does not give a minimum number of hours for foreign language teaching. The Basque Decree regulates compulsory education and not pre-primary education. As an example we can see the objectives for primary school (ages 6–12) according to the Spanish Decree in Table 5.1. The objectives set by the Spanish Decree are similar for primary and secondary school, particularly those regarding attitudes and strategies (the objectives for secondary can be seen in Decree 1631/2006, BOE 5-1-2007).

According to the primary school Decree (Decree 1513/2006) the objectives and content of the foreign language curriculum are a response to the need to prepare students to live in a more international, multicultural and

Table 5.1 Objectives for foreign languages in primary school according to the Spanish Decree 1513/2006 (BOE 8-12-2003)

1. To understand messages in different types of interaction so as to carry out different specific tasks.
2. To be able to interact orally in everyday situations.
3. To write different types of texts about topics already known.
4. To read different texts related to the children's own experience and interests so as to obtain general and specific information.
5. To learn to use different possibilities to obtain information and communicate in the foreign language including new technologies.
6. To have a positive attitude towards the language as a means of communication for different people and culture and a tool for learning.
7. To develop confidence about students' own ability to learn and use the language.
8. To use the knowledge of other languages so as to learn the target language more quickly and efficiently.
9. To identify phonetic, structural and lexical aspects and use them as basic elements of communication.

Table 5.2 Number of hours for the first foreign languages in primary and secondary school. Spanish and Basque Decrees

	Total number of hours		Average number of hours per year	
	Spanish Decree	*Basque Decree*	*Spanish Decree*	*Basque Decree*
Primary (6–12)	385	770	64.16	128.8
Secondary (12–16)	420	420	105	105

multilingual world and are based on the Council of Europe Common Framework of Reference for Languages (Council of Europe, 2002). It is also stated that given the very limited exposure to foreign languages outside the classroom it is necessary to focus more on communication at school. As it can be seen in the Table 5.1 the objectives are quite general and there are no specific aims equivalent to the CEFR levels.

The number of hours for first foreign languages is given in Table 5.2.

It can be seen that there is a big difference in the minimum number of hours for foreign language teaching in primary but not in secondary. The Decree for Compulsory Secondary Education (1631/2006) states that a second foreign language is optional in the fourth year of secondary (70 hours) but that it can be taught in other courses in primary and secondary. The minimum number of hours is approximately two hours per week in primary education and three hours in secondary education. In any case the exposure to the foreign language is very limited if there is no contact with the language outside the classroom.

Learning English as a Third Language in the Basque Country

The Basque educational system includes at least one additional language apart from Basque and Spanish. Until the 1980s, the most common foreign language studied at school was French. In the last two decades there has been an important shift in emphasis from French to English and, at present, English is studied as a foreign language by over 95% of Basque schoolchildren. So, the Basque Country has followed the same trend as the rest of Spain and Europe where English is the first foreign language at school. French and German are the other foreign languages used at school but they are usually learned optionally as fourth languages except in some international schools where they are the medium of instruction.

English is a foreign language in the Basque Country and is hardly used at all in everyday life. In contrast to some European countries, there are very few opportunities to use English outside the classroom. Spanish and Basque television use dubbing and not original versions with subtitles and in spite of the possibility of accessing other televisions, in most cases the only exposure to English is at school. In other countries, children are exposed to original versions in English, and can acquire receptive vocabulary and better listening comprehension skills. Many adults in the BAC did not study English but French at school. This means that in many cases parents are much interested in their children learning English but cannot speak the language themselves. Many schoolteachers also studied French and not English as a foreign language and cannot speak English.

The ability to speak English is perceived as an important tool in modern society. Increasing contact between different areas of Europe and between Europe and other countries make proficiency in English an important goal of education. Parents in the Basque Country are aware of this need. For example, according to a study conducted by the Basque Institute of Educational Evaluation and Research, parents believe that it is important for their children to learn several languages and they think that English will be useful for travelling and for getting to know people and countries as well as for their future jobs (ISEI-IVEI, 2007).

Traditionally, students in the BAC have not reached a good command of English by the end of secondary education (Cenoz, 1998). Even at the university level there are still few students who are ready to have some courses taught through the medium of English, as we will see in Chapter 10. Lasagabaster (2007) also reports that the level of English in a teacher training college where there is no specialization in English is remarkably low. These poor results have been attributed to a number of factors, including the use of outdated or traditional instructional approaches, the lack of well-trained teachers with adequate proficiency in English, the large class sizes, the position of foreign languages in the school curriculum, the parents' limited knowledge of English and general limited exposure to English in the social context (Cenoz, 1998, 2005). Some of these factors have changed in recent years and are changing nowadays. The size of the class is not a problem in general terms because of the extremely low birth rate in the BAC and the consequent drop in school enrolment. The position of English in the curriculum has become stronger in the last years and schools include multilingualism as one of their aims. Exposure to English is still very limited and most parents of schoolchildren do not speak English although the situation is changing slightly with the new generations. There have also been some changes regarding teachers' proficiency and instructional approaches. Many parents send their children to private classes of English or to language schools in the evenings. In some cases it is because children need the extra classes in order to pass the school exams and in others it is because they just want their children to learn more English. Teachers in these schools are in many cases native speakers of English and they prepare children for specific certificates (see Figure 5.1).

The spread of English has also reached the BAC but not to the same extent as other European countries. Exposure to English for communicative purposes is very limited but it seems to be changing in the new generations because of internet and computer games. English is also used in the linguistic landscape in international brand names or as a marketing strategy to give an idea of modernity. Figure 5.2 shows two examples from shops in the city center of Donostia-San Sebastian.

There are no studies of teachers' proficiency in English but it seems that it is not very high among primary school teachers. As we have already seen in Chapter 3, most primary school teachers are nowadays bilingual in Basque and Spanish and many of them are speakers of Basque as a second language. However, it is often the case that only teachers of English speak English. The shift from French to English as a third language and the early introduction of English in pre-primary and primary levels has increased

Figure 5.1 Example of a bilingual ad for English language courses

Figure 5.2 Commercial signs including English in Donostia-San Sebastian

the demand for teachers of English in primary schools. Teachers of English usually teach only English to different groups in pre-primary, primary and secondary school. Primary school teachers obtain a teacher's certificate at Teacher Training colleges and nowadays can get specialized in English. Secondary school teachers usually hold a BA in English Studies, which is not aimed specifically at teaching and take a professional masters course once they have finished their BA. In general, secondary school teachers have a higher level of English proficiency because they have studied most of the subjects (mainly literature and linguistics) through the medium of English but primary school teachers have more training in psychology and pedagogy. It is also possible to become a teacher of English by having a teacher's certificate or a BA in a different specialization and an official certificate of English. The decrease in the birth rate in the BAC has seriously limited the creation of new jobs for teachers of English. The early introduction of English has implied that English language teachers were needed in pre-primary and primary school while there was a general surplus of teachers. As a result, many teachers have taken in-service courses to become specialists in English in primary and pre-primary school. These courses include both language and methodology classes and the teachers can get leaves of absence for some months. Teachers can also get grants to go to English speaking countries or to attend conferences and get support from teachers' centers particularly when taking part in specific projects. These teachers have managed to achieve different degrees of proficiency in English but in some cases this proficiency is not very high. With very few exceptions, teachers are native speakers of Basque or Spanish both in public and private schools.

The number of native teachers is higher in foreign schools. There are a few French, English and German schools in the BAC and the foreign languages are taught as subjects and languages of instruction. Schoolchildren attending these schools are sometimes native speakers of the foreign languages who live in the Basque Country but many others are local students.

There are also several official Language Schools in the BAC. English, Basque, French and German and other languages are taught at these schools, which are supported by the government. The classes are for adults but schoolchildren over 14 can take specific exams so as to get an official certificate at different levels of proficiency. Many parents also send their children to English speaking countries in the summer or to summer camps where English is spoken. All these activities show that there is a great interest in the learning of English but they also show that the level obtained at the school is regarded as insufficient for the needs of modern society.

The Basque Government Department of Education along with other private networks and schools (Ikastolen Elkartea, Gaztelueta Foundation, Ahizke-Cim, etc.) have made a great deal of effort in recent years to reinforce and improve the teaching of English within the context of bilingual education. Apart from subsidizing intensive language learning courses for English teachers both in the Basque Country and abroad, there have been important changes in the methodology. Instructional approaches that emphasize communicative competence and the acquisition of oral skills and the use of learner-centered syllabuses were adopted already some years ago (Cenoz & Lindsay, 1994). Nowadays, English is in most cases the language of communication in the English classes and in the first years all the activities are oral. The methods used in kindergarten require the children's active participation by means of playing, singing or collective dramatization. In many cases the materials for the teaching of English include new technologies and have been created by teacher trainers and teachers to be experimented in the schools. The general policy is not to mix English with other languages. Teachers are supposed to use only English in the class and teaching materials are in English only with the exception of dictionaries (see Figure 5.3).

The interest has not only been on the teaching of English but on moving from bilingual education to multilingual education. Specific projects to develop trilingual education in Basque schools started in the nineties and they can be regarded as an extension of the bilingual educational system. These projects aim at achieving communicative competence in the three languages (Basque, Spanish and English) and also consider the

Figure 5.3 Basque-English picture dictionary
Source: http://www.aizkorri.com

importance of developing positive attitudes towards the languages. The interest in multilingual education is also reflected in the conferences organized on this topic in the last years so as to discuss the Basque situation as compared to other examples of bilingual and multilingual education. Some example of these activities are the seven conferences organized by the Gaztelueta Foundation (http://www.jornadasgaztelueta.org) or the six conferences organized by Getxoko Berritzegune (http://www.getxolinguae.net/). The Basque Government Department of Education supports the development of trilingual education and subsidizes different activities such as courses, seminars and projects.

The study of a foreign language is now compulsory from the first year of primary school but most schools in the BAC start teaching English in pre-primary at the age of four. As we have already seen in Chapter 2, most children in the BAC go to school at the age of two. In many cases the school language is Basque which is a second language for many children. English is introduced in the second or third year of pre-primary when children have already been exposed to Basque. The early introduction of English started in 1991 and it has become very popular in public and private schools. The characteristics of these projects and the effect of the early introduction of English will be discussed in Chapter 9 as related to the age factor.

Some schools also work in the integration of the curricula of Basque, Spanish and English so as to benefit from linguistic interdependence and transfer (Cummins, 1979). The idea is that the teachers of the three languages work together when planning their classes so that the contents and the different skills used in the language classes are related to each other (Arano *et al.*, 1996; Mugertza & Aliaga, 2005). Arano *et al.* (1996) propose to focus on form as well as on content and to reinforce production as well as comprehension. The rationale of these programs is that the language acquisition process will be enhanced as a result of transfer of learning processes including learning strategies among the different languages. Ruiz Bikandi (2005) adds that there are sociolinguistic, psycholinguistic and linguistic reasons to integrate the curricula. She also illustrates how the integration of the three languages can be beneficial for the development of metalinguistic awareness. The examples provided by Ruiz Bikandi (2005) show the differences between languages which can be compared by looking at the three languages at the same time (Table 5.3).

This comparison of the languages can raise metalinguistic awareness in the context of multilingual education.

The experience of teaching through the medium of Basque and the influence of Canadian immersion, content based instruction and CLIL have also influenced the teaching of English as a subject and as a medium of instruction. In 1996 the Basque Government Department of Education designed a project including three different possibilities: (1) to introduce English in pre-primary at the age of four for 2 or 3 hours a week; (2) to start English in the third year of primary school (at the age of eight) but having

Table 5.3 Examples of English, Basque and Spanish

English: *My old friends* ('old' can refer to the length of the friendship or to age)
Basque: *Nire aspaldiko lagunak/nire lagun zaharrak* (two different words are needed: 'aspaldiko' for length of friendship and 'zaharrak' for age)
Spanish: *Mis viejos amigos/Mis amigos viejos* (the position of the adjective 'viejos' before the noun refers to the length of the friendship and after the noun to age).
English: *Tomorrow we are going to Paris* (present continuous)
Basque: *Bihar Parisera joango gara* (future)
Spanish: *Mañana vamos a París* (present simple)

Source: Ruiz Bikandi, 2005

more intensity of exposure, 5 hours a week and using a content-based approach; (3) to start English in primary school and to have five hours of English per week in secondary school using a content based approach. Most of the schools taking part in the project decided to choose the first possibility but some primary and secondary schools have been using a content based approach and have even gone further and are using English as an additional language of instruction. The schools participating in the different projects receive support from the teachers' centers so as to get materials for the classroom and to discuss how to use them. Nowadays, approximately 25% of the primary schools in the Basque Country (about 20,000 students) and 9% of secondary schools (about 1600 students) are 'officially' participating in a special CLIL project but many other schools also use a CLIL approach to teaching English as a third language. In CLIL classes, content and language are taught at the same time and content can include subjects in social science, science and mathematics. The materials are designed by teacher trainers and consultants who also organize regular meetings with teachers and visit the schools. Some materials have been designed in collaboration with other countries for projects funded by the European Commission and the Council of Europe. In addition, there are language courses and courses on instructional methods subsidized by the Basque Government. Schools officially participating in the CLIL project get special funding. The selection of the content to be taught through the medium of English depends on different factors including the type of activities students can carry out, the level of abstraction and theorization and the specific language needed (see for example Arano & Ugarte, 2000).

English as an Additional Language of Instruction in the Basque Country

The integration of the curricula, CLIL or the early introduction of English can be important but taking into account the limited results of Basque as a second language in the A model, exposure to the language is also considered crucial. As Sierra (1997) already pointed out some years ago, starting early is not enough, it is necessary to teach subjects through the medium of English. Using English as an additional language of instruction is a lot more difficult to organize than the coordination between teachers of different languages or the early introduction of English. As usual, the main problems are related to the availability of trained teachers and appropriate materials. Who can teach science, mathematics or history through the medium of English: the subject teacher or the English language teacher? It is difficult to generalize and in many cases it depends on the school and the availability of teachers. Using English as an additional language can imply readjustments for teaching staff because of the new distribution of subjects. It depends on the characteristics of the school but in general it can be more difficult in secondary because the teachers are more specialized and the academic level is higher.

There is no shortage of learning materials in English but school-children in the BAC need to learn the same content if a subject is taught through the medium of English or through Basque and Spanish. This means that many materials, which are available in English, need to be adapted and in some cases the Basque or Spanish materials are translated into English.

In spite of these difficulties some schools have decided to intensify the role of English in the curriculum within bilingual education and are using English as the language of instruction at the end of primary school and in secondary school (Cenoz, 1998, 2005, 2008b).

Some of these schools were originally A model schools that had also English as a language of instruction and now have Basque as an additional language of instruction. For example, Gaztelueta school in Bizkaia and Erain and Eskibel schools in Gipuzkoa have already been using Basque, Spanish and English as languages of instruction for some years. Most of the students at these schools have Spanish as the home language but the aim of these schools is that they also achieve a high level of proficiency in the other two languages. The distribution of the subjects in the different languages is given in Table 5.4.

Table 5.4 Languages at Erain and Eskibel schools at primary level

Language of instruction	Subjects	Number of hours in each language
Basque	Basque language Science Handicraft	6.75
Spanish	Spanish language Mathematics Religion	9
English	English language Music/motor skills Physical Education	6.75

Source: Valero and Villamor, 1997

Children participating in this project have already been exposed to the three languages in pre-primary. The first contact with Basque and English is oral but literacy skills are introduced in pre-primary school. There are some special activities including music and games to stimulate the early acquisition of languages. Each teacher speaks only one language to the children. The use of different languages is also reinforced outside the classroom during the breaks and in the language used on boards and other elements of the linguistic landscape of the school. Literacy skills are taught in the three languages from the age of five (Valero, 2000).

Another A model school with a long tradition in the teaching of English as a medium of instruction is Gaztelueta school (Goyeneche, 1993; Bilbao, 1994). This school has been teaching several subjects (history, science and handicrafts) through the medium of English for over 20 years and added Basque as an additional language of instruction in the early nineties for subjects such as history, handicrafts, natural science or computer science. Spanish is the main language of instruction but trilingualism is also encouraged outside the classroom by using the three languages in the school television and the school newspaper. Most of the students at Gaztelueta school have Spanish as the first language and most of them have also the other two languages as languages of instruction provided that they have previously attained the necessary proficiency level. Basque and English are also taught as school subjects and specific activities are carried out so as to reinforce the linguistic areas to be used in the content classes.

A different possibility is to start from a D model with Basque as the main language of instruction and to use also English as an additional language of instruction. This is the 'Eleanitz' project of the network of Ikastolak which is *'a multilingual school project with the Basque language as its main axis'* (Elorza & Muñoa, 2008: 86–87). This project, which started in 1991, has approximately 22,500 students from 70 schools all over the Basque Country (Ball *et al.*, 2005). Basque is the main medium of instruction in these Ikastolak but children also study Spanish as a subject. In most cases, Spanish is not taught as a second language but as a language in which students are already fluent and the main focus is on literacy skills. The rationale for this project is that if Basque is going to survive it needs to be the main language in its context but that Basque speakers also need to speak Spanish and other languages, mainly English and French. The project highlights the advantages of multilingualism on cognitive development and social skills (Garagorri, 2000).

The materials for the project are prepared by the network of Ikastolak (Ikastolen Elkartea) in some cases in collaboration with external experts as part of European projects. A CD-Rom produced by the Ikastolen Elkartea

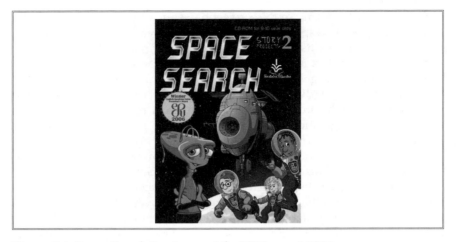

Figure 5.4 Space Search 2, winner of the ESU award 2006

'Space Search 2' obtained the English Speaking Union President's Award in 2006 (see Figure 5.4)

The network of Ikastolak organizes general courses of English and methodology and also specific sessions for teachers participating in the project. These sessions are organized to discuss specific techniques to be used in the classroom and some classes are also recorded so as to discuss the use of materials and the interaction with the students. The aim of the project is to reach level B2 (Independent user, vantage) of the CEFR in Basque and Spanish by the end of compulsory education, level B1 for English and level A2 for French as a fourth language. The description of these levels can be seen in Table 5.5 (Council of Europe, 2002: 24).

Children start learning English as a subject at the age of four (see also Chapter 9) and in secondary school they have a subject through the medium of English. Out of the 70 schools participating in the multilingualism project, the students of more than 20 schools have already reached the third year of secondary education and study Social Science through the medium of English in the third and fourth years (age 14–16). All the students in the Ikastolak taking part in the project have English as the language of instruction for this subject and in general, there is no selection of students to have English-medium instruction as it happens in some other schools. The students have already had a content based approach in their English classes in primary and secondary school and it is in the last two years of secondary when it is considered that they are ready for using English as the

Table 5.5 Aims of the Eleanitz project at the age of 16

Basque Spanish B2 Independent user: Vantage	– Can understand the main ideas of complex text on both concrete and abstract topics, including technical discussions in his/her field of specialization. – Can interact with a degree of fluency and spontaneity that makes regular interaction with native speakers quite possible without strain for either party. – Can produce clear, detailed text on a wide range of subjects and explain a viewpoint on a topical issue giving the advantages and disadvantages of various options.
English B1 Independent user: Threshold	– Can understand the main points of clear standard input on familiar matters regularly encountered in work, school, leisure, etc. Can deal with most situations likely to arise while traveling in an area where the language is spoken. – Can produce simple connected text on topics which are familiar or of personal interest. – Can describe experiences and events, dreams, hopes and ambitions and briefly give reasons and explanations for opinions and plans.
French A2 Basic user: Waystage	– Can understand sentences and frequently used expressions related to areas of most immediate relevance (e.g. very basic personal and family information, shopping, local geography, employment). – Can communicate in simple and routine tasks requiring a simple and direct exchange of information on familiar and routine matters. – Can describe in simple terms aspects of his/her background, immediate environment and matters in areas of immediate need.

language of instruction. The students have three hours of Social Science taught either by a teacher of Social Science who is fluent in English or an English teacher and two hours of English taught by an English teacher. The materials used include a Basque textbook which has been translated into English and adapted for these classes. There are also some guidelines for the teacher and an activity book for the students. The two hours devoted to the study of English are used to work on the cognitive and linguistic needs in the area of Social Science. The use of English as the language of instruction gives the possibility of working with different types of text: descriptive, narrative, expositive or argumentative. Some Ikastolak have their own model of multilingual education. For example, Lauro Ikastola is a D model school with a longer tradition in the teaching of subjects though the medium of English (see Martínez, 1997; Cenoz, 1998, for more information).

Apart from these projects which are taking place mainly in private schools, the Basque Government Department of Education has also organized a specific project to use English as an additional language of instruction in public schools since 2003. Schools participating in these projects are already over 30 and they receive specific funding and training from teachers' centers. The subjects taught through the medium of English include social sciences, natural science, arts, music, computer science, handicrafts, religion and chemistry. The choice of the different subjects and the levels to teach through the medium of English depends on the school organization and the availability of teachers in the schools. The support teachers can receive is less specific when they teach different subjects. In this case the selection and development of appropriate materials has been a real challenge. This project has been evaluated by the Basque Institute of Educational Evaluation and Research (ISEI-IVEI) and the results are reported in Chapter 6.

Conclusion

This chapter summarizes the teaching of English as a third language within bilingual education and the move towards multilingualism by adding English as an additional language of instruction. This need to move from bilingual to multilingual education is also felt in other contexts (for example Bolivia, Catalonia, Friesland). The teaching of English and through English faces important challenges in the BAC but different projects indicate that it is possible to combine the protection and development of the minority language with the need to be proficient in languages of wider communication. The use of different languages has, among others, specific challenges regarding the goals to be achieved for each of the languages and the boundaries between languages. In this respect, Shohamy (2007: 80) points out that establishing hard boundaries between languages *'perpetuates issues of language correctness, of using the language with native-like proficiency .... It also creates artificial boundaries among the different languages, does not encourage cooperation of the language teachers ...'.* Multilingual education does not only mean making room in the curriculum for more languages or improving teachers' proficiency in English. It implies having a multilingual perspective at the conceptual level that is reflected when establishing goals, planning lessons and assessing students. Some of the projects in the BAC have already given the first steps in this direction.

Key Points

- The teaching of English as a third language is widely spread in bilingual communities in Europe and all over the world.
- There are different possibilities to teach a third language in the school context either as a subject or as an additional language of instruction.
- The integration of language and content can be an efficient way to counterbalance the limited exposure to the target language.
- The integration of the curricula for different languages as part of a multilingual perspective in language teaching can soften the boundaries between languages at schools and probably foster the benefits of multilingualism.

Chapter 6

Learning English and Learning through English: Research Outcomes

Introduction

The spread of English as an international language has some implications for its assessment in bilingual and multilingual programs. In this chapter we will focus on the outcomes of instruction in English as a third language in the BAC both when it is a school subject and a language of instruction. Comparisons between monolinguals and bilinguals learning English will be discussed in Chapter 7 and the effect of the age factor on the acquisition of English in Chapter 9.

When evaluating the outcomes in educational contexts we can think of a continuum that ranges from standardized testing to teacher-based assessment. As Davidson and Cummins (2007: 416) point out, standardized testing established specific types and levels of achievement. Some examples of international standardized tests are the PISA and TIMSS we have already seen in Chapter 4. A variation of standardized testing is the competency-based Common European Framework of Reference (CEFR). The studies discussed in this section are more exploratory rather than standardized tests. They are not teacher-based either but they all try to analyze the level of English obtained when English is a third language in the Basque educational system.

Assessing Proficiency in English

The learning of English within bilingual education is linked to the specific educational, linguistic and sociolinguistic context in which it takes place as it can be seen in the '*Continua of Multilingual Education*'. In this section we are going to focus on three aspects that have to be taken into account when assessing English in bilingual and multilingual programs:

(1) *Exposure to English in the social context.* Assessment of English in bilingual and multilingual programs has to take into account the sociolinguistic context in which the school is located because this can have an important influence on the learning process, particularly in the case of English. It can be said that, with a few exceptions, English is always part of the social context where bilingual and multilingual schools are located. The spread of English is due to many different factors as we have seen in Chapter 1 but there are important differences between countries. For example, in Europe, there is more exposure to English in countries such as Sweden, Denmark, Finland or the Netherlands than in France, Spain or Italy. English is also penetrating in the BAC as it can be seen for example in studies of the linguistic landscape in which there are no big differences in the use of English in street signs between the Basque Country and Friesland although there are important differences in proficiency in English (Cenoz & Gorter, 2006).

(2) *The role of English as a lingua franca.* English is used for communication not only with native speakers but also among non-native speakers. In this context, speakers use English as a tool to communicate. English is a lingua franca when 'is chosen as the means of communication among people from different first language backgrounds, across linguacultural boundaries' (Seidlhofer, 2005: 339). If English is going to be used to communicate with other speakers of different languages, the aim of teaching English should be intelligibility rather than native-speaker norms (see Seidlhofer, 2007). English as a lingua franca can be more neutral and therefore, less linked to a specific culture and without having the native speaker as a necessary referent (see Llurda, 2005). This perspective has important consequences for testing and assessment but, at least in the context of the BAC is not often taken into consideration in educational contexts.

(3) *The concept of multilingual proficiency.* Acquiring communicative competence involves the acquisition of linguistic, sociolinguistic, discourse, pragmatic and strategic competence. When several languages are part of the curriculum it is unrealistic to expect learners to acquire a native-like level of competence in all these different components. Perfectly balanced multilingual speakers are an exception. Language competence in the case of multilinguals does not have to be necessarily regarded as simply the sum of three or more monolingual competences, and can be judged in conjunction with the users' total linguistic repertoire, that is adopting a holistic view of multilingualism. Even though these ideas have been proposed and discussed at a theoretical level for several years now (Grosjean, 1992, 2008; Cook,

1992, 1995, 2007) monolingual norms and comparisons with monolingual speakers are still very common in bilingual and multilingual schools. Assessment of multilingual education needs to take this issue into account.

Learning a Third Language as a Subject: Research Findings

When the bilingual educational models were established in the early eighties foreign languages were included in the curriculum but they were not considered as important as they are now. As we have already seen in Chapter 5 there have been important changes in the curriculum regarding English. English is nowadays introduced from pre-primary school and it is even used as an additional language of instruction. For a long time there has been a worry about the potential negative effect that an increasing presence of English in the curriculum could have on Basque and Spanish or other subjects. Moreover, there is a concern about proficiency in English achieved at school.

The main concern of research on learning English in the BAC has been English proficiency and research studies and evaluations have focused on areas such as:

- the interaction between competences in the three languages;
- the influence of teaching styles;
- the effect of extra classes of English outside school;
- the effect of using English as an additional language of instruction;
- the influence on individual and contextual variables; and
- the influence of age, particularly regarding the early introduction of English in pre-primary school.

Apart from students' proficiency in English other studies have focused on the following areas:

- Parents' and teachers' assessment of new programs.
- The influence of bilingualism on third language acquisition.
- The analysis of attitudes towards the three languages and their influence on the acquisition of English.
- Cross-linguistic influence from previously learned languages on the acquisition of additional languages.

In this chapter we look at studies focusing on English proficiency both as a school subject and as the language of instruction and at cross-linguistic influence from Basque and Spanish into English.

Evaluations of English in pilot programs

The first study by Sierra (1995) looks at English proficiency of children in the 5th year of primary school and the 2nd year of secondary school. At the time, there was a change in the introduction of English from the 5th year of primary to the 3rd year of primary and the teaching of English in pre-primary was very limited. Participants in the primary school group were in their third year of English and participants in the 2nd year of secondary school were in their 4th year of English. Both groups participated in a special project focusing on the development of communicative skills and the primary group was special at the time because children were learning English from the age of eight (3rd year of primary) instead of 11 (5th year of primary). Sierra (1995) included some control groups who had not started in the 3rd year of primary and were not using a special methodology.

The skills tested were listening and speaking tests for primary education and listening, reading and writing for secondary. The results in primary indicate that there were no differences in listening comprehension in primary but there were some significant differences in speaking. The best results correspond to children who had taken part in the Project and were also having extra classes of English outside the school. The second best were children who were taking part in the Project but had no extra classes and the worst results were obtained by students in the control group. In secondary there were only significant differences in the listening test. The best results corresponded to the students in the Project who also attended English classes outside school, followed by students in the Project who did not attend classes and by the control groups. Therefore the results of this evaluation indicate that the extra classes of English outside school have an important influence on some aspects of English proficiency and also that students taking part in the Project got better results in some skills than other students. Table 6.1 summarizes the characteristics of this study and another one carried out by Cenoz and Gallardo (2000).

Cenoz and Gallardo (2000) carried out an evaluation in the 6th year of primary and the 4th of secondary school in five schools. The schools had taken part in a special program using a content based approach at different ages. At the time of testing all students were in their 4th year in the Project. Students in the 6th year of primary had started learning English in the 3rd year of primary and students in the 4th year of secondary in the 5th year of primary. So, students in the secondary group were in their 6th year of English but in the 4th year in the Project while students in the primary group had only studied English during the four years of the Project.

Table 6.1 Characteristics of the evaluations

	Sample	*Tests*	*Results*
Sierra, 1995	5th year of primary 54 experimental + extra English 101 experimental 12 control	Listening Speaking Background Questionnaire	Listening: no differences Speaking: experimental + extra
	2nd year of secondary 105 experimental + extra English 167 experimental 14 control + extra English 20 control	Listening Speaking Writing Background Questionnaire	Listening: experimental + extra Speaking: no differences Writing: no differences
Cenoz and Gallardo, 2000	6th year of primary N = 68	Listening Speaking Writing Attitudes Background Questionnaire	Lower scores in oral and written tests
	4th year of secondary N = 27	Listening Speaking Writing Attitudes Background Questionnaire	Higher scores in oral and written tests

The results of the two groups were compared and it was observed that secondary school students obtained significantly better results in all the dimensions of oral production (vocabulary, grammar, fluency and content) except in pronunciation. Students in secondary also obtained significantly higher results in all the dimensions of written production (content, organization, vocabulary, use of English and mechanics of writing). Secondary school students obtained significantly higher scores in the reading and writing test and in the cloze test but not in the oral comprehension test. These results are to be expected because the total number of hours of instruction for secondary schoolchildren was higher and because older children progress faster in formal contexts (see also Chapter 9; Mayo & Lecumberri, 2003; Muñoz, 2006a). This study also collected data from teachers and parents about the special project to teach English through content. The questionnaires included information about their attitude and the children's attitudes towards the project.

Teachers value children's attitude towards English as positive or very positive and their attitudes towards the project as very positive. When teachers involved in the project were asked whether this type of project could have an influence on Basque, Spanish, cognitive development or other subjects they responded that if there was an effect it would be positive. In general teachers consider that learners have made a lot of progress mainly in comprehension skills. According to the teachers, the most important factor affecting success was the method and the material used, the teacher's proficiency in English, his/her training and the ability to work with the specific age groups. The factor teachers considered less influential was to have a specific classroom for English and they gave intermediate scores to factors such as the attitudes of other teachers towards the project. Teachers consider that taking part in the project has been very useful for their professional development because they have practiced their English more and they have also acquired more knowledge about methodology and other subject areas. Teachers added that the materials they have used are in general appropriate and the support of the teacher educators has also been very helpful. They would have liked to have more support, more meetings with the coordinators and more materials to be used with the students but they thought that they got enough support from the school.

General evaluations of English

The Basque Institute of Educational Evaluation and Research has conducted two general evaluations of English in the 6th year of primary school (ISEI-IVEI, 2002) and the second year of secondary school (ISEI-IVEI, 2004b). Table 6.2 includes the characteristics of the samples and the tests.

Table 6.2 Evaluations of primary and secondary school

Sample	Tests	Schools
6th year of primary $N = 1555$	Listening, Reading, Writing Background questionnaires, Attitudes	Public and private
2nd year of secondary $N = 2142$	Listening, Reading, Writing, Oral production (sub-sample) Metalinguistic aptitude, Background questionnaires, Sociocultural aspects, Attitudes	Public and private

These evaluations are not focused on a specific project and do not have control groups but aim at describing levels of competence so as to get a general knowledge about the situation in the BAC regarding competence in English. The results of the primary school tests indicate that the weakest area is written production and the strongest oral comprehension. The results in secondary school are also similar and students have more difficulties with writing and metalinguistic awareness. Students who have some exposure to English outside school obtain better results and also those who are in classes with teachers who use more English. The results are also better when students have to do some homework in English at home and they are confident that they will be going to the university.

Studies on specific aspects of multilingualism

The two studies included in this section are not general evaluations but try to answer some research questions in the study of multilingualism in education. The instruments used in by Azpillaga and Goikoetxea can be seen in Table 6.3.

Table 6.3 Measuring instruments used by Azpillaga, 2005 and Goikoetxea, 2007

	Azpillaga	*Goikoetxea*
Basque proficiency		Written skills: description of a picture, formal letter; letter to a friend Oral skills: story telling with a cartoon and role-play in groups
Spanish proficiency		Written and oral skills: the same as in Basque
English proficiency	Oral comprehension and oral production (story)	Written skills: to write a message Oral skills: description of a picture and Frog story
Classroom variables	Interviews with teachers Videos of the classes Researcher's diary	
Other Variables	Background questionnaire for parents including attitudes Intelligence	Background questionnaire Intelligence

Azpillaga (2005, see also Azpillaga *et al.*, 2001) focused on competence in English as linked to teaching styles. Her study is one of the few examples of classroom research on the acquisition of English in the BAC. In this study children were taking part in a European Lingua project developed by several European universities and networks including the University of the Basque Country and the network of Ikastolak (Ikastolen Elkartea).

Azpillaga had a sample of 10 teachers and 213 students who were in the 3rd year of primary. All the children were in the D model and studied English for three hours a week. All the students had started to learn English from scratch and data were collected at different times. The data collected in this research study are based on triangulation. Azpillaga videotaped 200 classes and she interviewed the teachers so as to observe the teaching styles and the teachers' conceptualization of the methodology used in the classroom. The analyses of the classes focused on the didactics and the analysis of interaction and included the identification of the type of activity carried out in the class, the time devoted to each activity, the organization of the classroom, the level of difficulty and the quantity and quality of the interaction between the teacher and the students.

Azpillaga measured the level of English of the students by using oral comprehension and oral production tests. Oral production was analyzed by looking at verbal fluency, the complexity of structures and discourse devices that indicated narrative ability. Other measurements included in this study are a Raven test to measure general intelligence and a background questionnaire for parents. The questionnaire included items on their knowledge of languages, SES and the children's attitude towards the specific project. Azpillaga also kept a diary so as to write down additional observations.

The results of this research study indicate that some teaching strategies are associated with better scores in the English tests. Teachers who are more successful provide more comprehensible input, reinforce meaning when communicating with their students, have a better relation with their students and understand the theoretical background of the teaching method they use better. This research study shows that classroom research is necessary to have a full understanding of bilingual and multilingual education. In this research, factors such as intelligence or SES were not associated with the English scores. The study shows that the same project, including the same materials and training, can result in different levels of achievement, depending on teachers' skills to implement it.

Goikoetxea (2007) conducted a detailed analysis of the different dimensions of communicative competence in Basque, Spanish and English. Her sample included 24 students in the D model with either Basque or Spanish as their first language. All the students were in the same school and had Basque as the language of instruction. Half of the students had started learning English at the age of five and the other half at the age of eight.

Goikoetxea used different tests to measure Basque, Spanish and English proficiency (see Table 6.3). The materials include different types of oral and written tests so as to be able to analyze the following dimensions of communicative competence: linguistic, strategic, sociolinguistic, actional and discourse competences. The same type of tests was used for Basque and Spanish but the test for English was less demanding. The results of the research study were the following:

- The levels of Basque and Spanish are similar and much higher than the level of English.
- There is a correlation between the levels of different languages. Students who have higher competence in one language also have higher competence in the other languages.
- In general, students have more problems with sociocultural and discourse competence than with strategic, actional and linguistic competence. Students have problems to distinguish and use different levels of formal language and also showed limitations at the discourse level.
- Students are better at linguistic competence in their first language (either in Basque or Spanish) but there are no differences in other dimensions of communicative competence.

This study is an important step to considering multilingual competence from a more holistic perspective because it relates competence in the different languages.

Learning through a Third Language: Research Findings

As we have seen in Chapter 5, other projects involve the use of English as an additional language of instruction. The extent of the use of English as the language of instruction is relatively limited when compared to the extent of Basque-medium instruction. The number of research studies on English as an additional language of instruction is also limited in the Basque Country and elsewhere. This type of research is really important because of the additional challenges of using several languages as languages of instruction and not only as school subjects.

One of the projects with English as an additional language of instruction is the multilingual project developed by the network of Ikastolak

(Ikastolen Elkartea) we have already discussed in Chapter 5. This project, which starts with the early introduction of English in pre-primary school, uses English as the language of instruction for Social Science in the 3rd year of secondary school. The Ikastolak network has carried out an evaluation of this project so as to see if it is effective to learn English and Social Science (Ikastolen Elkarteko Eleanitz-Ingelesa Taldea, 2003). All the students in the schools participating in this project had English as an additional language of instruction.

Another evaluation has been carried out in different secondary public schools by the Basque Institute for Research and Evaluation in Education (ISEI-IVEI, 2007). This evaluation looked at the results of a special project to teach different subjects in English in 12 schools (see also Chapter 5). This project was not open to all students because only those who passed a specific test of English could take part. The teaching of different subjects through the medium of English depended on the availability of the teachers in the different schools taking part in the project. Table 6.4 gives information about the sample in both evaluations.

The Ikastolak evaluation included over 400 students in the 3rd year of compulsory secondary school. The students are divided into experimental and control groups. All the students took the English written tests and most of them the Social Science test. A sub-sample of 143 students also undertook the oral English test. The students in the experimental group had had classes of English since the age of four while the children in the control group had started learning English at the age of eight. The teachers in the experimental group had had specific training and methodological support. Both experimental and control groups had three hours of Social Science per week but the experimental group had English as the language of instruction (with the exception of two schools that also teach some

Table 6.4 Characteristics of the sample in studies on English-medium instruction

	Sample	*Groups*
Ikastolak 2003	3rd secondary $N = 476$ (143 oral)	Experimental and control
ISEI-IVEI 2007	$N = 229$ 1st–2nd secondary (87) 3rd–4th secondary (64) 5th–6th secondary (78)	Experimental and control

Social Science in Basque) and the control group had Basque as the language of instruction. Teachers in experimental groups were language teachers and teachers in control groups were Social Science teachers. The materials for social science were similar in English and Basque.

The ISEI-IVEI evaluation has a more complex design because they had three different cohorts who were tested at the beginning and the end of two academic years. As it can be seen in Table 6.4, these years were the 1st and 2nd of secondary for the first cohort, the 3rd and 4th of secondary for the second cohort and the 5th and 6th of secondary for the third cohort. This evaluation only looked at achievement in English and participants were 229 students including the experimental and control groups. The control groups had similar academic achievement, similar distribution according to gender and similar motivation according to their teachers. The data were collected between 2004 and 2006 (ISEI-IVEI, 2007). In this evaluation there was more diversity regarding the subjects taught through the medium of English and only proficiency in English was measured. The tests used in the two evaluations are in Table 6.5.

The tests used in the ikastolak evaluations to measure English proficiency included the four skills plus a test of grammar. Social Science was measured by using a test of comprehension and production in Basque although some students had used English as the language of instruction. Students in the experimental group with English as the language of instruction were expected to have better results in English because they had had more exposure to English. These students had started learning English earlier and they had had more hours of English when English was used as a language of instruction. It was expected that there would be no

Table 6.5 Tests used in the evaluations

	Ikastolen Elkartea (network of Ikastolak)	*ISEI-IVEI*
English Proficiency	Listening, Reading, Speaking, Writing, Grammar	1–2 Secondary Flyers A2/ KET A2 3–4 Secondary KET A2/ PET B1 5–6 Secondary PET B1/FCE B2
Subject	Social Science in Basque: Comprehension and Production	Different subjects
Other Variables	Background questionnaire	Questionnaires: School managing team, students, family, teachers, teachers' diaries

differences between the groups in Social Science in the case of basic concepts but that the control group would be better when more difficult concepts were assessed because they had learned them in Basque and the Social Science test was in Basque for all the students.

The results show that the experimental group was better than the control group in all the tests of English which included listening, reading, writing, speaking and grammar. The results also indicate that the experimental group was better than the control group in all the Social Science tests even in the ones that were measuring more difficult concepts and content. Students in the experimental group are able to transfer the knowledge acquired through the medium of English into Basque even when the content is more abstract. According to the results, using English as the language of instruction is not only possible but even beneficial to acquire content. In fact, some teachers remarked that students had to pay more attention when Social Science was taught through the medium of English than through the medium of Basque as a possible cause for these results. A group of 122 students from the experimental group took the 7th level of the Trinity College oral tests (http://www.trinitycollege.co.uk/site/?id=368) at the end of 4th year of secondary and 69.7% of them passed this test which is equivalent to the B2 level of the Common European Framework.

The ISEI-IVEI evaluation focused only on English proficiency because different schools were using English as the medium of instruction for different subjects. The tests used were Cambridge tests of different levels. These tests are equivalent to three levels of the Common European Framework: Flyers and KET are roughly equivalent to the A2 level, PET to the B1 level and FCE to the B2 level. The tests were administered twice to the same groups, at the beginning of the first year of the project and at the end of the second year so that the students had different tests at the beginning and the end of the two year project. The results can be seen in Figure 6.1.

The experimental group obtained better results than the control group at the beginning of the project and these differences were maintained and even increased by the second year of the project. The abilities tested were listening, reading comprehension and writing and oral production and the best results are in most cases in oral production tests.

No data were collected on the acquisition of content in the different subjects taught through the medium of English but questionnaires and interviews were used to obtain further information about academic achievement and other aspects of the project. According to the teachers academic achievement is as good as when Basque or Spanish are the medium of instruction. The results of this evaluation show that there are very important differences in the level of English as compared to the

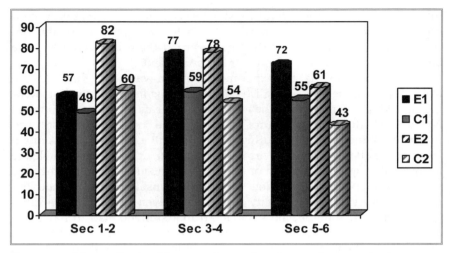

Figure 6.1 Means obtained by experimental and control groups in the ISEI-IVEI evaluation (2007)

E1 = Experimental Test 1; C1 = Control Test 1; E2 = Experimental Test 2; C2 = Control Test 2

control group but only good students of English could take part in this project and many of these students also studied English outside school. The students consider that learning subjects through the medium of English implies an additional effort but that it is worth it. The project is valued very positively by the teachers, the school management, the students and their families.

Another research study based on using English as an additional language of instruction is reported by Jiménez Catalán *et al.* (2006). These researchers carried out a study with 130 students in the 6th year of primary who were studying English in two different educational and sociolinguistic contexts. Specifically they looked at general achievement, receptive and productive vocabulary when English was taught as a subject in a monolingual context outside the Basque Country in La Rioja and as an additional language of instruction in a bilingual context in the Basque Country. Students were asked to complete a battery of tests to assess their English knowledge and vocabulary was measured by means of the Vocabulary Levels Test (VLT) (Schmitt *et al.*, 2001), and a written composition. The compositions were evaluated using scales to measure content, organization, vocabulary, use of the language, and mechanics of writing (Jacobs *et al.*, 1981) and a textual analysis was carried out by using the program WordSmith Tools (Scott, 1996). The cloze test and reading comprehension scores indicate that there is a difference in favor of using English as the language of instruction. Students with English as a language of instruction also had better results in some measures of the receptive vocabulary test. In order to measure productive vocabulary the number of tokens, types and the type/token ratio of the compositions were analyzed. The students with English as the language of instruction produced fewer tokens and types than the non-content group but the type/token ratio was higher. These students also used a larger number of lexical verbs. The results of this study indicate that having English as an additional language of instruction can result in more lexical richness. The most extensive exposure to English is very likely to be a strong predictor of vocabulary acquisition but other factors including the influence of bilingualism on third language acquisition, motivation or cognitive ability could also play a role. In fact, some studies on the acquisition of English that will be reported in Chapter 7 confirm the influence of bilingualism on third language acquisition but also show that factors such as socio-economic status, motivation and intelligence are strong predictors of English proficiency (Cenoz, 1992; Lasagabaster, 1998; Sagasta, 2002).

Cross-Linguistic Influence in Multilingual Acquisition

An area of research that is particularly interesting when considering the acquisition of several languages is cross-linguistic influence. Do learners acquiring a third language transfer from the other languages they know? When looking at transfer from previously known languages it can be interesting to see the specific linguistic context in which the interaction takes place. We could distinguish two main possibilities (see Cenoz, 2003a): interactional strategies and transfer lapses. _Interactional strategies_ are intentional switches into languages other than the target language and they are linked to factors such as the knowledge of other languages by the interlocutor or the topic of the conversation. Intentional switches are usually preceded by a pause in oral production. _Transfer lapses_ are non-intentional switches which are not preceded by a pause or false start and can be regarded as automatic. Transfer lapses are accidental and not intended by the speaker. The main indicator to distinguish between interactional strategies and transfer lapses is the existence of pauses before the element from another language is produced.

Some studies have looked at the influence of Basque and Spanish on the acquisition of English as a third language. Specifically they have tried to identify the conditions in which speakers transfer terms from the other languages they know and the factors that can potentially predict the relative weight of cross linguistic influence. Among the most common factors identified by researchers are typological distance, proficiency in the different languages and factors related to the use of the language such as frequency and recency (Hammarberg, 2001; Cenoz, 2001b, 2003a). Speakers tend to borrow more terms from languages which are typologically closer to the target language. However, as Odlin and Jarvis (2004) and Ringbom (2007) point out, there are a large number of factors that can influence cross linguistic influence from the first language or from other languages known by the speaker. For example, cross linguistic influence is related to factors such as the level of proficiency in the source and the target language, the level of formality, the order of acquisition of the languages or the specific context of the interaction can influence the amount of transfer. Another factor that can predict cross linguistic influence is the so called 'foreign language effect', that is the trend to use languages other than the L1 as a source language of cross linguistic influence (see Clyne, 1997; Williams & Hammarberg, 1998; De Angelis, 2007).

The combination of languages in the Basque educational system is very interesting because of the important differences between the languages at the lexical and syntactic level. As we have already said in Chapter 1, Basque is a non-Indo-European language of unknown origin; English is an Indo-European Germanic language and Spanish an Indo-European Romance language. Therefore Spanish and English are relatively closer than Basque and English or Basque and Spanish. This can be seen in the following example where we can see that the word order for Basque is SOV and it is SVO in English and Spanish. We can also see that as a subject of a transitive verb the subject 'Iñigo' needs the ergative 'k' in Basque but not in the other languages.

1. *Iñigok izozkia jan zuen* (Basque)
2. *Iñigo ate the icecream* (English)
3. *Iñigo se comió el helado* (Spanish)

The three languages have important differences in the lexicon as it can be seen in the noun *'icecream'* (*'izozkia'* in Basque and *'helado'* in Spanish) but language contact also plays an important role in this case. Both English and Basque have a strong influence from Romance languages and nowadays English has an influence on Basque and Spanish and Spanish on Basque. Cenoz (2003a) reports the results of a study on the role of typology in cross linguistic influence in third language acquisition. She analyzed all the cases of cross linguistic influence in two stories told by 18 primary schoolchildren in English. The stories were the Frog story (Mayer, 1969) and a specific story the children had been told in class. She found that 80% of the utterances in one story and 91% of the utterances in the other story were in English without any words in Basque or Spanish. This study also showed that Basque children use Basque and Spanish in different ways in spontaneous oral production in English. Basque was used for interactional strategies, that is, for intentional switches when asking for help from the interlocutor as in the following examples:

1. ... *the dog and the boy was # aurkitzen? (the dog and the boy was # 'find'?)*

It is interesting to observe that in some cases the student is asking for help in Basque but says the term he needs in Spanish. In the following example there is a pause before the question (#) but the term 'bosque' (forest) is inserted in a Basque question instead of the Basque term 'basoa'.

2. ... *then Alex # bosque nola da? (how is 'forest'?)*

Spanish is more common in the case of transfer lapses, that is when the switches are non-intentional, there are no pauses before the switch and they can be regarded as automatic (see Poulisse & Bongaerts, 1994)

3. ... *### and # in the door middle hay the crocodiles (there are)*

Why do children give different roles to Basque and Spanish as source language of cross linguistic influence? A possible explanation for the use of Basque is that Basque is the school language; it is the language they use to ask questions to the teachers and in the context of telling a story they also use it to ask questions to their interlocutor. In the case of more automatic transfer lapses it seems that Spanish is more accessible than Basque. The availability of Spanish as the source language of transfer seems to be common both for students with Basque and Spanish or both languages as a first language. Cenoz (2001b) conducted a study with 90 primary and secondary school subjects and analyzed all cases of cross-linguistic influence in transfer lapses according to the L1 when telling the Frog story in English. The percentages corresponding to the terms transferred from Basque and Spanish into English are given in Figure 6.2.

The results indicate that the subjects who have Basque as the first language do not use Basque more often than Spanish as their source language and that they do not use Basque as the source language more often than the other two groups. Subjects with Spanish as L1 tend to use Basque as the source language more often than the rest of the subjects but the main source language is Spanish for the three groups. One possible explanation for the results of both studies is that schoolchildren can perceive linguistic distance

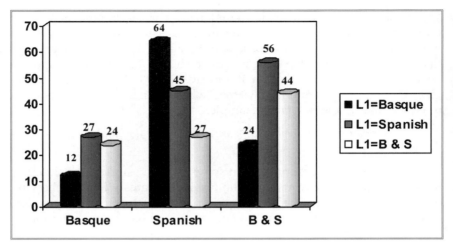

Figure 6.2 Source language of transfer in English oral production according to L1

Source: Adapted from Cenoz, 2001b

and realize that Basque is less likely to work as a source language of transfer. These children have two possible sources of transfer and use the one that is more likely to work so as to benefit from positive transfer which is an important process in L2 and L3 acquisition (Ringbom, 2007). The fact that older children use even less Basque as the source language could be related to their higher metalinguistic awareness that makes them more aware of the linguistic distance between Basque and English. Odlin and Jarvis (2004) reported that Finns and Swedes used their knowledge of Swedish, which is typologically closer to English to form hypothesis about English.

However, the influence of other factors cannot be dismissed. Learners in these studies are in the D model in a school located in a town where less than 50% of the population speaks Basque. Basque is a minority language and as we have seen in the study conducted by Erriondo *et al.* (1998) in Chapter 4, the number of words activated in Spanish by Basque speakers in the D model is higher than the number of words activated in Basque by the same speakers. The Basque speakers in these studies could have a higher level of activation of Spanish relative to Basque in all situations unless the speaker intentionally uses Basque when interacting with Basque-Spanish bilinguals in a context in which Basque is the required language. For example, D model children learn from a very early age that Basque is the language for interaction with their teachers and that could be the reason they use more Basque in the case of interactional strategies, for example to ask for help in Basque. But even in the case of interactional strategies sometimes there are terms in Spanish which indicate that Spanish is highly activated at all times, even when the speaker has decided to use Basque as the language to address his/her interlocutor (see also García Mayo, 2006). Spanish is continuously co-activated and when a learner lacks a specific word in English or Basque, the Spanish term is more available than the Basque term.

Conclusion

Research on proficiency in English in the BAC shows that using English as an additional language of instruction can provide the opportunity for more exposure to English in a context in which contact with English outside the classroom is very limited. One of the challenges of the educational system in the BAC is that students achieve proficiency in English without having the need for extracurricular classes of English that imply extra hours and cannot be afforded by all families. Even though research on CLIL and the use of the target language as an additional language of instruction in bilingual programs is limited in the BAC as it is elsewhere, it seems that they are the most effective ways to increase proficiency in foreign language contexts (Genesee, 1998; De Graaff *et al.*, 2007). More studies to assess the different projects in multilingual education in the BAC are needed and they have to take into account not only the specific characteristics of the school (number of hours of English, integration of subjects) but also the sociolinguistic context in which learning takes place including exposure to English outside the school.

Key Points

- Proficiency in a language is multidimensional and can be evaluated in different ways such as skills (listening, reading, speaking, writing) or competences (can describe, can communicate, can produce, etc).
- Studies on English achievement in the BAC have focused on the measurement of skills and the description of different aspects of proficiency and not on teacher-based assessment.
- Studies on cross-linguistic influence in the BAC indicate that Spanish is the main source of transfer. This could be due to the typological distance between Basque and English and also to the minority status of Basque that makes Spanish the default language.

Chapter 7
The Influence of Bilingualism on L3

Introduction

When a bilingual person and a monolingual person face the challenge of acquiring a language they are not on equal footing. The bilingual person already has access to two linguistic systems with their lexicons, syntax, phonetics, pragmatic and discourse properties. With the exception of early bilinguals, bilinguals are potentially aware of the process of acquiring a second language and this experience could have impact on the acquisition of additional languages. In many cases, bilinguals are active users of the two languages they know and switch between languages according to the situation or the interlocutor. This experience in communication is also different when comparing monolinguals and bilinguals because monolinguals do not have to switch languages.

Research on the influence of bilingualism on third language acquisition is not only important for studies on multilingualism and language acquisition in general but also has specific interest in the educational context of BAC. As we have seen in Chapter 4, the use of Basque as the language of instruction (models B and D) results in more balanced Basque-Spanish bilingualism than the use of Basque as a subject (model A). In this chapter we are going to see if Basque-Spanish bilingualism has a positive effect on English.

The Effect of Bilingualism on Third Language Acquisition

According to folk wisdom, the more languages one knows, the easier it becomes to acquire an additional language. If this is the case, bilinguals would have advantage over monolinguals when learning an additional language. It could also be possible that bilinguals learn languages in different ways, that is, that they follow a different route from that followed by second language learners. This chapter will focus on the rate of acquisition and the studies in which monolinguals and bilinguals have been compared when acquiring an additional language. It will also look at the influence of acquiring a third language on the other languages known by the speakers. This is a relatively new perspective which has been explored in the case of second language acquisition by looking not only at the influence of the L1 on the L2 but at how acquiring an L2 can affect the L1 (see Cook, 2003). Third language acquisition can similarly affect the other languages already known by the learner as it has been shown by Kecskes and Papp (2000). Second and third language acquisition are complex phenomena involving a large number of individual and contextual factors. Different theoretical approaches and methodologies have been used when analyzing the effect of bilingualism on third language acquisition. Some studies have been carried out in educational contexts while others are laboratory studies. Some studies focus on the effect of bilingualism on general proficiency in the third language while others only look at very specific aspects of proficiency or specific aspects of language processing.

The idea that bilinguals could have an advantage over monolinguals when learning a third language was already proposed by researchers in the sixties and seventies (see Cenoz, 2003b for a review). Some of these early studies reported that bilinguals were better than monolinguals at phonetic discrimination skills and auditory discrimination tests and that more balanced bilinguals make fewer errors than less balanced bilinguals.

Laboratory studies using artificial linguistic systems compared monolinguals and multilinguals in the completion of learning and processing tasks. In general, these studies report that multilingual subjects were superior to monolinguals in three different ways because: (1) multilinguals demonstrated greater flexibility in switching strategies according to the demand characteristics of the task; (2) they were more likely to modify strategies that were not effective in language learning and (3) they were more effective using implicit learning strategies. The superiority of bilinguals in these domains was attributed to their richer experience as language learners (Nation & McLaughlin, 1986; McLaughlin & Nayak, 1989; Nayak *et al.*, 1990).

In the rest of this section we are going to review studies on the effect of bilingualism on third language acquisition carried out outside the Basque Country. First, we will look at the studies in bilingual education programs and then we will focus on those in regular programs.

Third language acquisition in bilingual education programs

Immersion education in Canada has resulted in a large number of evaluations of academic and non-academic outcomes. Most research studies focus on academic achievement and the measurement of French and English proficiency. In some cases researchers have also paid attention to the influence of bilingualism on the acquisition of a third language.

Bild and Swain (1989) compared the level of French proficiency attained by three groups of grade-8 learners in the English-speaking city of Toronto: English-speaking monolingual children, bilingual children who could speak English and a Romance language and bilingual children who could speak English and a non-Romance language. The results indicate that both groups of bilingual children obtained higher scores on the French tests than monolingual children. There were no significant differences between the two bilingual groups in spite of the typological relation between the L1 of one of the groups (Italian) and the target language. There was a positive significant influence of the number of years of instruction in the heritage language. So, according to this study bilingualism is associated with advantages in the acquisition of another language and being bilingual seems to be more influential than being a speaker of a Romance language when learning French.

Another study conducted by Swain *et al.* (1990) goes a step further and examines the relationships between literacy skills and typology and the influence of bilingualism (heritage language and English) in the acquisition of French. The sample comprises grade-8 learners who were in their fourth year of French immersion and the four skills were measured: listening comprehension, reading, writing and speaking. The results of this study indicate that literacy in the heritage language has a positive effect on third language learning but no differences were found as related to language use. The effect of typology was not as important when speakers of Romance and non-Romance languages were compared. The only significant measures in which speakers of Romance languages had advantages were global understanding and fluency.

It is also interesting to look at the results of double immersion programs in Canada. Genesee (1998) reports the results of the evaluations conducted in three French-Hebrew double immersion schools as compared to children in early French immersion and children in regular English programs. The results of early double immersion students in French were as good as those of early French immersion. The results of the evaluation also indicate that double immersion in French and Hebrew did not have any negative effect on the development of English or mathematics as the scores were not different from those of the English regular group.

Outside Canada, another study on the influence of bilingualism on third language acquisition included Catalan-Spanish bilinguals from Catalonia and Spanish monolinguals from another Spanish area outside

Catalonia. Catalan and Spanish are the official languages in Catalonia but Catalan is the main language of instruction at school (Sanz, 2000). Catalan students in this study learned English as a third language and the non-Catalan Spanish students also learned English but as a second language. All the participants took tests of grammar and vocabulary to measure English proficiency. The results clearly indicated that bilingualism had a significant effect on English proficiency so that bilinguals had advantage over monolinguals.

An interesting European project in trilingual education is the Foyer project involving immigrant languages, Dutch and French. Jaspaert and Lemmens (1990) analyzed the acquisition of Dutch as a third language by participants in this project who were Italian immigrant children and had also received instruction in Italian and French. The tests used to measure proficiency in Dutch included tests of grammar, writing, vocabulary, dictation, reading and a cloze test. When the level of proficiency in Dutch of Italian-French bilinguals was compared to that of French-speaking monolinguals, no significant differences were observed. These results were considered positive taking into account that Dutch was a third language for immigrant children. Another study on the effect of bilingualism on third language acquisition is that of Brohy (2001). She analyzed the acquisition of French as a third language by Romansch-German bilinguals and German-speaking monolinguals in Switzerland. Brohy measured general proficiency in French by using tests to measure the four abilities. She found that bilinguals obtained significantly higher scores in the acquisition of French than monolinguals.

In sum, the studies carried out in immersion programs and in other bilingual programs indicate that bilinguals have advantages over monolinguals in the acquisition of an additional language.

Studies on third language acquisition in regular programs

The results of studies on third language acquisition in regular programs are not as conclusive. Sanders and Meijers (1995) found no differences between monolinguals and bilinguals when they compared immigrant Turkish-Dutch and Arabic-Dutch bilingual speakers to monolingual Dutch speakers learning English. Schoonen et al. (2002) focused on proficiency in written English by native speakers of Dutch and immigrants who were bilingual in their L1 and Dutch. The results of the study indicate that there are no significant differences in the different measures of writing proficiency between the two groups in spite of the general trend for immigrant learners to present poor school achievement. In another study with the same participants Van Gelderen *et al.* (2003) reported that bilingual speakers obtained significantly lower scores in the reading comprehension measures. These results are explained by linguistic distance between the L1 and the L3 in the case of immigrant learners, but the authors also consider that socioeconomic status could have some influence.

Some studies conducted in Sweden have also compared immigrant bilinguals and monolinguals learning English. The participants in Balke-Aurell and Lindblad's (1982) study were monolingual Swedish speakers and bilingual immigrant speakers. The tests of English proficiency included grammar, listening, word comprehension and reading and indicated that there were no differences between the groups. The second study was conducted by Mägiste (1984) who compared English proficiency by monolingual Swedish speakers, passive bilinguals (who only use Swedish in everyday life) and active bilinguals (who use Swedish and another language in everyday life). She found that the best results in English were obtained by the passive bilinguals, followed by the monolinguals and the active bilinguals.

Another study conducted with immigrants in the USA focused on the acquisition of French by monolingual English-speakers and bilingual English-Spanish speakers (Thomas, 1988). The results indicate that bilingual learners obtained significantly higher scores in French than their monolingual peers. Thomas also observed that those bilinguals who had literacy skills in their first language (Spanish) obtained better results than those who were fluent in the first language but only had literacy skills in English. These results were not confirmed by a study conducted by Wagner *et al.* (1989) in Morocco. The results of this study indicate that instruction in a second language without literacy in the first does not hinder the acquisition of a third language.

Bilingual learners acquiring a third language obtained good results in other contexts. For example, Clyne *et al.* (2004) observed a general tendency for L3 learners to perform better than L2 learners in Australia when learning Greek or Spanish as a third language.

Some studies have focused on very specific aspects of language proficiency rather than trying to measure general proficiency in the language. For example, Enomoto (1994) compared the discrimination of single and geminate stops in Japanese by five bilingual and five monolingual subjects and observed that bilinguals had advantages over monolinguals. Okita and Jun Hai (2001) compared monolingual Chinese-speakers to bilingual Chinese-English speakers in the acquisition of the Kanji writing system in Japanese. The results of the study indicate that the scores obtained by Chinese-speaking monolinguals were higher than those obtained by Chinese-English-speaking bilinguals. One possible interpretation for these findings is that the bilinguals, who were from Singapore, did not have a strong command of the Hanzi Chinese writing system and therefore could not transfer it to Japanese as the Chinese monolinguals did.

Zobl (1993) used a grammaticality judgment test to measure several structures such as adjacency of verb and object, indirect and direct object passive, indirect and direct object and wh-movement in English. Multilinguals formulate wider grammars, that is, they accept as correct more incorrect sentences than monolinguals. Monolinguals tend to formulate grammars that are just powerful enough to fit the input data, that is, their grammars are more restricted but include fewer errors. Multilinguals generate larger grammars which include incorrect sentences but allow them to progress faster. According to Zobl this difference between monolinguals and bilinguals could explain why bilinguals have advantages when learning additional languages. Another study focusing on grammar was conducted by Klein (1995). In this study, multilinguals obtained significantly higher scores in both constructions, but both groups had the same types of errors and this is interpreted as a difference in rate but not in route.

Gibson *et al.* (2001) examined the acquisition of German prepositions by learners who were studying German as an L2 or as an L3 (or L4). They found no statistical differences between the two groups. They consider that the specific characteristics of the task and interference from other languages could explain these results. A clearer pattern favoring bilinguals was reported by Keshavarz and Astaneh (2004) who conducted a study in Iran with Armenian-Persian and Turkish-Persian bilinguals and Persian monolinguals. They found that native speakers of Turkish and Armenian as a first language who could speak Persian as a L2 obtained better results in oral production and a vocabulary test.

Safont (2005) compared the acquisition of requests in English by Spanish-monolinguals and Catalan-Spanish bilinguals. She found that bilinguals obtained significantly higher scores than monolinguals on the different measures used to analyze the formulation of requests. They also demonstrated a higher degree of pragmatic awareness.

In sum, results of studies on the influence of bilingualism on third language acquisition carried out in regular programs are more mixed. In some contexts, bilinguals obtain better results but in others, particularly in the case of immigrant students, bilinguals do not progress faster in third language acquisition. There is also a difference between studies focusing on general proficiency that are usually more favorable for bilinguals and those studies on specific aspects of proficiency which do not show so favorable results.

The Influence of Basque-Spanish Bilingualism on the Acquisition of English: Research Findings

In this section we will look at research studies conducted in the Basque Country which focus on the influence of bilingualism on the acquisition of English as a third language. These studies compare bilingual Basque-Spanish-speaking learners to monolingual Spanish-speaking learners or bilingual learners with different degrees of proficiency in Basque. In the context in which these studies were carried out the higher proficiency in Basque implies a higher level of bilingualism because all the students were proficient in Spanish. Some of these studies focus on general proficiency in English and others on very specific aspects of grammar or phonological competence. The focus of the studies can be seen in Table 7.1.

Table 7.1 Studies conducted in the Basque Country

Level of Bilingualism	L3 Proficiency measured	Level
Bilinguals vs. monolinguals More balanced bilinguals vs. less balanced bilinguals	General proficiency Specific aspects	Primary school Secondary school University

The research studies comparing the acquisition of English by monolinguals and bilinguals are basically cross-sectional comparisons between models. As we have already seen in Chapter 4, students in model A have Basque as a school subject in primary and secondary school but generally achieve a very limited level of proficiency in Basque. On the other hand, model D students, instructed through the medium of Basque, can be considered bilingual or at least the most bilingual of the three models. Some students in the B model also achieve a high level of proficiency in Basque but on average it is lower than in model D.

Some of the studies comparing the different models (Cenoz, 1992; Lasagabaster, 1998) have looked at different areas of proficiency in English and used a battery of tests to measure the different oral and written dimensions of proficiency while others have only focused on very specific areas and have used very specific tests (Gonzalez Ardeo, 2000; García Mayo, 1999).

Comparing general proficiency

The studies on general proficiency (Cenoz, 1992; Lasagabaster, 1998) have not only measured different skills but have also included bigger

Table 7.2 Participants in studies comparing English proficiency in different models

	Sample	*Models*	*Location*	*Schools*
Cenoz 1992	N = 321 Age range: 17–19 Secondary 6	A 154 D 167	Tolosa and Donostia-San Sebastian	Public and private
Lasagabaster 1998	N = 252 Age range: 10–11 and 13–14 Primary 5, Secondary 2	A 84 B 84 D 84	Vitoria-Gasteiz	Public and private

samples. Cenoz (1992; see also Cenoz & Valencia, 1994) conducted a study which included 321 secondary school students and Lasagabaster (1998, 2000) included 252 primary and secondary school students. Both studies include approximately the same number of male and female students. The distribution of the sample in these two studies can be seen in Table 7.2.

Both studies, taken together cover different ages and models in primary and secondary education. They measured English proficiency at different stages from the second year of English instruction in primary school to the last year of secondary school. They compare the existing models (Cenoz's study does not include model B because it did not exist in secondary school at the time). Lasagabaster's study compared two different grades in the three models using groups of 42 students for each grade and model. The different location of the schools participating in this research studies is very interesting regarding the use of Basque. Donostia-San Sebastian is the capital of the province of Gipuzkoa and the most Basque-speaking city in the Basque Country with 32.6% of the population who is proficient in Basque. Tolosa is a town in Gipuzkoa with 65.5% of the population proficient in Basque. Vitoria-Gasteiz, the capital of the province of Araba is mainly Spanish-speaking with 13.6% of Basque speakers. Both studies include public and private schools. These two studies also include different age groups in primary and secondary education. The youngest group is between 10 and 11 and started to learn English in the 4th year of primary and has been tested in the 5th, the intermediate group is 13–14 years old started to learn English in the last year of primary school and were in their 2nd year of secondary. The oldest group was 17–19 years old and these students were in most cases in the seventh year of English in the last year of secondary school. As the age of the introduction of English has gone down, the youngest group started to learn English at a younger age than the other groups, in the 4th year of primary (9–10) but still much later than children in the Basque Autonomous Community nowadays. Both studies use a similar battery of tests which are included in Table 7.3.

Table 7.3 Tests and questionnaires used in the comparative studies

	Cenoz, 1992	*Lasagabaster, 1998*
English proficiency	*Listening*: three texts and multiple choice (MC) questions *Reading*: 10 pages to read and MC, True-False and open questions *Speaking*: Interviews on two topics to provide information and give opinions *Writing*: Composition 200–250 words *Lexis & grammar*: 3 tests of including auxiliary verbs, tenses, subordinate clauses, vocabulary, prepositions	*Listening*: one text and MC questions (different primary and secondary) *Reading*: matching pictures and sentences in primary; text and MC (primary and secondary) open questions (secondary) *Speaking*: tell a story using pictures, same both groups *Writing*: letter (only in secondary) *Lexis & grammar*: two levels vocabulary, word order, sentence completion, tenses, interrogatives
Other variables	*Intelligence*: Otis-Lennon Mental *Background*: gender, age, SES, cultural background, location of school, rural/urban, private vs. public *Psychosocial*: attitude towards British, American, towards learning English, motivational intensity, capacity to learn English, satisfaction with English classes *Socioeducational*: Extra lessons of English, parents' knowledge of English, number of years of English, grade in English the previous year, stay in English-speaking country *Bilingualism*: Model, L1, knowledge of Basque father, mother, subject, siblings, use of Basque at home, friends, school, to read, to watch TV.	*Intelligence*: two levels Raven *Background*: gender, age, SES, cultural background, private vs. public *Psychosocial*: Motivation: attitude, effort, wish, importance of English *Socioeducational*: Extra lessons of English, parents' knowledge of English *Bilingualism*: Model, L1, knowledge of Basque father mother, use of Basque with father, mother, at home, with friends, TV, Basque and Spanish tests *Metalinguistic awareness*: adapted THAM-2. *Creativity*: Torrance Creativity test

As we can see in Table 7.3, Cenoz (1992) and Lasagabaster (1998) used a battery of tests to measure the four skills of language proficiency and an additional test of syntax and vocabulary. The tests are different because the participants belong to different age groups, pre-university students in Cenoz's study and primary and secondary students in Lasagagaster's. Testing English in higher levels allows for the use of longer tests that cannot be used in primary school. For example, the writing production of primary schoolchildren is not measured because the primary school-children who participated in Lasagabaster's study were not used to write in English.

A number of cognitive, general background, psychosocial, linguistic and socioeducational variables were also measured in these studies. Different tests are used to measure general intelligence because of the age group differences. Cenoz uses the Otis-Lennon test and Lasagabaster the Raven's Progressive Matrices Test A, Ab, B in the primary group and the Raven B, C, D in the secondary group. Cenoz includes the difference between rural and urban areas and more psychosocial and socioeducational variables. She includes two towns in her study but as many of the participants attending the schools in Tolosa came from smaller towns and villages the students are divided into three groups: those living in towns and villages with less than 10,000 inhabitants, those living in towns that have between 10,000 and 20,000 inhabitants and those living in towns and cities with more than 20,000 inhabitants. The use of Basque is much more common in everyday life in the smaller towns and villages. Lasagabaster measured proficiency in Basque and Spanish by using tests and also controls for metalinguistic awareness and creativity. He uses an adapted shorter version of the Basque and Spanish tests used in the EIFE studies that were used by Sierra and Olaziregi (1989, 1991) in former evaluations discussed in Chapter 4. In the case of primary school these tests measure three skills: oral comprehension (10 points), reading comprehension (10 points) and written production (60 points) and in the case of secondary school students they measure reading comprehension (15) and writing (60). Lasagabaster uses a shorter version of the THAM-2 test to measure metalinguistic ability (Pinto & Titone, 1995). He includes synonymy, acceptability and ambiguity for both groups and also phonetic segmentation for the secondary school students. In order to measure creativity Lasagabaster uses Torrance's test (1990) and he measures for fluency, flexibility and originality. A variable which is controlled in both studies is the extra lessons of English outside school.

The studies by Cenoz and Lasagabaster analyze the effect of different variables on the acquisition of English but the results presented here will

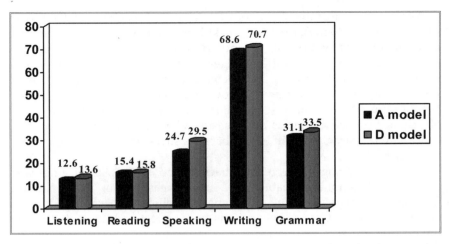

Figure 7.1 English proficiency at the end of secondary school (Cenoz, 1992)

only focus on the effect of bilingualism on the acquisition of English. Figure 7.1 shows the means obtained by model A (Spanish as language of instruction) and model D (Basque as language of instruction) students in English tests in Cenoz's study. The maximum scores for these tests were the following: listening (max 19), reading (max 26), speaking (max 50), writing (max 100) and grammar (max 75).

The results in Figure 7.1 indicate that bilingual students (model D) obtained higher scores than monolingual students (model A). The differences are significant for listening comprehension (F = 6.11; S = .00) and speaking (F = 19.55; S = .00) and marginally significant for the lexis and grammar test (F = 3.19; S = .09). There were no significant differences in the case of reading and writing.

Table 7.4 shows the results of the Analyses of Variance comparing the results obtained in the English tests by the students in the different models in Lasagabaster's study. Students in model D have Basque as the language of instruction and are the most balanced bilinguals.

The results of comparing the different models in the 5th year of primary school and the 2nd year of secondary show that the model D students got the best results in all the tests with the exception of the lexis and grammar test in the case of secondary school students. In the case of primary school, model D participants obtained significantly higher scores than model A in reading, speaking and grammar and significantly higher scores than model B in speaking and grammar. Model B obtained better scores than

Table 7.4 English proficiency in models A, B and D (Lasagabaster, 1998)

Primary School				
	Model A	*Model B*	*Model D*	*F*
Listening (max 5)	2.28	2.38	2.64	.939
Reading (max 11)	6.97	8.52	8.59	6.595**
Speaking (max 50)	24.57	26.19	28.80	3.569*
Grammar (max 38)	28.00	28.09	30.92	2.461#
Secondary School				
Listening (max 9)	4.95	4.59	5.88	4.716*
Reading (max 10)	4.42	5.52	6.30	6.149**
Speaking (max 50)	27.21	28.40	29.90	3.219*
Writing (max 100)	72.11	70.77	76.59	5.314*
Grammar (max 40)	25.80	23.73	25.30	.733

**p < .001, *p < .05, #p < .09

model A only in the case of reading comprehension. In the case of secondary school, model D participants obtained significantly higher scores than model A in listening, reading, speaking and writing and significantly higher scores than model B in listening and writing. Model B obtained better scores than model A only in the case of reading comprehension. Therefore, model D students obtain the best scores and the main differences are between model D and the other two models.

The results of Cenoz's and Lasagabaster's studies confirm that students who have Basque as the language of instruction obtain better scores in English than students instructed through Spanish, the majority language. These two studies included different individual and contextual variables in their design and they also looked at the effect of bilingualism once the influence of these variables was controlled. That is, they isolated the effect of bilingualism so as to make sure that the differences between monolinguals and bilinguals were not caused by other variables. In both studies, variables such as general intelligence, motivation, SES and extra lessons of English are controlled. Cenoz also conducted Analyses of Variance to check the mediating effect of bilingualism when the influence of individual and contextual variables on English proficiency is analyzed. In order to do that she divided the subjects into two or three groups depending on their scores on the specific independent variable and compared the

Table 7.5 Differences between monolinguals and bilinguals in English proficiency controlling for SES

	Monolinguals	*Bilinguals*	*F bilingualism*
SES Lower	−0.50	0.18	23.68[**]
SES Intermediate	−0.24	0.48	
SES Higher	0.43	0.84	

[**]$p < .001$

scores in English of monolinguals and bilinguals belonging to the different groups. For example, all the participants in the study were divided into three groups according to their socioeconomic status: lower, intermediate and higher. Then monolingual and bilingual students were separated and the differences in the mean scores in all the skills in English were compared. Table 7.5 shows the results for the total score of the English proficiency test by monolinguals and bilinguals belonging to the three SES groups. The results are in Z scores because the different tests of proficiency had different maximum and minimum scores.

The results indicate that students coming from lower socioeconomic backgrounds obtained the lowest scores in English and students coming from intermediate and higher socioeconomic backgrounds obtained better scores but they also show that bilinguals obtained better results than monolinguals when the effect of SES is controlled. These analyses were conducted with all the independent variables and the effect of bilingualism was significant in almost all the analyses. Cenoz and Valencia (1994) conducted further analyses of the data and reported that when the weight of the most influential variables (intelligence, age, motivation and extra lessons of English) is analyzed in a multiple regression analysis adding bilingualism did significantly improved the level of explained variance of English proficiency. These results confirm that bilingualism has a positive mediating effect on the acquisition of English. Bilingualism in this study was measured by using an index which included not only the language of instruction but also the first language, the sociolinguistic context and the knowledge of Basque by the subject.

Comparing specific areas of proficiency

After looking at studies on general proficiency in English in this section we look at two studies that compare the results obtained in English by

Table 7.6 Information about the sample in studies on specific areas

	Sample	*Models*	*Location*	*Schools*
García Mayo, 1999	N = 120 Age range: 11–12/ 14–15 Grade = 6th year of primary 3rd year of secondary	A 60 D 60	Town near Bilbao Town in Gipuzkoa	Private
Gonzalez Ardeo, 2001	N = 48 Age range: 21–25 University students of engineering	Monolingual 12 Bilingual 36	Bilbao	Public university

Table 7.7 Tests and questionnaires used in studies on specific areas

	García Mayo	*Gonzalez Ardeo*
English proficiency	*Syntax*: 30 sentences on pro-drop parameter	*Lexis*: Two cloze tests Phonetics: Reading aloud Perception of proficiency
Other variables	*Background*: Gender, age, location of school *Socioeducational*: Extra lessons of English, stay in English speaking country *Bilingualism*: Model	*Background*: Age, SES, *Psychosocial*: Motivation intensity, attitudes towards classes, communication need *Aptitude*: Perception of codification ability *Bilingualism*: Model, L1

monolingual and bilingual students but they focus on specific aspects of language proficiency and include a limited number of independent variables. Table 7.6 provides information about the samples.

As we can see in Table 7.7 these studies include primary, secondary school and university students who are studying in the different models in the case of primary or secondary schools. These can be classified as monolingual or bilingual according to their model before going to university and according to their first language in the case of university students. The variables considered in these studies can be seen in Table 7.7.

The variables included in Table 7.7 indicate that there is a very important difference between these studies and those conducted by Cenoz and Lasagabaster. The measurements of English proficiency in García Mayo's and Gonzalez Ardeo's studies are limited to specific aspects and the number of variables measured are also very few as compared to the other studies. García Mayo using a generative approach analyzes some aspects of a specific parameter, the pro-drop parameter and asked students whether 30 sentences were correct or not and to correct them accordingly. Gonzalez Ardeo tested 20 vocabulary words related to Engineering by using two cloze tests and looked at mistakes in pronunciation in a reading aloud activity. The number of background, socioeducational and psychosocial variables as well as the measurement of bilingualism included very few variables as compared to the previous studies. Both García Mayo and Gonzalez Ardeo controlled for extra lessons of English but Gonzalez Ardeo faces the problem shared by many research studies involving adult speakers. Adults' experience in language learning is longer than that of schoolchildren and it is very difficult to control for all the exposure to English that they had before going to the university; the control of this variable only affects extra classes of English at the time of testing and the number of hours of English at the university.

García Mayo (1999) reported that monolinguals (model A) could identify a higher number of sentences as incorrect than bilingual (model D) students in both age groups. She also found that monolinguals obtained higher scores than bilinguals when correcting those sentences identified as incorrect. As García Mayo explains this study is limited to a very specific type of task. It is also interesting to see that when asked if a sentence is correct or incorrect the preferred categories are different for bilinguals and monolinguals. Bilinguals in both age groups respond 'I don't know' as their preferred answer while monolinguals in general do not choose 'I don't know' and choose mainly between 'correct' or 'incorrect'. In this way, bilinguals make more mistakes than monolinguals by not recognizing incorrect sentences but monolinguals make more mistakes than bilinguals when saying that correct sentences are incorrect. It is very difficult to know why monolinguals and bilinguals followed a different strategy. One possibility is that bilinguals had not been used to grammar exercises because they were taking part in a special project to develop communication skills (Elorza & Muñoa, 2008) and monolinguals, who were not taking part in this project, were more used to grammar exercises in which they had to give a specific answer. Another possible explanation is that as Zobl (1993) points out, multilinguals formulate wider grammars and they accept as correct more incorrect sentences than monolinguals. According to Zobl this can make multilingual progress faster in the acquisition of an additional language. The basic idea is that as bilinguals and multilinguals have a larger repertoire of grammar structures, they are more likely to accept new structures as grammatical while monolinguals only accept as grammatically correct the structures they are sure they know. A lower score in identifying incorrect structures could indicate a wider grammar that makes multilingual learners progress faster even if they make mistakes. García Mayo's study confirms that there are some interesting differences between monolinguals and bilinguals and the next step could be to conduct longitudinal studies to examine the relationship between wider grammars and the general rate of acquisition.

Gonzalez Ardeo reported that bilinguals got slightly higher scores in the lexical tasks but that the differences did not reach significance. There were some differences favoring bilinguals in the pronunciation test but they did not reach significance either. Further analyses of phonetic ability indicate that bilinguals with Basque as their first language outperformed those with Spanish as their first language and that the differences reached significance. A possible explanation for the lack of differences can be that the phonetic systems in Basque and Spanish are very similar and different from English. The fact that the knowledge of Basque does not add many phonemes to the phonetic repertoire of monolingual Spanish speakers and that even monolingual speakers are exposed to Basque pronunciation at school and outside school can explain the lack of significant differences between monolinguals and bilinguals. According to Gonzalez Ardeo, one of the conditions to select participants in this study was that they had obtained equal results in a written test in the previous term. This study confirms that no differences between monolinguals and bilinguals exist in a specific lexical and phonetic task one term later. Even if there had been significant differences, the small size of the sample and the uniformity of the results in the previous written examination would have made it difficult to explain whether the possible differences were related to bilingualism.

These two studies focus on very specific aspects of language proficiency and show that bilinguals do not always obtain significantly better results than monolinguals. These results are compatible with those obtained in the studies conducted by Cenoz and Lasagabaster because they reported significantly higher scores for bilinguals in most tests but not in all the tests. The effect of bilingualism is not as strong as the effect of other variables such as intelligence or motivation and it cannot be shown in all aspects of third language acquisition. It can be expected that if we focus on a very specific aspect of proficiency the effect of other variables such as the teaching methodology, SES, motivation or intelligence can hide the effect of bilingualism. Nevertheless, the contribution of these studies of specific areas is important not only to analyze the effect of bilingualism on third language acquisition but also to analyze the different strategies used by bilinguals and monolinguals when performing specific tasks (see also Kemp, 2007).

Comparisons between more and less balanced bilinguals

The studies included in this section do not compare the acquisition of English by monolinguals and bilinguals but focus on bilinguals with different levels of proficiency in Basque. As Basque is the minority language a higher level of proficiency in Basque equals a higher level of bilingualism in Basque and Spanish. Therefore, it would be expected that balanced bilinguals do better in English. Table 7.8 shows the characteristics of the samples in these studies.

The study by Sagasta includes 155 model D secondary school students who are divided into two groups: D-maintenance and D-immersion. All the participants have Basque as the language of instruction at school but they were in two different classes because these two varieties of the model D are distinguished in the specific school where the data were collected. The D-maintenance group includes 78 students who have Basque as their first language or used mainly Basque at home, at school and in social contexts. The D-immersion group includes 77 students who have Spanish as their first language or used more Spanish than Basque in everyday communication. All students study Spanish and English as school subject from the 3rd year of primary (age eight).

Table 7.8 Characteristics of the samples in comparisons between bilinguals

	Sample	*Models*	*Location*	*Schools*
Sagasta, 2002	$N = 155$ Age range: 12–16 Grade = 1,2,3,4 secondary	D L1 = Basque 78 L1 = Spanish 77	Town in Gipuzkoa	Public
Gallardo, 2005	$N = 60$ Age range: 9–18 Grades: 4, 5 primary; 2, 3, 5, 6 secondary	D More bilingual = 30 Less bilingual = 30	Town in Gipuzkoa	Private
Goikoetxea, 2007	$N = 24$ Age range: 13–14 Grade = 2 secondary	D L1 = Basque 12 L1 = Spanish 12	Town in Gipuzkoa	Private

The study by Gallardo includes 60 model D primary and secondary school students who are also divided into two groups according to the use of Basque (Gallardo, 2005, 2007). These students are in different grades in primary and secondary school and started to learn English at different ages but have the same amount of exposure to English. They have all had Spanish as a school subject from the 3rd year of primary. The most bilingual group got a 9.53 score (max = 10) regarding the use of Basque at home, at school and with their friends. The less bilingual group got a score of 3.33 in this questionnaire. The items and questionnaires used in these two studies are listed in Table 7.9.

The study by Goikoetxea (2007), which has already been discussed in Chapter 6, includes 24 model D secondary school students who had either Basque or Spanish as their first language. Half of the sample started to learn English when they were 5–6 and the other half when they were 8–9. In Chapter 6, we have already seen that Goikoetxea used at background questionnaire, an intelligence test and oral and written tests of the three languages.

Table 7.9 Tests and questionnaires used in the comparisons between bilinguals

	Sagasta (2002)	*Gallardo (2005)*
English proficiency	*Writing*: letter and recipe	*Phonetics*: Auditory discrimination test for vowels and consonants
Other variables	*Intelligence*: Domino D-48 *Background*: gender, age, SES, cultural background, rural/urban *Psychosocial*: Attitudes towards learning three languages, speakers, multilingualism, teacher; attitude towards own capacity *Socioeducational*: Extra lessons of English *Bilingualism*: model, L1, use of Basque father, mother, siblings, friends, school, television, reading *Basque proficiency*: letter and recipe *Spanish proficiency*: letter and recipe *Metalinguistic awareness*: adapted THAM-2	*Background*: gender, age, SES, cultural background, rural/urban *Socioeducational*: Extra lessons of English, stay in English speaking country, years of instruction *Bilingualism*: L1, use of Basque with father, mother, siblings, friends, school

Sagasta analyzes only one of the four skills of language proficiency, written production but the analysis is quite comprehensive. She uses two types of test and looks at differences between the two groups of bilinguals regarding the following variables: global competence which includes content, organization, vocabulary, use of the language, and mechanics of writing (Jacobs *et al.*, 1981) and other aspects of written production following Wolfe-Quintero *et al.* (1999): fluency (number of words divided by number of T units), syntactic complexity (number of finite and non-finite verb clauses), lexical complexity (types and tokens) and error index (number the errors divided by T unit). She also includes a large number of independent variables and participants completed the same writing tasks in Basque, English and Spanish.

Gallardo focuses on the perception of English phonemes by the two groups of bilinguals and used minimal pairs of identification tasks for vowel and consonant phonemes. The stimuli amounted to 45 phoneme contrasts. The stimuli were carefully selected taking into account the different phonetic systems of Spanish/Basque and English. The tests were administered individually and subjects had to choose the card with the drawing and the orthographical transcription corresponding to the word they heard. Gallardo also includes some independent variables but the main aim of the study is to analyze the effect of bilingualism and the effect of age on the perception of English phonemes.

Sagasta compared the mean scores of the indexes obtained in the different dimensions of English oral production by model D-maintenance (L1 = Basque) and model D-immersion (L1 = Spanish) as it can be seen in Figure 7.2 (see Sagasta, 2002, for more details).

The results indicate that model D-maintenance students (L1 = Basque) obtained significantly higher scores in fluency (T = 2.93; S = .05). These students also obtained higher scores in grammatical complexity and lexical complexity but the differences are only marginally significant. The error index is higher in model D-immersion (L1= Spanish) but in this case the differences are marginally significant. Students with Basque as their L1 have an overall mean score of 53.91 and those with Spanish as the language of instruction 48.09 (max = 100). These differences were significant (T = 2.99; S = .05).

Sagasta also conducted other analyses by dividing the students into three groups according to the results of their Basque and Spanish written productions. These groups were the highest bilingual, the medium and the lowest bilingual. When comparing the means obtained in the different measures of English writing by these three groups she observed that the highest level of competence in the two languages had a significant effect on English written production (see Sagasta, 2003).

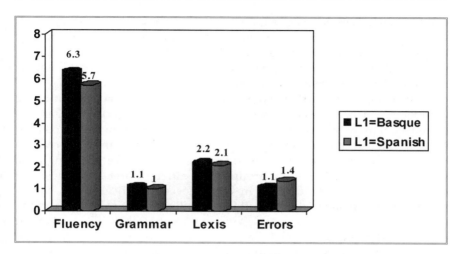

Figure 7.2 Results obtained in writing tests (Sagasta, 2002)

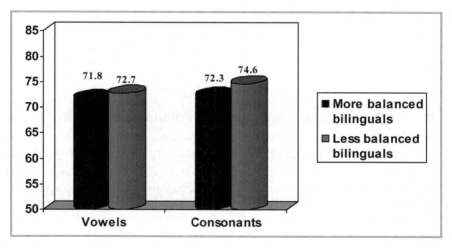

Figure 7.3 Results in phonetic discrimination (Gallardo, 2005)

Figure 7.3 includes the right discrimination means for the two bilingual groups in Gallardo's study (see also Gallardo, 2005).

Gallardo (2005) reports that there were no significant differences between more and less balanced bilinguals in vowel and consonant discrimination. Less balanced bilinguals obtained slightly higher scores but the difference does not reach significance. As we have already seen before, Spanish and Basque are very similar with regard to segmental phonology, they have the same vowel system and very similar consonantal inventories so if there are differences between more and less balanced bilinguals they are more likely to be seen in other areas.

Goikoetxea (2007) analyzed the different dimensions of communicative competence in the three languages using a qualitative approach. Regarding the effect of more or less balanced bilingualism on communicative competence in English she found that there were no differences in action competence, sociocultural competence, discourse competence and linguistic competence between the two groups with different first languages. She found some slight differences in strategic competence. When facing difficulties to go ahead with an utterance, bilinguals with Spanish as the first language stopped the conversation more often than bilinguals with Basque as the first language. Bilinguals with Basque as the first language used more code switching and invented more words by foreignizing them than those with Spanish as a first language.

The results of these three studies do not provide enough evidence to generalize about the differences between more and less balanced bilinguals in third language acquisition because they look at different dimensions of proficiency at different ages. However, Sagasta (2003) and Goikoetxea (2007) found some differences that have to be confirmed with further research.

Language Interaction and the Effect of the L3 on the L1 and the L2

As we have already seen, the L2 can have influence on the L1. As Cook (2003) says, acquiring a second language could be a way of training the brain with positive effects for the L1 but acquiring a L2 can also result in attrition of the L1 when there is not enough exposure to it. Is Basque or Spanish affected by the acquisition of English? Is proficiency in the three languages related? The main interest regarding the effect of learning English on Basque and Spanish is related to the age factor because there have been some worries about the effect of a very early introduction of English as a third language in the Basque educational system. We will discuss these studies related to the age factor in Chapter 9. In this section we will only report the results of a study about the effect of English on some aspects of Spanish pragmatic competence and look at the relationship between proficiency in the three languages in some of the studies already discussed in the previous section.

Cenoz (2003c) considered the effect of the L2 on the L1 in studies of other aspects of proficiency (Kecskes & Papp, 2000) and the multicompetence model (Cook, 1992, 1995) to look at the interaction between the L1 and the L2 at the pragmatic level. She wanted to check if the 'Intercultural Style Hypothesis' (Blum-Kulka, 1991; Kasper & Blum-Kulka, 1993) defined as the development of an intercultural pattern which reflects bi-directional interaction between the languages in pragmatic competence was confirmed. Specifically, the study analyzes whether intensive instruction in English has an effect on the formulation of requests in Spanish.

Participants were 69 university students with a mean age of 20.68. They were all students at the University of the Basque Country and they all had Spanish as their L1, Basque as their L2 and English as their L3. Forty-nine subjects were specializing in English Studies and the other 20 were Psychology students with a very low command of English who had not studied English in the last three years. The data were obtained via a general background questionnaire and a discourse completion test (DCT) including four situations to elicit requests (Blum-Kulka *et al.*, 1989). The group with a higher command of English completed the DCT both in English and Spanish and the other group only in Spanish. The elements of the requests analyzed were alerters, request strategies, syntactic downgraders, lexical downgraders and mitigating supportives.

The results indicated that with the exception of syntactic downgraders in one of the utterances, there were no significant differences between requests formulated in English and Spanish by the students specializing in English. This group uses a very similar number of elements of the same type in English and Spanish. When the Spanish requests formulated by the two groups were compared, it was observed that there were significant differences between the two groups in some of the measures corresponding to some of the requests. A qualitative analysis showed that participants who were proficient in English used their interlocutors' first name more often, more indirect strategies and a wider range of syntactic downgraders, lexical downgraders and mitigating supportives. These findings indicate that participants who are fluent in English have developed an 'intercultural style' and that there is an effect of the L3 on the L1.

The interaction between languages has been proposed by Cook (1992, 1995) when discussing the concept of multicompetence and also by Herdina and Jessner's dynamic model of multilingualism (2002). Some of the studies included in the previous section have analyzed the relationship between proficiency in Basque, Spanish and English. These studies do not prove the effect of the L3 on the L1 or L2 but they indicate that proficiency in the three languages is related. For example, Lasagabaster (1998) and Sagasta (2002) conducted correlation analyses and found that the correlations between the three languages were significant. Egiguren (2006) and Goikoetxea (2007) also reported that proficiency in Basque, Spanish and English was related. Outside the Basque Country, the correlation between the results in three languages was also reported by Muñoz (2000) who found significant correlations between tests of Catalan, Spanish and English.

Conclusion

In general, research indicates that bilingualism has a positive effect on third language acquisition and this outcome is confirmed in the Basque Country where the languages involved are relatively distant. These advantages can be related to metalinguistic awareness (see Jessner, 2006, 2008; Ransdell *et al.*, 2006), to the abilities bilinguals may have for specific tasks and their advantages in cognitive control (Bialystok, 2001, 2003, 2005). Bilingualism is a factor affecting the acquisition of additional languages but language acquisition is a complex phenomenon and other factors can have a more important influence and hide the effect of bilingualism. This can be the case when language acquisition takes place in subtractive contexts or when the effect of teaching practices is seen in studies focusing in very specific skills and sub-skills. If metalinguistic awareness associated with bilingualism has positive effects it can be important to develop this awareness so that bilinguals can benefit from it to a larger extent. As Moore (2006: 243) says, the idea would be to consider multilingualism as a principle for language education, as a transversal project. As we have seen in Chapter 5, some Basque schools are working in this direction but it is important to conduct research so as to identify the specific teaching practices that can enhance metalinguistic awareness and efficient language learning strategies. Research on the influence of bilingualism on L3 should adopt a 'multilingual perspective' and look at the multidirectional interaction between all the languages that form part of the multilingual speaker's repertoire. It is necessary also to conduct research to identify the individual and contextual conditions for bilingualism to have a more positive effect on the acquisition of additional languages. Moreover, longitudinal studies are needed to analyze with more detail the process of acquiring third or additional languages.

Key Points

- In general, bilingualism has a positive influence on the acquisition of a third language.
- Language acquisition is a complex process and bilingualism is only one of the factors involved, there are other factors, such as motivation or learning aptitude, that can be more influential.
- It is necessary to identify the specific conditions for bilingualism to have a more positive effect on the acquisition of additional languages so as to have a maximum benefit from bilingualism.
- The interaction between languages is multidirectional so that the influence is not only from the L1 or L2 to the L3 but also from the L3 to the other languages known or from the L2 to the L1. A holistic approach to the study of multilingualism is necessary to take this whole constellation into account.

Chapter 8
Identities and Attitudes

Introduction

Bilingual and multilingual education practices have outcomes that go beyond language proficiency or academic development. As Jaffe (2007) says when referring to bilingual education in Corsican schools, bilingual schools not only provide a model of bilingual behavior but also display that the minority language is a legitimate language in society. This second role has important socio-political implications in bilingual and multilingual contexts.

Learning and using a second and a third language has a potential effect on identity and attitudes because language learners and users negotiate identities in multilingual and multicultural contexts (Pavlenko & Blackledge, 2004: 3). In this chapter we will discuss the socio-political dimension of multilingual education in the BAC and we will focus on studies on identity and attitudes.

The Socio-Political Dimension

Multilingual education does not take place in a social vacuum but in a specific political, ideological, social and cultural context. Bilingual and multilingual schools are influenced by social and political factors as Lo Bianco (2007: 47) points out: '*Like all educational practice, bilingual education is inextricably bound up with the socio-political context in which it arises and the purposes it serves*'.

Basque education is dynamic and as we have already seen in Chapter 3 there has been a major shift of the language of instruction from Spanish to Basque. At the same time, the spread of English has resulted in a shift from bilingualism to multilingualism. In the last years this multilingualism has been enhanced by the arrival of immigrant speakers of other languages. There is a strong policy in the BAC to support the learning and use of Basque at different levels. Apart from the Basque Government, the county halls and the town halls, the promotion of Basque is part of the agenda of universities, associations, private agencies and some companies. The strength of this policy depends but only to a certain extent on the political parties in power. There is a general idea that Basque political parties encourage the maintenance and revival of Basque more than Spanish political parties in the Basque Country but in some institutions it is difficult to see a difference in everyday life as the result of a change of power.

According to the most recent sociolinguistic survey (Basque Government, 2008) 64.7% of the population supports the policy to promote the Basque language, 24% are indifferent and 11.2% are against it. There is an important difference according to language proficiency. Most Basque speakers (89.3%) support these measures but only half of those (50.8%) who do not speak Basque do.

Controversies over languages in education in the BAC are very common and there are hot debates on different issues in the Basque Parliament, the media, internet and other forums. Examples of heated debates are the 2006 PISA evaluation results (ISEI-IVEI, 2008) and the future of the three linguistic models. As we have already seen in Chapter 4, the BAC results in the PISA evaluation were just intermediate in comparison to other countries but higher than the Spanish average. These results have been highly controversial because of the language of the test. The Basque Government agency ISEI-IVEI decided that students should be tested in their family language and not in their language of instruction. According to the Basque Government, this decision was taken because Spanish is clearly dominant for L1 speakers of Spanish even if they are in model D (El Correo, 20 May 2008, see also http://www.isei-ivei.net/blog/). This procedure could have had a negative effect in some of the results of model D because the subjects are taught in Basque but it could have been an advantage for other students. The most negative criticisms took this procedure as evidence to prove that Basque-medium instruction is a failure and even went further to question the whole methodology of the evaluation (Montero, El Correo, 11 December, 2007).

Another controversial issue is the future of the models (see also Zalbide & Cenoz, 2008). A body of opinion considers that many students only get a very limited level of proficiency in Basque by the end of compulsory schooling. This low level in Basque is confirmed by the results of an evaluation reported in Chapter 4 in which only 32.8% of the students in model B and 68% in model D achieved the CEFR B2 level (ISEI-IVEI, 2005d). The proposal is to eliminate model A and to replace the models by a single model with Basque as the main language of instruction for all students

(Etxeberria, El Diario Vasco, 9 November, 2008). Others consider that parents have the right to choose the language of instruction and that the intensive use of Basque in education is producing negative academic results and go against the proposal of a single model (El Correo Digital, 2 October, 2008).

These controversies show that when discussing multilingual education there are different 'imagined communities' and different 'imagined schools' in the BAC. Based on the idea of the *'Continua of Multilingual Education'* it is possible to apply the continuum that ranges from 'less multilingual' to 'more multilingual' to the type of communities which are desirable for Basque citizens. Figure 8.1 shows the different possibilities: monolingual (either Basque or Spanish), bilingual or multilingual.

The bilingual position 'Basque-Spanish' has been the official position because both languages are official in the Basque Country but while for some using some Basque is enough, others think that because the situation of the two languages is asymmetrical only a very strong policy can help to achieve some balance. The bilingual positions can also exclude one of the official languages and include English. The multilingual position includes three languages or even additional languages and is spreading more in the last years. In the case of monolingual positions, the extreme position of 'Basque only' has as its opponent the 'no Basque' position that includes both 'Spanish only' and 'Spanish/English'. The 'no Basque' position can be seen in the following example (see Table 8.1).

This position sees Basque as a rural language which is not appropriate for the modern world. It gives as an example that Basque has borrowed words from other languages.[1] This vision of the language is incompatible with its use in modern society and particularly with its use as the language of instruction at school and at the university. This position can be monolingual (Spanish only) or bilingual (Spanish and English).

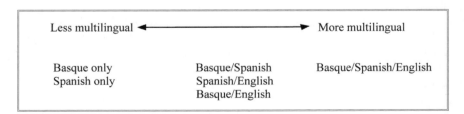

Figure 8.1 Imagined communities

Table 8.1 Example of the 'no Basque' position

> "Euskera just isn't used in real life," says Leopoldo Barrera, the head of the center-right Popular Party in the Basque regional Parliament. Though it has existed for thousands of years – there are written records in Basque that predate Spanish – it is an ancient language little suited to contemporary life. Euskera has no known relatives, though theories abound linking it to everything from Berber languages to Eskimo tongues.
>
> Airport, science, Renaissance, democracy, government, and independence, for example, are all newly minted words with no roots in traditional Euskera: *aireportu, zientzia, errenazimentu, demokrazia, gobernu, independentzia.*

Source: Wall Street Journal, 6 November 2007

Table 8.2 Example of the 'Basque only' position

> If English becomes a language of instruction for University Studies, the right to learn through Basque will diminish because it can be seen that University masters and PhD programs will be in other languages (English, Spanish, French, …).
>
> Every year we see that there are more foreign students at the university. This will be good for the prestige of the university but it cannot be denied that it is bad for the Basque language. All these students are coming to Spain or France, not to the Basque Country and they speak Spanish or French.

Source: http://www.ikasleabertzaleak.org/ (translated from Basque)

The 'Basque only' position is a monolingual view which excludes Spanish and English. An example of this view is the comments of a student organization about the Bolonia process (Table 8.2).

The first comment is about the language of instruction at the university and the Multilingualism Plan at the University of the Basque Country (see Chapter 10). The second comment refers to students on the Erasmus program who come from other European universities to the Basque Country (including the Northern Basque Country, Iparralde) and can be a risk for the Basque language.

A different position is the more multilingual position which combines the promotion of Basque with the knowledge of other languages. There are different possibilities within this position depending on the relative weight of Basque. One example of this multilingual position comes from Ikastolen Elkartea, the network of Basque language schools. Ikastolak are Basque-medium schools where the learning of Spanish, English and French is promoted (see Table 8.3).

Table 8.3 Example of a multilingual position

Society in the 21st century is multilingual. In modern-day society, in the century of globalisation, where communicative resources, personal mobility and international relations are on the increase, it is impossible to maintain and revitalise a minority language such as Basque by considering it to be the only language of a society. The future of Basque speakers is, therefore, multilingual. If Basque is to survive, it must become the dominant language in its linguistic area, but Basque speakers also need to be able to speak other languages, since otherwise Basque itself will be in danger. As a result, our main aim must be to combine both elements: on the one hand, to attain the maximum degree of development that Basque requires in its linguistic area and, on the other, to ensure that Basque speakers are able to learn and use other languages.

Source: Elorza and Muñoa, 2008: 85

As we can see this position defends multilingualism but gives a prominent role to Basque in Basque society.

Identities

In contrast to a traditional view of identity as a fixed category, post-structuralist and postmodernist approaches see identities as '*multiple, complex, context contingent, varied, overlapping, sometimes fragmented and even contradictory along different contexts*' (Baker, 2006: 138). According to this view individuals continually construct and reconstruct multiple identities. These identities, which are fluid and mutable, not only change over time but also across situations. As Niño-Murcia and Rothman (2008: 16) point out '*language becomes the conduit for constructing identity*' because identities are negotiated through social interaction (see also Pavlenko & Blackledge, 2004). Although Basque schools can be a very interesting context to analyze the construction of multiple identities by using ethnographic research and critical discourse analysis, this tradition is not strong in the BAC yet.

Studies on identity in the BAC have focused mainly on ethnolinguistic identity along the Basque-Spanish continuum. Research related to education has been based on questionnaires and surveys and has focused on different categories rather than on the way identities are built and negotiated in school. The study of identities has been based on specific categories such as 'being Basque' but also include in some cases bilingual categories such as 'being Basque and Spanish'.

Azurmendi *et al.* (2008) report a study based on ethnic and ethnolinguistic identity and look at two identity types, Basque and Basque-Spanish,

Table 8.4 Differences between university students who identify themselves as Basque and Basque-Spanish

Basque identity	– Knowing and speaking Basque – Knowing Basque culture and defending it – Participating in Basque culture – Adhering to the Basque Country's democratic values – Having Basque as a first language – Being in favor of the Basque Country's sovereignty – Participating in the Basque Country's association movements
Basque-Spanish identity	– Living and working in the Basque Country – Being a voter in general and autonomous community elections

Source: Azurmendi *et al.*, 2008

in the case of university students. This study was based on questionnaires and significant differences were found in several items as it can be seen in Table 8.4.

The results indicate that the Basque language and culture are more important for Basque than for Basque-Spanish identity. These results are consistent with those reported by Etxeberria-Sagastume (2006) about the reasons students have to learn Basque. Etxeberria-Sagastume found important differences between models A and B (Spanish-medium or Basque and Spanish-medium instruction) and model D (Basque-medium instruction). For secondary school students in models A and B, the main reasons to recommend learning Basque are social (emotions, uses and spaces of use) and practical (for jobs). In the case of model D the predominant reasons are cultural (identity, part of heritage) and political (language rights, revitalization, power relationships).

The increasing number of L2 speakers of Basque is having an effect on identity. According to a survey conducted a few years ago, bilingual identities are increasing among young people (Basque Government, 2004). The data also indicate that the most important condition to be Basque is to live and work in the Basque Country (69%) while speaking Basque was a condition for being Basque only in 18% of the cases. Young people think that the future situation should be 'bilingualism' (88%), as compared to 'monolingual Basque' (9%) or 'monolingual Spanish' (2%). Unfortunately the survey does not give information about other languages. Identities are fluid and dynamic and the equations '*Basque identity = speaker of Basque*' vs '*Spanish identity = speaker of Spanish*' have given way to more complex multiple identities. However, as Boix-Fuster and Sanz (2008) say in the case of Catalan, these new L2 speakers who have built bilingual and Catalan identities (or bilingual and Basque in the BAC), are not necessarily perceived as Catalan or Basque speakers by L1 speakers.

Language Attitudes in Multilingual Education

Attitude is a hypothetical construct used to explain the direction and persistence of human behavior (see Baker 1992). Ajzen (1988: 4) defines attitude as '*a disposition to respond favourably or unfavourably to an object, person, institution or event*'. In the case of languages we can understand attitudes as evaluative reactions towards a specific language or a specific language group (an object), or the activity of learning languages (event). Attitudes have been viewed as having three components: cognition, affect and readiness for action (Ajzen, 1988; Baker, 1992).

Why is it interesting to look at attitudes in multilingual education? Positive attitudes and motivation are often mentioned as necessary for language learning and the development of positive attitudes is often seen as one of the aims of teaching languages. To know what attitudes are like in multilingual educational contexts can be useful to know how the status of different languages (minority, majority, English) is perceived. Attitudes provide information to teachers about learners' reactions to the learning process and to language planners about the support for the use of different languages in the curriculum. Language attitudes can also influence achievement and this relationship can be bidirectional as learners with a good level of proficiency in one language could have better attitudes towards this language. As it is the case with identities, attitudes do not develop in a social vacuum either. Children are raised in a social context and they can be influenced by the attitudes of their parents, teachers or friends. Traditionally the study of attitudes has adopted a social psychological perspective and has looked at attitudes as related to group identity and inter-group relations (Gardner & Lambert, 1972; Giles & Byrne, 1982) but this approach has been challenged by poststructuralist approaches understood '*as an attempt to investigate and to theorise the role of language in construction and reproduction of social relations, and the role of social dynamics in the process of additional language learning and use*' (Pavlenko, 2002: 282). Poststructuralist approaches can provide a better explanation for the dynamics of attitudes and their relation to social practices.

Different methodological approaches have been used to measure attitudes (see Garrett *et al.*, 2003 for a review). The most common instrument to collect data is the questionnaire. Questionnaires can have open questions or closed questions and scales are very frequent in the measurement of attitudes. Some of the most common scales are Likert and Osgood scales. Likert (1903–81), an American educator and psychologist, devised an attitude scale in which participants were given a statement such as '*Speaking English is good to find a job*' and they were asked to indicate the degree of agreement or disagreement on a scale with five positions ranging from '*totally agree*' to '*totally disagree*'. The scale can also use 7 or 9 positions but the number has to be uneven so as to be able to identify a central position. Osgood (1916–91), an American psychologist, developed bipolar scales based on semantic opposites. For example, the respondent is asked about Basque speakers by choosing a position between two opposites such as '*hard working-lazy*' or '*intelligent-unintelligent*'. There are uneven number of positions between the two adjectives which is usually 5, 7 or 9. The use of scales gives the opportunity of adding up the items, obtaining frequencies or conducting statistical analyses. Scales have some problems and may be subject to some biases. Open questionnaires give the opportunity to obtain information about thoughts and beliefs not previously designed by the researchers but they have more problems to quantify the results.

Another technique used for the measurement of attitudes is the matched-guise technique (Lambert *et al.*, 1960). In this case, participants are asked to evaluate the personal qualities of the speakers they hear on a recording with the same speaker using different languages or language varieties. The advantage of this technique is that the responses can be quite spontaneous because the participants do not have to realize that attitudes are being measured. This technique also has some limitations and it has been pointed out that the recording can encourage the use of stereotypes. The discussion group is another instrument to get information on language attitudes. It tries to see the relationship between different types of social discourse and the characteristics of specific groups. Another technique used is in-depth individual interviews.

All these measuring instruments have been used in the BAC but questionnaires are the most common. According to Garrett *et al.* (2003: Chapter 2), this direct approach is more obtrusive because respondents have to report their attitudes. In the next two sections research studies on attitudes in the BAC will be reported by focusing mainly on the effect of the language of instruction on attitudes towards Basque and Basque and other languages.

Attitudes towards the Minority Language in Basque Education

When a minority language such as Basque has an important place in the curriculum and becomes the language of instruction, it is interesting to analyze students' attitudes towards this language (see also Baker, 1992; Garrett *et al.*, 2003). A first step is to compare the attitudes of students in the different models of education so as to see whether students take Basque as an obligation or if they enjoy learning it. It can be expected that those students with Basque as the language of instruction will have more positive attitudes towards this language than those students who have the majority language as the language of instruction. An important issue here is that the potential better attitudes towards the minority language do not have to be necessarily the result of bilingual and multilingual education as it could be that attitudes towards the minority language are more positive in the student's family and social networks. Another issue to consider is that attitudes can be related to the specific sociolinguistic context where the school is located and there can be important differences in the use of the minority language in different contexts. The '*Continua of Multilingual Education*' considers this interaction between schools and the macro and micro levels (see Chapter 2). For this reason it is important to consider the sociolinguistic context when analyzing the results of research on attitudes towards the minority and the majority language and to be particularly careful about the generalization of these results.

The first two studies to be discussed were carried out by Madariaga (1994) and Aiestaran (2003) in schools in the provinces of Bizkaia and Araba. Both studies have samples of over 200 students from primary and secondary schools and their distribution can be seen in Table 8.5.

The two areas are quite different regarding the percentage of Basque speakers. The Bizkaian town, Mungia, where Madariaga conducted his research has 58.8% of bilingual speakers and 12.36% of passive bilinguals.

Table 8.5 Characteristics of the samples

	Sample	*Models*	*Location*	*Schools*
Madariaga, 1992	$N = 212$ Primary 5 and secondary 2	A = 96 D = 116	Town in Bizkaia	Public school
Aiestaran, 2003	$N = 232$ Secondary 3, 4 and 5	A = 112 B = 21 D = 99	Three towns in Araba	Public and private

The percentages corresponding to the three towns in Araba where Aiestaran conducted his research are much lower and the number of bilinguals ranges from 6.33% to 21.42% and the number of passive bilinguals from 5.66% to 9.46%.

Madariaga had primary and secondary school students in his sample, 83 from primary school (36 in the model A and 47 in the model D) and 129 from secondary school (61 in the model A and 68 in model D). Aiestaran included secondary school students from four different years. Most of these students had Spanish as the first language. Even in model D, 79.8% of the students had Basque as their first language.

Both research studies focus on attitudes and the variables measured can be seen in Table 8.6.

Both researchers use the Likert-type questionnaires to find out information about attitudes. In both cases the students are asked to choose one of the five options that go from 'totally agree' to 'totally disagree'. Madariaga distributed all the questionnaires in Spanish. Aiestaran had two versions of the questionnaire; model A students completed the Spanish version and model B and D students the Basque version.

Table 8.6 Instruments

	Madariaga, 1992	*Aiestaran, 2003*
Attitudes Basque	*Questionnaire*: 42 questions to measure attitude towards Basque and attitude towards Basque speakers	*Questionnaire*: 23 questions to measure attitudes towards bilingualism and 24 to measure attitudes towards Basque *Group interviews* mothers
Other variables	*Basque proficiency*: Cloze test and perception of competence in Basque *Background*: Knowledge and use of Basque in social networks, gender, age, age of acquisition, use of resources in Basque *Psychosocial*: Importance of Basque, parents' attitude, subject's opinion of parents' attitude IQ: Raven. (non-verbal), TEA-1, TEA-2 (verbal) *Bilingualism*: Model	*Basque proficiency*: Perception of competence in Basque *Background*: Knowledge and use of Basque in social networks, gender, age, SES, cultural background, private vs public school *Psychosocial*: Ethnolinguistic vitality, ethnolinguistic and ethnocultural identity, inter-group relations between Spanish speaking monolinguals and Basque speaking bilinguals *Bilingualism*: Model

Table 8.7 Attitudes towards the Basque-speaking group

Affective – Affective value of the language – Personal attitude towards Basque	– *When I study Basque I think I am wasting my time* – *One day I will know a lot of Basque*
Cognitive – Personal experience of the use of Basque in the sociolinguistic context – Basque and future career	– *I would like to live in a town where more Basque was spoken* – *It is easier to get a job if you speak Basque*
Behavioral – The use of Basque and its resources	– *I watch the Basque television channel whenever I can*

Madariaga identifies five types of attitudes towards the Basque-speaking group as it can be seen in Table 8.7.

Aiestaran used attitude questionnaires based on Baker (1992) to measure attitudes towards Basque and attitudes towards bilingualism. The items are given in Table 8.8. Both studies also measured a number of background variables and other social psychological variables apart from attitudes. Madariaga measured proficiency in Basque by means of a cloze test and both researchers measured the perception students had of their own proficiency. Madariaga (1992) found that attitudes towards Basque were significantly more positive in the case of students with Basque as the language of instruction (model D) than in the case of model A students, who had Spanish as the language of instruction. Madariaga also analyzed the effect of different variables and found that the sociolinguistic context is the most important predictor of Basque proficiency and that the effect of attitudes on Basque proficiency is also significant.

Aiestaran gives specific results about what attitudes are like for all the items in the questionnaire to measure attitudes to Basque and attitudes towards bilingualism. The results corresponding to attitudes to Basque are given in Table 8.8 and those corresponding to attitudes to bilingualism later in this chapter. Table 8.8 shows the percentages corresponding to the positions '*totally agree*' and '*agree*'.

It can be observed that in the Spanish speaking area in the south of Araba where the data were collected, attitudes towards Basque are in general terms very positive. We can see that the highest figure, 89.6%, corresponds to agreement with the item '*Basque is a language worth learning*' and the lowest (3.1%) to the item '*Basque is a language to be spoken only within the*

Table 8.8 Percentages of students who agree and totally agree

Items	%
1. Basque is a difficult language to learn	31.6
2. It is more important to know English than Basque	40.5
3. Basque is a language worth learning	89.6
4. There are far more useful languages to learn than Basque	33.5
5. I don't want to learn Basque as I am not likely to ever use it	6.5
6. I would like to be able to speak Basque if it were easier to learn	43.6
7. I like to hear Basque spoken	70.5
8. It is particularly necessary for the children to learn Basque in the schools to ensure its maintenance	75.8
9. Basque is an obsolete language	17.9
10. I should like to be able to read books in Basque	64.4
11. Learning Basque is boring but necessary	18.0
12. I would like to learn as much Basque as possible	80.5
13. The learning of Basque should be left to individual choice	63.6
14. I like speaking Basque	71.2
15. Basque is a language for farmers	17.8
16. I would like to learn Basque because my friends are doing that	24.4
17. Learning Basque is a waste of time	7.0
18. Basque should be used more in government services	60.4
19. I dislike learning Basque	10.7
20. I am learning Basque because my parents want me to	16.6
21. I enjoy learning Basque	61.2
22. Basque is a language to be spoken only within the family and with friends	3.1
23. The Basque language is something everybody should be proud of	66.6
24. I like listening to TV/radio programs in Basque	63.0

family and with friends'. It is interesting to see that the students themselves are interested in Basque and not because of their parents or friends. Both the status and the solidarity dimensions get high scores. So, most students agree with items such as '*I like to hear Basque spoken*' or '*I like speaking Basque*' that refer to the solidarity dimensions but also with items about the status of the language: '*It is particularly necessary for the children to learn Basque in the schools to ensure its maintenance*' or '*Basque should be used more in government services*'.

Aiestaran also looked at the differences between the models and found out that there were significant differences in only 6 of the 24 items. The attitudes of students in models B and D are more positive than the attitudes of model A students. For example, more students in model A agreed with the item '*It is more important to know English than Basque*' but more students in models B and D agreed with the items '*I enjoy learning Basque*' or '*I should like to be able to read books in Basque'.* The more positive attitudes towards Basque in model D have also been reported in other studies (Larrañaga, 1995; Urrutia *et al.*, 1998; Urrutia, 2005; Etxeberria-Sagastume, 2006).

The differences between the models have also been confirmed by studies using other methodologies. Jausoro *et al.* (1998) reported that model D students had more positive attitudes towards Basque in focus group discussions.

Attitudes towards Basque, Spanish and English

As we have seen, several studies have looked at attitudes towards Basque and compared them to attitudes towards Spanish or towards Spanish and English. Some other educational studies have looked at attitudes towards Basque at the university level. There are no models at the university but some courses have Basque as the language of instruction as we will see in Chapter 10.

The studies conducted with university students have focused on different aspects. For example, Amorrortu (2001a, 2001b) examined the attitudes of 157 students towards Basque and Spanish using a matched-guised technique and a semantic differential. All these university students had Basque as the language of instruction at the university and 66% had Basque as their first language. Attitudes towards Basque were more favorable than towards Spanish in the status dimension but similar in the solidarity dimension. Students with Basque as their first language had more favorable attitudes towards Basque in status. Echeverria (2005) also used a matched-guised technique to see whether the use of Basque as the language of instruction had the effect of feeling more identified with Basque. Echeverrria reported that all learners considered that the vernacular variety of Basque, which is not standard Basque used at school, demoted solidarity. She also reported some differences between students coming from Basque and Spanish speaking backgrounds who had Basque as the medium of instruction. The former gave higher scores to standard Basque than to Spanish while the latter did not make a difference. This study shows that the non-standard variety of Basque is highly appreciated on a solidarity scale probably because it is seen as different from the school languages. It also shows the effect of the home language. This study is focused on a specific aspect of attitudes, solidarity, and results on other aspects could be different.

Other studies have looked at attitudes towards the three languages: Basque, Spanish and English. Cenoz (2001c) and Sagasta (2001) looked at attitudes towards the three languages in model D. Cenoz (2001c) used semantic differentials to compare different school grades (4th of primary and 2nd and 4th of secondary) and found that attitudes towards the three languages were significantly more positive in the case of primary school students than in the case of secondary school students. The results also indicate that all students had more positive attitudes towards Basque than towards Spanish or English but it is important to remember that the study was conducted in a model D school. Sagasta (2001) measured different dimensions of attitudes and reported that attitudes towards the three languages were quite positive. Attitudes towards Basque speakers, attitudes towards Basque and confidence in their own ability to learn Basque were slightly higher than for the other two languages. Attitudes towards learning the language and towards the teacher were slightly higher in the case of English.

Other studies comparing attitudes towards Basque, Spanish and English have looked at the attitudes of learners according to their first language (Lasagabaster, 2001, 2003). Participants in these studies were university students and the questionnaire was adapted from Baker's (1992) but included only 10 of the original 20 questions. In both studies, Lasagabaster found that students with Basque as their L1 had the most positive attitudes towards Basque. Students with Spanish as their L1 had the most positive attitudes towards Spanish. Students with Spanish as a first language had more favorable attitudes towards English than students with Basque as a first language.

Huguet and Lasagabaster (2007) reported the results of a comparative study conducted in teacher training colleges in different European bilingual communities. They observed that Basque participants ($n = 222$) rated the minority language quite high as compared to students in other countries. The percentages of favorable attitudes were 71% in the case of Basque, 41% in the case of Spanish and 24% for English. These results do not necessarily correspond to the general population because there were more Basque speakers than in the general population (55% vs. 30.1%) and they were all from a specific sector, education, where Basque is highly valued.

Attitudes towards Bilingualism and Multilingualism

Some studies have aimed at analyzing students' attitudes towards bilingualism and multilingualism rather than towards each of the languages one by one. This is a very interesting dimension of research into attitudes that was adopted by Baker (1992).

Aiestaran (2003) adapted Baker's questionnaire to measure attitudes towards Spanish and Basque in a combined way. He used 23 items and, as

Table 8.9 Percentages of agreement (Aiestaran, 2003)

Item	Agree (%)
1. It is important to be able to speak S. and B.	88.8
2. To speak one language in the BAC is all that is needed	22.1
3. Children get confused when learning B. and S. at the same time	20.7
4. Speaking both S. and B. helps to get a job	84.0
5. Being able to write in S. and B. is important	80.9
6. All schools in the BAC should teach pupils to speak in B. and S.	68.8
7. Road signs should be in S. and B.	51.7
8. Speaking two languages is not difficult	75.0
9. Children in the BAC should learn to read in B. and S.	73.8
10. There should be more people who speak both S. and B. in the Government services	64.5
11. People know more if they speak in S. and B.	41.1
12. Speaking both S. and B. is more for younger than older people	18.0
13. The public advertising should be bilingual	56.7
14. Speaking both B. and S. should help people get promotion in their job	53.5
15. Young children learn to speak S. and B. at the same time with ease	76.6
16. Both B. and S. should be important in the BAC	77.4
17. People can earn more money if they speak both S. and B.	32.3
18. In the future, I would like to be considered as speaker of B. and S.	62.8
19. All people in the BAC should speak S. and B.	53.5
20. If I have children, I would want them to speak both B. and S.	78.6
21. Both the S. and the B. languages can live together in the BAC	79.6
22. People only need to know one language	14.4
23. All the civil servants in the BAC should be bilingual	53.7

we have already seen in this chapter, the study was conducted in the South of Araba with students in models A, B and D. The percentages of 'agreement' and 'total agreement' taken together are given in Table 8.9.

In general, attitudes towards bilingualism are positive. The items with the highest scores are '*It is important to be able to speak Spanish and Basque*', '*Speaking both Spanish and Basque helps to get a job*' and '*Being able to write in Spanish and Basque is important*'. The positive attitudes towards bilingualism are also shown in the low scores of items such as '*Speaking both Spanish and Basque is more for younger than older people*' or '*Children get confused when learning Basque and Spanish at the same time*'. It is interesting to observe that the items related to the use of Basque in the linguistic landscape, both on road signs and public advertising, do not get high scores. It is also interesting to see that the students in this research study do not think that speaking two languages makes them more knowledgeable.

There were significant differences between the models in the following items:

7. *Road signs should be in Spanish and Basque*
9. *Children in the BAC should learn to read in Basque and Spanish*
13. *The public advertising should be bilingual*
18. *In the future, I would like to be considered as speaker of Basque and Spanish*

Model A students showed less favorable attitudes towards the two items related to the linguistic landscape (7 and 13). It is more surprising that even though 73.8% of the students agreed with item 9, 19% of the students in model B disagree with this statement. In the case of item 18, it is model D students who disagreed more than students in the other models. The results for these items are more difficult to explain and it could be that the students also want other languages such as English to be included or in the case of model D students some of them may want to be considered mainly as Basque speakers. It could be interesting to obtain more information on this issue.

Cenoz (2001c) included a questionnaire about multilingualism in her study comparing attitudes towards the three languages in three age groups and reported significant differences for the total score. As it was the case with attitudes towards the three languages the most positive attitudes correspond to primary school. Learners also completed a questionnaire on attitudes towards multilingualism based on Baker's (1992) questionnaire on attitudes towards bilingualism and adapted it so as to measure attitudes towards multilingualism. This questionnaire adopts a holistic approach towards multilingualism and not towards each of the languages, that is, it takes into account the co-existence of the languages instead of the specific attitudes towards each of the languages.

Lasagabaster (2003), in the study we have already discussed in the previous section, also used a questionnaire based on Baker (1992). The mean scores for all the items according to the first language are given in Table 8.10.

The results indicate that attitudes towards multilingualism are in general positive as most of the scores are higher than 3. The highest scores correspond to items that reflect the importance of speaking the three languages and the wish to do so, children learning languages and the possibility of getting a job (items 1, 5, 6, 8, 18, 20 and 22). The lowest scores

Table 8.10 Mean scores according to first language (Lasagabaster, 2003)

Item	Mean scores		
	Basque* L1	Spanish* L1	Both*
1. It is important to be able to speak S, B and E	4.66	4.64	4.68
2. To speak one language in the Basque Country (BC) is all that is needed	3.69	3.81	4.05
3. Knowing B. S and E. makes people cleverer	3.68	2.96	3.54
4. Children get confused when learning S., B. and E.	3.86	3.70	3.99
5. Knowing S., B. and E. helps to get a job	4.62	4.73	4.65
6. All schools in the BC should teach pupils to speak in S. B and E.	4.20	4.34	4.32
7. Speaking three languages is not difficult	3.37	3.03	3.32
8. Knowing B., S. and E. gives people problems	4.04	4.23	4.16
9. People know more if they speak S., B and E.	2.87	3.13	3.15
10. People who speak B., S. and E. can have more friends that those who speak one language	2.85	2.77	3.10
11. Speaking S., B., and E. is more for younger than older people	3.54	3.63	3.59
12. Young children learn to speak B., S. and E. at the same time with ease	3.76	4.01	4.03
13. B., S. and E. are important in the future of the BC	3.57	4.05	4.02
14. People can earn more if they speak B., S. and E.	3.32	3.70	3.68
15. I should not like E. to take over from the B. and S. languages	4.40	3.96	4.15
16. I should not like B. to take over from the E. and S. languages	2.07	3.48	2.60
17. I should not like S. to take over from the B. and E. languages	4.26	3.11	3.75
18. I would like to be a speaker of B., S. and E.	4.40	4.57	4.53
19. All people in the BC should speak B., S. and E.	3.24	3.29	3.47
20. If I have children, I'd want them to speak S., B. and E.	4.30	4.44	4.56
21. The B., S. and E. languages can live together in the BC	3.41	4.31	4.10
22. Given the new European context it is very important to speak S., B. and E.	4.30	4.09	4.37

*Maximum = 5

correspond to items which refer to multilinguals being cleverer, knowing more, having more friends (items 3, 9 and 10). Some differences can be observed if we look at the scores according to the first language. Students with Spanish as a first language and both Spanish and Basque as first languages seem to have more positive attitudes towards multilingualism. Each of these groups obtained the highest score in 9 of the 22 items. The Basque L1 group obtains the highest score in 4 of the 22 items. Three of these (items 7, 15 and 17) do not necessarily imply positive attitudes towards multilingualism but easiness to speak the languages or being against the replacement of their own language by others.

Conclusion

Bilingual and multilingual schools are part of society and as such are affected by the socio-political context. Education and in particular bilingual and multilingual education can reflect power relationships (see for example Heller, 2007). Controversies on language-related issues in Basque education clearly show that bilingualism and multilingualism in education cannot be separated from political power and ideologies. The study of identities in the BAC shows a trend to more fluid bilingual or even multilingual identities which are different from the traditional association between one language and one identity. Both the study of power relationships in critical discourse analysis and identities have received a lot of attention by scholars working in multilingual education in other settings (Heller & Martin-Jones, 2001; Creese & Martin, 2003; Norton & Toohey, 2004; Heller, 2007; Blackledge & Creese, 2009), but this approach, generally based on ethnographic studies, still has a poor tradition in the BAC.

The studies conducted in the BAC reported in this chapter show that the most common approach to the study of identities and attitudes is social psychological. The studies report some interesting findings regarding the relationship between Basque language and identity and also indicate that attitudes towards Basque are generally quite favorable. A consistent result is that subjects who have Basque as a first language or/and have Basque as the main language of instruction (model D) generally have more positive attitudes towards Basque. Spanish L1 students have more positive attitudes towards Spanish and in some cases towards English. An interesting aspect of attitudes that has received some attention in the Basque Country is the study of attitudes towards multilingualism in Basque, English and Spanish which is based on attitudes towards bilingualism as measured by Baker (1992) in Wales. This approach focuses on multilingualism instead of separating the different languages and give interesting results. The social psychological perspective of these attitude studies has contributed to the knowledge of attitudes but has some theoretical and methodological problems (Pavlenko, 2002; Baker, 2006). It is considered very superficial, static and descriptive. It is necessary to go beyond this descriptive social psychological approach into a more explanatory account of attitudes. The trend towards a more multilingual and more multicultural society due to the arrival of immigrants to the Basque Country can make this study even more interesting.

Key Points

- The socio-political context is directly linked to many aspects of bilingual and multilingual education.
- There are different imagined communities and schools in the BAC ranging from monolingualism in Basque or Spanish to multilingualism in Basque, Spanish, English (and other languages).
- Speaking Basque is an important indicator of identity for Basque speakers.
- Learners have more positive attitudes towards their L1 and their main language of instruction than towards other languages.
- In general, attitudes towards multilingualism are positive in studies conducted in the BAC.

Note

1. English and Spanish have also borrowed the same words from Latin and Greek.

Chapter 9
The Age Factor in Bilingual and Multilingual Education

Introduction

The effect of age on second language acquisition (SLA) is a controversial area which has received much attention in SLA research (Harley & Wang, 1997; Hyltenstam & Abrahamsson, 2003; De Keyser & Larson-Hall, 2005; Singleton & Ryan, 2004). The idea that children pick up languages more easily than adults is very popular. It is not only based on research studies but also on anecdotal evidence of young children learning languages faster than their parents when a family moves to a country where another language is spoken. These contexts with a lot of exposure to the target language both at school and outside school are considered natural language environments as compared to formal contexts where exposure to the target language takes place only at school. In this chapter, we summarize very briefly the Critical Period Hypothesis and the main findings in natural contexts to focus on the age factor in formal contexts and particularly in Basque schools.

The Age Factor in Language Learning at School

Research studies conducted in natural language environments tend to support the idea that 'earlier the better' (De Keyser, 2000). These studies tend to prove that older learners present initial short-term advantages in morphology and syntax but in the long run, younger learners achieve higher levels of proficiency than younger learners (see Singleton & Ryan, 2004 for a review). Krashen *et al.* (1979) already pointed out long ago that there is the need to distinguish between rate of acquisition and ultimate achievement. The early exposure to the second language has advantages on ultimate achievement, but not on the rate of acquisition in the early stages. For example, Snow and Hoefnagel-Höhle (1978) proved that younger learners outperformed adolescents and adults after approximately one year of exposure in a natural environment.

The most popular explanation for the effect of age on second language acquisition has biological foundations and it is known as the Critical Period Hypothesis (CPH). Critical periods refer to periods of time in life when human beings or animals are sensitive to external stimuli and can explain some aspects of human and animal behavior. Penfield and Roberts (1959) and Lenneberg (1967) were the first to apply this hypothesis to language acquisition. There is no basic agreement about the necessary conditions for supporting or rejecting the CPH. For some researchers the CPH would exist only if *'there is a discontinuity in the slope of decline in L2 proficiency situated around the terminus of the critical period and no second language learners starting after the terminus period should demonstrate achievement of native-like levels'* (Bongaerts, 2005: 259). Several research studies have found that this is not the case and it has been pointed out that not all learners acquiring the second language before the age of seven acquire native proficiency. However, early starters usually achieve higher levels of proficiency than late starters, at least in natural contexts but the age factor in second language acquisition is still a very controversial issue (Birdsong, 2004; Bialystok, 1997; Bialystok & Miller, 1999; Long, 2005; De Keyser, 2000, 2006).

New psycholinguistic approaches to the study of language processing that can contribute to the study of the CPH are neuroimaging technologies such as functional magnetic resonance imaging (fMRI). Abutalebi *et al.* (2005) consider that the level of proficiency attained in a language can be more important than the age of L2 acquisition when looking at some aspects of language processing but there can be specific differences linked to the age of onset in others. Franceschini *et al.* (2003) point out that a high proficiency in the L2 can mask the differences with respect to the onset time of acquisition. There is a great diversity and individual differences involved in the acquisition of several languages regarding factors such as time of onset, level of proficiency or language use and it is difficult to isolate their effect. At the same time there are many different dimensions in communicative competence and psycholinguistic tests usually focus on the processing of limited stimuli. Although neuroimaging technologies do throw new light on the age factor issue and many other areas of language acquisition, the diversity and complexity of the processes involved make it necessary to conduct a large number of studies so as to provide evidence that can be generalized.

Research supporting the existence of sensitive periods for second language acquisition has important implications for formal contexts, and particularly for the early introduction of foreign languages, in the school curriculum. If there are sensitive periods for language acquisition, schools should introduce second and third languages earlier so as to provide optimal conditions for language learning.

The distinction between natural and formal contexts of language acquisition is important and most research supporting sensitive periods has taken place in natural contexts where extensive natural exposure to the language is combined with formal learning. This situation is quite different from acquiring a second or foreign language in situations in which exposure to the language is limited to the school context and usually to a very limited number of hours per week. Learners with a minority language as their L1 are exposed to the majority language from an early age outside school and are in a situation which is closer to that of natural contexts. On the other hand learners with a majority language as their L1 are very often exposed to the minority language at school and may find it more difficult to attain a very high level of proficiency in the minority language. In these situations, the amount of exposure and the type of input are very important.

When discussing different types of immersion programs for language-majority students, Genesee (2004: 557) refers to age differences when comparing early and late immersion. He says that early immersion learners can benefit from natural language learning ability, their open attitudes to new languages and cultures, the opportunity for extended exposure and an optimal fit between learning styles of young learners and effective L2 pedagogy. On the other hand, older students can benefit from a more developed knowledge of the L1, particularly literacy skills, and self-selection because those who opt for later immersion are usually highly motivated. Immersion in Basque for Spanish speaking children in the BAC is, with a few exceptions of late arrivals, early immersion with little variation regarding age so in this chapter we will discuss the age factor as related to the teaching of English at different ages.

Taking into account that research conducted in natural settings has found out that older learners progress faster in the first stages of language acquisition it can also be expected to find advantages on part of older learners in school contexts. If young children have advantages after the first stages, it is possible that these advantages are not clearly seen at school because the number of hours of exposure in primary and secondary school is not high enough to get to a stage in which the advantages can be observed. The initial advantages associated with older learners in natural settings are usually in morphology and syntax, but it can be expected that because learners in foreign language contexts tend to have non-native teachers, younger learners will not present better pronunciation skills than older learners.

Most studies conducted in formal settings confirm the advantages presented by older learners (Singleton & Ryan, 2004; Muñoz, 2006b). The good results obtained by older learners have also been confirmed by Canadian immersion programs. Genesee (1987) and Harley (1986) report that learners who experience intensive exposure to the second language in late immersion in the first year(s) of secondary school present similar levels of proficiency in the second language as children who have experienced more exposure to the second language in early immersion programs.

Early Introduction of English in the Basque Educational System

The increasing role of English in Europe has developed a growing interest in learning English which is reflected in demands for more English instruction and better quality English instruction in schools. One of the consequences of this need to acquire higher levels of proficiency in English is the trend to introduce English in kindergarten or primary school in several European countries (Eurydice, 2008).

Pre-primary education in the BAC is divided into two stages: stage for ages 0–3 and stage for ages 3–6. Between the ages of zero and two some children stay at home and others go to a day care centre. Most of these schools have Basque as the language of instruction and some even introduce a few sessions in English. As we have already said in Chapter 2, school starts very early in the BAC and nowadays most children go to school at the age of 2. The classrooms are equipped for the needs of these children and they have a shorter school day. Basque is the main language of instruction and as we have seen in Chapter 3, Basque is the language of instruction for the whole day (model D) or part of the day (model B) for almost 95% of the children aged two to six. Most schools introduce English at the age of four but some even introduce English earlier.

The early introduction of English in kindergarten was initiated on an experimental basis in several 'ikastolak' in 1991 (see Artigal, 1993). These model D schools, with Basque as the language of instruction, developed a multilingual project that goes from the age of four to the end of compulsory education, at the age of 16 (see Elorza & Muñoa, 2008). English is taught in kindergarten for approximately two hours a week in four 30-minute sessions but the number of hours of English increases in later years. This early introduction of English has spread to most schools in the BAC.

As we saw in Chapter 5, a few years later the Basque Government Department of Education carried out a project in other schools so as to compare the results of the early introduction of English to more intensive exposure to English in later years. This comparison was not possible because most schools wanted the early introduction of English rather than having the same number of hours at the end of primary or in secondary. Thirteen public schools started to introduce English at the age of four officially in 1996 but many others also did the same without taking part in the project and without specific counseling and economic support. The Basque Government had to extend the counseling to other schools and in the following years English language teachers from more than 150 schools attended specific workshops for teaching English to younger learners. Teachers met every two weeks with their advisors so as to get materials for use in the classroom and discuss teaching practices (Aliaga, 2002). The methodology was basically content-based. The English language teachers participating in this project only use English in the classroom and all the activities are oral. The methodology used is based on story-telling, songs and other oral activities and requires the children's active participation by means of collective dramatization and playing.

Nowadays, 90% of the schools in the BAC teach English from the age of four although it is not compulsory until the age of six. This very early introduction of English has also taken place in some areas in Spain but it is not as common in other parts of Europe. One of the main reasons for this early introduction of English is the pressure from parents who want their children to learn English and think that an early introduction necessarily results in a higher level of competence. Before the early introduction of English was spread to the whole system, individual schools had an interest in offering something 'special' because they needed to attract students in a context in which the birth rate is very low. Introducing English at an early age has some difficulties but can be easier than using English intensively in later years when academic content is more important. According to a survey carried out by Cenoz and Gallardo (2000) English language teachers thought that the early introduction of English was a good idea because it increases the amount of hours of instruction and because more exposure is very necessary in the case of a foreign language. The questionnaires addressed to parents also indicate that they have very positive attitudes towards early instruction in English in primary schools and kindergarten (Cenoz & Lindsay, 1994).

The early introduction of English has spread all over the BAC but it has also been criticized. It is considered that the increasing role of English in the curriculum could be an obstacle for the revitalization of the Basque language (Etxeberria, 2002, 2004; Ruiz Bikandi, 2002). The hours devoted to English are hours that in many schools were previously taught in Basque. English is considered just as a fashion by some people. Another criticism is that there are not enough qualified teachers and that the money spent in teacher education and material development could be used for other purposes.

The Development of English Competence at Different Ages

In this section, we will discuss in detail a research project conducted at the University of the Basque Country which aims at analyzing the effect of the age of introduction of English as a third language. Apart from the results on general proficiency (see also Cenoz, 2003d), this section will include some results on specific aspects of language proficiency obtained in the same research project (García Mayo, 2003; García Lecumberri & Gallardo, 2003; Ruiz de Zarobe, 2005; Lasagabaster & Doiz, 2003). The next section will discuss data from the same project on attitudes and motivation.

This longitudinal research project started in 1996 and has been conducted in a specific school in which English is taught as a third language to all the students. Traditionally, the English language was introduced in the 6th year of primary school (11 years old) but when the Spanish Educational Reform was implemented in 1993, foreign languages were introduced in the 3rd year of primary school when children are eight years old (Cenoz & Lindsay, 1994). The school collaborating with this study took part in a specific project to introduce the teaching of English in the second year of kindergarten at the age of four. This program started in 1991. Therefore, this school provides the possibility of comparing groups of children who have started their English classes at three different ages within the same bilingual program and school curriculum. All the children in this research study come from the same geographical area and similar social backgrounds. The subjects included in this research study were selected on the condition that they did not receive instruction and were not exposed to English outside school (private classes, academies, summer courses, etc).

Taking into account that third language acquisition is a very complex phenomenon and that the influence of age can be related to other factors such as the amount of exposure, cognitive development or teaching methodology, the study of the age factor has been approached from different perspectives and covered different areas of proficiency.

Comparisons controlling for age of testing

The first perspective we are going to discuss here compares subjects who are the same age but have experienced different amount of exposure. The research question is the following: *Do learners who are the same age but have had different amounts of exposure achieve the same level of proficiency in English?* In order to answer this research question we are going to present data corresponding to comparisons made in the 6th year of primary school, in the 4th year of secondary school and in the 6th year of secondary school. These comparisons have been carried out with a specific sample from the project.

All the participants in this research study (N = 184) were primary and secondary schoolchildren from a school in Gipuzkoa. This school has Basque as the language of instruction (model D). Spanish and English are taught as school subjects but Basque is the main language of communication at school. Some students used only Basque at home, others only Spanish and others both Basque and Spanish. On a scale of three points (1 = only Spanish; 3 = only Basque) the students in this sample obtained 2.28 points when asked about the language they used with their mothers and 2.22 points for the language used with their fathers. These scores indicate that the use of the Basque language is slightly more common than the use of Spanish at home for the students in our sample. The distribution of male and female is quite balanced: 48.6% male and 51.4% female. The other characteristics of the sample are given in Table 9.1.

The data were collected at four different times between 1997 and 2005. Before the tests were administered all the students in each of the classes in which data were going to be collected completed a short questionnaire so as to know if they had received additional instruction in English or had been exposed to English outside school. Only students who had not received additional instruction in English were included in the sample. The instruments used are given in Table 9.2.

The background questionnaire was designed to obtain information about sociological and sociolinguistic variables. The listening comprehension test consisted of three parts. In the first part, participants listened to a song and had to put some pictures in order. In the second part participants were asked to listen to a passage and identify eight characters and in the

Table 9.1 Characteristics of the sample

Model	Hours of English	Starting age		Course when data were collected	
D	400–700	Pre-school	(4–5)	Primary 6	(11–12)
		Primary 3	(8–9)	Secondary 4	(15–16)
		Primary 6	(11–12)	Secondary 6	(17–18)

Table 9.2 Tests of English proficiency

	Questionnaire/Test
Background	Gender, age, socioeducational background, competence in Basque and Spanish, use of Basque and Spanish.
Listening comprehension	3 parts (max 36 points)
Reading comprehension/grammar	3 parts (max 31 points) (different scales)
Oral production	Frog story/another story
Writing	Composition 250 words (max 100 points)
Cloze	34 blanks (max 34 points)
Placement test (in the 6th year of secondary)	Listening (max 100 points) Grammar/voc (max 100 points)

third part they had to choose an adverb to describe the eating habits of four characters. The maximum score in this test was 36 points. The reading comprehension/grammar test had three parts. In the first part, participants were asked to look at four pictures and to match the different parts of a dialogue. In the second part, participants were asked to fill in some blanks by using the appropriate word (auxiliaries, pronouns, quantifiers, etc.). The third part is similar to the first and participants were asked to put the different parts of a dialog in order. The maximum score of the grammar test was 31 points.

Oral production was measured individually with each of the students. Students were asked to tell two stories: the Frog story and a story they had already worked with in class. The picture story *'Frog, where are you?'* (Mayer, 1969) consists of 24 pictures with no text and the interviewer asks the learner to describe the pictures. It has been used in a large number of contexts all over the world with different languages both with children and adults (Berman & Slobin, 1994; MacWhinney, 2000). Participants were also asked to tell another story that was related to the learners' class activities. This story was different in the different age levels.

In order to measure students' writing ability, participants were asked to write a composition with a maximum length of 250 words. In the composition, students were asked to write a letter to an English family and they had to tell them about their own family, their school and their hobbies (max = 100 points).

The two other tests of English proficiency were more holistic. In the cloze test participants were asked to fill in 34 blanks by using the appropriate words in a test. The test is the well-known story 'Little Red Riding Hood'. This test measures lexical, grammatical and discursive aspects of language production (max = 34 points). Participants in the 6th year of secondary also completed a standardized placement test, the Oxford Placement Test. This test had listening and grammar/vocabulary sections (max = 100 points for listening and 100 points for grammar/vocabulary).

The stories were recorded, transcribed and analyzed in order to examine different aspects of oral production. First, the number of tokens, types, utterances and words per utterance produced by the three age groups when re-telling the two stories were obtained. Then an overall evaluation of the oral production including pronunciation, vocabulary, grammar, fluency and content was carried out. The composition was graded according to the holistic approach proposed by Jacobs *et al.* (1981). This system uses scales corresponding to content, organization, vocabulary, language use and mechanics. Once the oral tests were fully transcribed, analyses were conducted by using the Childes Clan program to estimate the number of word tokens, word types, utterances and words per utterance. The different measures of proficiency were used to measure different dimensions of oral and written production and also the different linguistic levels: phonetic, lexical, morphosyntactic, pragmatic and discourse.

In order to find out whether there were differences between the different groups several statistical analyses were carried out in the 6th year of primary and the 4th and the 6th years of secondary.

Sixth year of Primary (11–12 years old)

The first analyses include two different groups of learners who were in the 6th year of primary school but had started learning English at different ages: the 2nd year of kindergarten and the 3rd year of primary school. At the time of testing, subjects who had started learning English at the age of four had received approximately 700 hours of instruction and subjects who had started learning English in the 3rd year of primary had received 400 hours of instruction. The results on the different dimensions of oral proficiency are given in Figure 9.1 (max 10).

The results of the T-tests indicate that there are significant differences in two of the measures of oral proficiency: pronunciation (T = 5.3, S = .00) and vocabulary (T = 4, S = .00). The scores obtained by the learners who started in the 3rd year of primary (400 hours of exposure) are significantly higher than the scores obtained by the subjects who started in kindergarten (700 hours of exposure) in these two measures. There are no significant differences between the two groups in grammar, fluency and content.

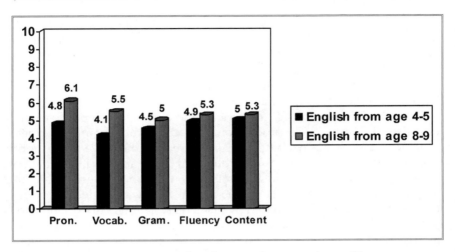

Figure 9.1 Oral proficiency in the 6th year of primary (age 12)[1]

Table 9.3 The Frog story and the second story in the 6th year of primary (11–12 years old)

	Starting in kindergarten (4–5 years old)		Starting in primary 3 (8–9 years old)	
	Frog	*Second story*	*Frog*	*Second story*
Tokens	260.4	388.1	179.4	129.3
Types	74.9	127.4	52.9	45.4
Utterances	33.7	49.7	26.2	18.2
Words/utterance	7.9	7.2	6.7	6.9

The scores in Table 9.3 correspond to the mean number of tokens, types, utterances and words per utterance obtained by the same groups in the Frog story and the story related to the classroom activities.

The results of the T-tests indicate that there are significant differences in the four measures in the case of the Frog story: tokens ($T = -4.5$, $S = .00$), types ($T = -4.6$, $S = .00$), utterances ($T = -3.3$, $S = .00$) and words per utterance ($T = -3.2$, $S = .00$). The subjects who had started in kindergarten (700 hours of exposure) obtained significantly higher scores in these four measures than learners who had started in the 3rd year of primary (400 hours of exposure). When comparing the stories students had practiced in class the results of the T-tests indicate that the differences between the means obtained by the two groups are significant in three of the four measures: tokens (T = –10.2; S = .00), types (T = –12.9; S = .00) and utterances (T = –12.1; S = .00). Learners who started in kindergarten obtained significantly higher scores than learners who started in the 3rd year of primary in the three measures. There were no significant differences between the two groups in the number of words per utterance. So in all these measures of oral production and for both stories the early starters were better than the late starters. However, learners who started in primary 3 obtained significantly higher results than learners who started in kindergarten in one of the written tests, the cloze test (T = 3.1, S = .00).

Fourth year of Secondary (15–16 years old)

The second comparison was carried out in the 4th year of secondary. In this case we have data from three groups of learners. They were all in the 4th year of secondary school but had started learning English at different ages: kindergarten, 3rd year of primary school and 6th year of primary school. At the time of testing subjects who had started in kindergarten had received approximately 1100 hours of exposure, those who started in the 3rd year of primary approximately 800 hours of exposure and subjects who started in the 6th year of primary had received 500 hours of exposure. The results of the analyses of variance for oral proficiency in the Frog story are given in Figure 9.2 (max = 10).

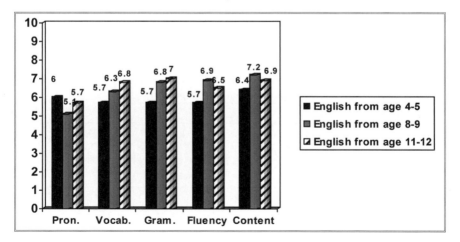

Figure 9.2 Oral proficiency in the 4th year of secondary (15–16 years old)

The results indicate that there were significant differences in all the dimensions of oral proficiency except in content but the results do not always go in the same direction. The students who had started to learn English late, in the 6th year of primary school obtained the best scores in vocabulary (F = 3.91; S = .02) and grammar (F = 8.37; S = .00) and the differences were significant when compared to the ones who started in kindergarten but not when compared to the subjects who started in the 3rd year of primary. The group who started in kindergarten obtained the highest scores in pronunciation (F = 4.31; S = .01) and the differences were significant as compared to the group who had started in the 3rd year of primary but not when compared to the group who started in the 6th year of primary. The intermediate group, those who started in the 3rd of primary obtained the best scores in fluency (F = 4.31; S = .01) and these scores were significantly higher than the ones of the group who had started learning English in kindergarten.

The results corresponding to the same three groups in tokens, types, utterances and words per utterance in the Frog story and the results of the Oxford Placement test are given in Table 9.4.

Regarding the Frog story, the results indicated that there were no significant differences between the groups. The results of the Oxford Placement Test indicate that there were no significant differences in the case of listening comprehension but the results of the students who started in the 6th year of primary were significantly higher than those of the other two groups in the vocabulary and grammar test (F = 15.35; S = .00).

Table 9.4 The Frog story and the Oxford Placement Test in the 4th year of secondary

	Starting in kindergarten	*Starting in 3rd primary*	*6th primary*
The Frog story			
Tokens	264.35	306.50	276.73
Types	89.53	95.22	86.86
Utterances	31.82	37.89	33.68
Words per utterance	8.73	8.28	8.21
Oxford Placement Test			
Listening (max = 100)	62.65	61.11	63.44
Vocabulary / grammar (max = 100)	52.82	37.44	56.56

Sixth year of Secondary (17-18 years old)

More comparisons were carried out at the end of secondary school. In this case we have data from two groups, those who started in the 3rd year of primary (1000 hours of instruction) and in the 6th year of primary (700 hours of instruction). The results of the comparisons on oral production can be seen in Figure 9.3 (max = 10).

The results indicate that there are no significant differences and that the differences in four of the five dimensions are only marginally significant. In these cases, students who started in the 6th year of primary obtained higher results in vocabulary (T = −1.78; S = .08), grammar (T = −1.87; S = .06) and fluency (T = −1.83; S = .07) and students who started in primary 3 in pronunciation (T = 1.86; S = .06).

The results corresponding to the same two groups in tokens, types, utterances and words per utterance in the Frog story and the results of the Oxford Placement test are given in Table 9.5.

In the case of the Frog story the differences are significant for three of the measures: tokens (T = 2.15; S = .03), types (T = 4.39; S = .00) and utterances (T = 4.18; S = .00). Subjects who started in the 3rd year of primary obtained better results than those who started in the 6th year of primary. In the case of number of words per utterance the differences are only marginally significant and the subjects who started later obtained better results

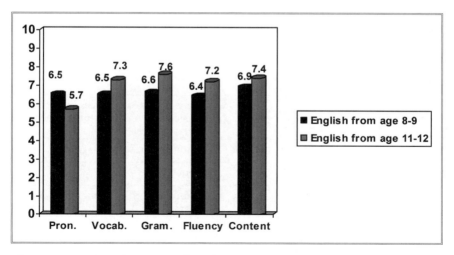

Figure 9.3 Oral proficiency in the 6th year of secondary (17–18 years old)

Table 9.5 The Frog story and the Oxford Placement Test in the 6th year of secondary (17–18 years old)

	English from 3rd primary (age 8–9)	**English from 6th primary (ages 11–12)**
The Frog story		
Tokens	368.72	296.47
Types	114.39	85.88
Utterances	46.17	32.82
Words/utterance	7.94	8.99
Oxford Placement Test		
Listening (max = 100)	65.67	67.79
Vocabulary/Grammar (max = 100)	59.28	53.12

(T = –1.81; S = .07). The results of the Oxford Placement Test indicate that there were no differences in listening comprehension and that learners who started in the 3rd year of primary obtained better results in vocabulary and grammar (T = 1.96; S = .05).

The analyses shown compare the results of English tests of students with a different number of hours of instruction that were in the same course. As we have seen in the different tables, the results are quite mixed. Table 9.6 provides a summary:

Table 9.6 Summary of the comparisons

Level	*Groups/hours*	*Results*	*Measurement*
6th primary (11–12 years old)	E 700 hours I 400 hours	I > E	Pronunciation, vocabulary (oral)
		E > I	Tokens, types, utterances in both oral stories, words per utterance in Frog, cloze test
4th secondary (15–16 years old)	E 1100 hours I 800 hours L 500 hours	E best	Pronunciation (oral)
		I best	Fluency (oral)
		L best	Vocabulary and grammar (oral and placement)
6th secondary (17–18 years old)	I 1000 hours L 700 hours	I > L	Tokens, types, utterances (Frog) and vocabulary and grammar (placement test)

E = early starters, age 4–5; I = intermediate, age 8–9; L = late starters, age 11–12.

These findings do not show a clear positive effect of the early introduction of English. There is no clear pattern showing advantages on part of the learners who have received more hours of instruction. The early starters (from age 4–5) only obtained significantly higher results in vocabulary in the 6th year of primary and in pronunciation in the 6th year of primary and the 4th year of secondary. The late starters obtained better results in vocabulary and grammar both in the oral test and the placement test but the 'intermediate' group got the best results in the placement test in the 6th year of secondary. Some of these results may reflect the different methodological approach that highlights oral proficiency in the case of the early starters compared to the other two groups. The results of the analyses indicate that learners who started later (either in the 3rd year of primary or the 6th year of primary) obtained better results in vocabulary and grammar than learners who started learning English in kindergarten. The differences between starting in the 3rd year of primary and the 6th year of primary are not that clear in the last year of secondary school. Learners who started in kindergarten seem to do quite well in oral skills but the number of hours of exposure is much higher than for other learners. The general conclusion is that learners are better at the skills they have practiced more in class and that the differences between the 3rd and the 6th level are not clear by the end of secondary school. It will be interesting to see how far learners who started in kindergarten get when they finished secondary school.

In a comparison of writing skills of a group of 'intermediate' starters with a late starters group reported by Doiz and Lasagabaster (2004) some mixed results were also found in the 4th year of secondary education. In general terms, the intermediate group obtained better results in holistic measures of writing (organization, vocabulary and language use), in the total number of words and sentences and in the use of different types of verb tenses. The late starters group obtained significantly better results in the total number of non-finite verbs and also made fewer errors.

Ruiz de Zarobe (2006) compared early starters and intermediate in the 6th year of primary after approximately 700 hours and 400 hours of English. She focused on the use of the negative in oral production by analyzing the Frog story. She found that in general terms the acquisition of the negative was for both groups at a very early stage and that there were no significant differences between the two groups.

Egiguren (2006) carried out a study in a different school which also focused on the comparison of learners who were in the same grade but had started learning English at different ages. Participants were 86 students with a mean age of 9.27 who had Basque as the language of instruction (model D) in three different schools in Gipuzkoa where Basque was spoken by 36–39% of the population. Egiguren conducted her study in the 4th year of primary and selected students who had no contact with English outside school. Forty-one students (47.7%) had studied English from the second year of kindergarten (four years old) and were in their 6th year of English and 46 (52.3%) had started learning English in the 3rd year of primary (eight years old), that is one year before the data were collected. The early starters had three hours of English per week while the late starters had four hours: two English classes, and two art classes taught through the medium of English.

Egiguren tested listening, reading and writing skills in Basque, Spanish and English. The Basque and Spanish tests (Galbahe E2 and C2) were standardized and used in the EIFE studies (Sierra & Olaziregi, 1989, 1991). The English tests were based on materials used in class. The reading and vocabulary test of English had several parts where students were asked to match pictures and sentences, choose the correct answer or fill in the blanks. The listening tests had three parts and students had to listen to a tape and complete some tasks. In the oral production test children were asked to tell *'The three little pigs story'*. The dimensions of oral production evaluated were pronunciation, vocabulary, grammar accuracy, fluency and content. Other variables measured were age in which participants started learning the foreign language, gender, intelligence, socioeconomic status, attitudes and use of Basque and Spanish.

Egiguren (2006) analyzed whether more hours of instruction in English corresponded to a higher level of competence. The results of this comparison are shown in Table 9.7.

The differences between the two groups were not significant for any of the four areas measured: vocabulary ($T = -1.12$; $S = .26$), reading ($T = 1.21$; $S = .22$), listening ($T = 1.39$; $S = .16$) and speaking ($T = .99$; $S = .32$).

Another comparison of results was carried out by Ikastolen Elkartea, the network of ikastolak that had first introduced English from the age of

Table 9.7 Comparison of early and late starters in the 4th year of Primary

	English from kindergarten (age 4–5)	*English from 3rd year of primary (age 8–9)*
Vocabulary (max = 408)	352.2	367.48
Reading (max = 144)	88.15	80.55
Listening (max = 18)	16.50	15.73
Speaking (max = 50)	29.61	27.75

Table 9.8 Comparison of early and later starters in the 2nd year of secondary (13–14 years old) (Garagorri, 2002)

	English from the kindergarten (age 4–5)	*English from 3rd primary (ages 8–9)*
Writing	8.93	5.62
Reading	8.62	6.90
Listening	15.76	11.90
Grammar test 1	9.47	7.10
Grammar test 2	4.47	2.37
Speaking	13.10	9.48

four in 1991 and coordinated the project of the early introduction of English in the ikastolak. The comparison was made when the students were in the second year of secondary school (Garagorri, 2002). The tests taken included writing, reading, listening, speaking and two tests of grammar. The means for the two groups can be seen in table 9.8.

Garagorri (2002) does not refer to statistical differences but students who had started learning English from the age of four obtained higher scores in all the tests. These results are remarkable as compared to the mixed results obtained in other comparisons. One possible explanation is the type of test used that could be closer to the methodology used with younger children while the more external comparisons used standardized tests.

Comparisons controlling for number of hours of instruction

The comparisons reported so far look at different aspects of proficiency by students who are the same age but have received different amounts of instruction and started learning English at different ages. The advantage of making this type of comparison is that learners are at the same stage of cognitive development at the time of testing. Another possibility is to control for the number of hours of exposure and to compare the rate of acquisition at different ages. These comparisons have also been made and the results are given in Table 9.9.

The results controlling for the amount of instruction and comparing students who are not the same age clearly indicate that older learners

Table 9.9 Studies comparing the number of hours of exposure

	Area	*Results*
Cenoz, 2003d	*General proficiency*: oral proficiency, writing, listening, cloze, reading	E, I, L: After 600–700 hours Late starters significantly better in most measurements
García Lecumberri & Gallardo, 2003, 2006	*Pronunciation*: vowels, consonants, foreign accent, intelligibility	E, I, L: After 600 hours Late starters significantly better in most tests, less differences between E and I.
García Mayo, 2003	Grammaticality judgement task to test Pro-drop parameter	E, I, L: After 400 hours Late starters better in identifying sentences with missing subjects and subject-verb inversion but not in the 'that' trace
Ruiz de Zarobe, 2005	Subject pronoun omissions, number of words, utterances, language use in oral and written production	E, I, L: After 400 to 800 hours E produce more subjectless sentences and obtain lower results in other measures. In the third measurement I obtained better results than L in some measures but also had about 100 hours more of instruction (800 vs 700).
Lasagabaster & Doiz, 2003	*Writing skills*: holistic, fluency, complexity, accuracy, errors	E, I, L: After 700–800 hours L best scores in holistic scores and most measures of fluency, complexity, accuracy and the E the lowest. Mixed results in errors.
García Mayo *et al.*, 2005	Insertion of placeholder 'is' and 'he' before lexical verbs	E, I, L: After 400 hours E use placeholder 'is' more often and I use placeholder 'he'.
Perales, 2004	Negative utterances	E, I, L: 300 to 800 hours The L the best scores, the I is that one that improves more between the two times of measurement

E = early starters, English from age 4–5; I = intermediate, English from age 8–9; L = late starters, English from age 11–12.

progress faster. Some possible explanations for these results are related to cognitive maturity and type of input. Cognitive maturity could explain the higher linguistic development of the secondary school-children as well as their higher scores in content and could also be linked to higher developed test-taking strategies. Another possible explanation of the results is linked to the type of input. The oral-based approach used with younger students could explain the fact that there are fewer differences when the groups are compared in pronunciation, tokens or utterances. The more traditional approaches used with older learners could explain the higher lexical and syntactic complexity of their production and their higher scores on the written tests (composition, cloze test, reading, grammar test). In sum, older learners seem to progress faster than younger learners or at least are able to show their progress in the tests better than younger learners when the amount of instruction is controlled. The differences are more important in those measures related to higher metalinguistic ability than in the quantitative measures of oral production or pronunciation and they could be related to cognitive development and input.

The results of these studies coincide with those obtain in a project on the age factor in a study conducted in Barcelona (Muñoz, 2006a). The Barcelona study has a larger sample and two age groups, those that have been called intermediate starters (starting at age 8–9) and the late starters (starting at 11–12). Late starters obtained significantly higher results in academically oriented tests when the time of exposure was controlled. No differences were found between the two groups in the case of listening comprehension and aural recognition. Muñoz (2006b) provides comparison at three different times, after 200, 416 and 726 hours of instruction. The results indicate that in general the late starters obtain better results than the 'intermediate' starters.

What do these results tell us? Is the early introduction of English worth it? The results of these analyses reflect the complexity of measuring the age factor in this context (see also Muñoz, 2008a). When we compare children who are in the same grade we no longer have the problem of comparing different ages and different levels of cognitive development or test taking strategies but other methodological problems are still there. The type of input and instruction that learners have experienced is clearly different for two reasons. In recent years there has been an emphasis on the development of communicative skills and teachers have tried to focus much more on oral skills rather than written language and grammar rules. There has been a change in the whole methodological approach. Learners who started learning English at the age of 11–12 studied grammar rules and vocabulary and applied them by doing exercises while young learners do oral activities. Furthermore, the difference in the type of instruction between older and younger learners does not depend only on the general change of methodological approach but on the stage of development of the children. When

English is introduced at the age of four children have not acquired literacy skills yet and they have not reached the stage in which they can reflect about the metalinguistic aspects of language. They cannot possibly receive instruction based on grammar rules and vocabulary.

Attitudes and the Age Factor

Language planners, advisors and teachers think that children are very happy in the English classes and that the early introduction of English can have a positive effect on attitudes (Cenoz & Gallardo, 2000). Some studies conducted in other contexts have associated the early introduction of foreign languages with more positive attitudes and motivation (Hawkins, 1996; Burstall, 1975) but in others no differences have been observed (Tragant & Muñoz, 2000).

Studies on the effect of age conducted in bilingual settings have reported that attitudes towards the minority language become less favorable when age goes up (see Baker, 1992 for a review). For example, Baker (1992) found that attitudes towards Welsh became less favorable between 11 and 14 years of age and the most significant change took place between 13 and 14 years of age. This trend has also been observed by Nikolov (1999) in the case of learning English as a foreign language in Hungary.

Among the different possibilities of looking at the relationship between attitudes and age in the Basque context, the specific question that we are going to discuss in this section is the following: *Do learners who are the same age but have had different amount of exposure present similar attitudes towards English?* In order to answer this question we compared the means obtained by learners who were in the same course but have started to learn English at different ages. The data available correspond to the 4th (15–16 years old) and the 6th (17–18 years old) of secondary (max = 56). The results can be seen in Figure 9.4.

The results of the analysis of variance indicate that there are no significant differences in attitudes towards the English language in the 4th year of secondary (15–16 years old). The results of the T-tests indicate that in the 6th year of secondary (17–18 years old) the differences between the means are only marginally significant (T = 1.73, S = .09). It seems that more exposure to English does not necessarily result in better attitudes. In some cases, it could even happen that more exposure to the language has a negative effect unless learners achieve a basic command of English, that is, learners may get bored and tired of English classes because their proficiency is still very limited. It could also be that early starters (and even intermediate ones) had a very communicative approach based on story

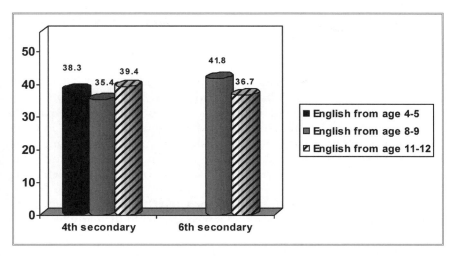

Figure 9.4 Attitudes towards English in the 4th year and the 6th year of secondary school

telling and projects in the first years and there is a contrast with a more grammar-based approach in later grades.

Egiguren (2006) also reported that there were no significant differences between early and intermediate starters in attitudes in the 4th year of primary school.

The results of the comparisons between learners of different ages who had received the same number of hours of exposure indicates that early starters present significantly more positive attitudes than older learners after 600 and 700 hours of instruction (see Cenoz, 2004). The most positive results correspond to the early starters who were younger than the other groups at the time of testing. Therefore, our results support the trend for younger learners to present more positive attitudes than older learners but this trend is not necessarily maintained in the long run.

The Influence of the Early Introduction of English on Basque and Spanish

As we have already seen in this chapter, one of the main worries related to the early introduction of English has been its influence on the development of Basque and Spanish. The main questions related to this issue are the following: Is the early introduction of English going to affect the development of the other two languages? Is the minority language going to suffer? Will three languages be too many? The number of research studies in this area is very limited and the spread of the early introduction of English practically to all children makes the comparison impossible in the future.

Cenoz *et al.* (1994) analyzed the linguistic competence in Basque and Spanish of 6–7 year old children who had started learning English at the age of four in the experimental group and had not been learning English in the control group. Children in the experimental group were in their third year of English. They measured listening comprehension and production in Basque and Spanish. They found no differences in Spanish but they found that children learning English were better in production in Basque.

In a follow-up of this study, Garagorri (2002) confirmed that there were no differences in Basque and Spanish related to the early introduction of English. He compared 195 students who started learning English at the age of four with 154 who started at the age of eight. Apart from the results in English that we have already referred to, the tests included reading comprehension in Basque and Spanish and a general intelligence test. The results indicate that there were no differences between the two groups of students. This means that the early introduction of English does not hinder the development of Basque and Spanish or cognitive ability.

Egiguren (2006) also looked at the possible influence of the early introduction of English on Basque and Spanish. She compared the competence in Basque and Spanish of students who had started to learn English at different ages as it can be seen in Table 9.10.

Table 9.10 Proficiency in Basque and Spanish in the 4th year of primary (15–16 years old)

	English from kindergarten (4–5 years old)	*English from 3rd primary (8–9 years old)*
Basque		
Listening (max = 20)	17.48	17.68
Reading (max = 20)	15.33	15.30
Writing (max = 100)	77.97	72.23
Spanish		
Listening (max = 20)	15.37	14.78
Reading (max = 20)	12.20	12.42
Writing (max = 100)	74.20	67.82

The only significant differences were found in writing skills both in the case of Basque (T = 2.30; S = .02) and Spanish (T = 2.48; S = .01). In both cases, learners who had started learning English at the age of four obtained significantly higher results.

These results are in agreement with those reported by Garagorri (2002) and by Goikoetxea (2007) and indicate that the early introduction of English does not have a negative effect on the development of the other two languages. The results are consistent with the proposal for interaction between languages in multilingual speakers made by some researchers and the results of other research studies (Kecskes & Papp, 2000; Cook et al. 2003; Jessner, 2006).

Conclusion

The early introduction of English as a third language is a relatively new phenomenon that has received a lot of attention in the last years in Basque education. In fact, the third language is introduced from a much earlier age in the Basque Country than in many other countries. One of the main worries parents and teachers had was that Basque and Spanish could be negatively affected by the early introduction of English. The results reported in this chapter indicate that the early introduction of English does not prevent the development of Basque and Spanish.

As we have seen in this chapter research studies have focused mainly on the development of linguistic proficiency in English by comparing students who are in the same grade but have started learning English at different ages or students who are in different grades but have received the same amount of exposure. In general terms, results are quite mixed. Early starters have some advantages in some areas only when they have received more hours of instruction than late starters and testing is carried out in the same grade. More exposure to the language can contribute to a higher level of proficiency but the results do not prove that this exposure has to take place from an earlier age rather than in a more intensive way in later grades (see Muñoz, 2006b, 2008b). The combination of an early start with a more intensive exposure by having English as an additional language of instruction will probably result in a higher level of proficiency. As we have seen in the *Continua of Multilingual Education*, the sociolinguistic context also plays a very important role and more or less intensive exposure will be needed depending on the use of the target language outside the school.

Research conducted so far has been useful to see the effect of the early introduction of English but more research is needed to get to know the way English, Basque, Spanish and other languages are used in the classroom, both in teacher-student interaction and student-student interaction at different ages. The research on the age factor reported in this chapter does not provide direct evidence for or against the existence of sensitive periods discussed earlier (Long, 2005; De Keyser, 2000, 2006, etc) because it does not measure final attainment in the target language when there is 'massive' exposure to the language. Exposure in the research studies reported in this chapter is minimal and limited to the classroom. In the case of Basque as a second language in the models B and D there is more exposure to the target language although in many cases it is limited to the school. However, as immersion in the models B and D is always early immersion in the BAC there is no possibility of comparing different times of onset for learning Basque.

Key Points

- The early introduction of second and additional languages in the school curriculum is becoming very popular in many parts of the world but it can be very limited when there is no additional exposure to the target language outside the classroom.
- When analyzing the influence of age on the acquisition of a second or additional language, there are important differences between natural and formal contexts.
- Studies in the BAC do not confirm in a consistent way that the early introduction of English with very limited exposure is the most efficient way to learn English.
- The early introduction of English has no negative effects on Basque and Spanish.

Note

1. When children in the BAC are assigned to different grades according the age, it is done according to the natural year (January to December), that is, all children born in the same year are in the same grade. In this chapter we give the ages the children along the academic year, for example 4–5 for kindergarten but the actual age of onset for English is four year because school starts in September.

Chapter 10

Bilingual and Multilingual Education at the University

Introduction

The extended use of Basque in primary and secondary school has important implications for university studies. If the minority language is the language of instruction for most children in secondary school there is a need to use the minority language, at least to an extent, in higher education. The BAC, along with other areas where minority languages are spoken such as Catalonia, uses Basque as one of the languages of instruction at the university level. At the same time, universities in the BAC are part of the general European and world trend to shift to English as the medium of instruction. This situation extends the trend to move from bilingualism to multilingualism, that we have already seen in pre-school, primary and secondary education in the BAC, to higher education. In this chapter we will look in more detail at the situation of the largest university in the BAC, the University of the Basque Country (Universidad del País Vasco-Euskal Herriko Unibertsitatea) and summarize the situation in other universities. The chapter also includes a section on the teaching and learning of Basque by adults outside the university.

Teaching through English at the University

The spread of English in higher education is related to general and specific factors. Universities are part of society and are affected by the same general processes that have influenced the spread of English as a language of wider communication. These include historical or political movements such as imperialism or colonialism or economic movements such as migration and globalization. Among the specific factors to promote the use of English at the university level we can find the following:

- English is the main language of science and technology and the use of English at the university can improve the opportunities to have access to knowledge. Scientific publications are rarely translated into different languages and proficiency in English is necessary so as to have access to them. This is also the case with international conferences. Students who are not proficient in English are very limited in the publications they can read and scholars are very limited not only in the access to international publications but also in the impact of their own work. One of the implications of this situation is that, as it is the case in other fields, native speakers of English have advantages over non-native speakers (Carli & Ammon, 2008).
- Student mobility has increased in the last years. In fact, according to a survey of 52 programs taught in English in Nordic universities in Europe, this is the first reason for setting up the programs (Hellekjaer & Westergaard, 2003). There are important differences in the number of international students in different countries and in some universities such as Maastricht University in the Netherlands they reach 25% of the students (Wilkinson & Zegers, 2006). In many cases international students do not speak the language of the country where they study and they expect all their courses to be in English. In the European context, these students are international students who have decided to attend European universities and students from European countries who spend one or two semesters in another university as part of the Erasmus program (http://ec.europa.eu/education/programmes/llp/erasmus/index_en.html). Universities offering courses in English can attract more students and can also prepare their own students to attend other universities.
- Proficiency in English is an important asset when looking for a job. Many advertisements in newspapers in many non-English speaking countries have English as a requirement for medium and high-paid jobs and there are some fields such as economics in which English is absolutely necessary. English is the main language of interaction for international business all over the world and students who have English as a language of instruction at the university are certainly in a better position.

The spread of English-medium education is taking place in many countries all over the world. For example, Yu (2007) reports that the Ministry of Education in China has a plan to teach at least between 5% and 10% of all the university courses all over the country in English. This spread of English is also taking place in many other countries and has important challenges related to the proficiency of instructors and students and the development of specific materials.

In the European context, an important factor favoring the spread of English is the Bologna process. The Bologna Declaration was signed by the ministers of education of 29 states in Bologna (Italy) in 1999. It was decided to standardize higher education and to create the European Higher Education Area (EHEA). The aim or this process is to increase the competitiveness of Europe, to increase the mobility of European students and to attract international students. The Bologna process aims at standardizing the number of years leading to the different degrees, the teaching methodology and also establishes a new credit transfer system. This new situation can encourage student and staff mobility and implies the increasing use of English as a lingua franca along with other languages (see Wilkinson *et al.*, 2006; Fortanet-Gómez & Räisänen, 2008). The use of English in higher education in Europe is not homogeneous. There are universities in countries such as the Netherlands or Denmark where English-medium education started several years ago and is well established (Wilkinson & Zegers, 2006; Kling, 2006). In many Southern European universities this is not the case yet.

Teaching through the Minority Language at the University

Teaching through a minority language at the university level implies many more challenges than teaching thorough the medium of English. It certainly shares some challenges with the teaching through a second language such as the proficiency level of students and teaching staff or issues related to the evaluation of content and language or teacher training. On top of all this, teaching through a minority language faces more challenges such as the lack of textbooks and other materials or the limited use of most minority languages in science and technology. In many cases, the use of a minority language as a language of instruction and for research activities implies developing the corpus of a language so as to include technical and scientific terms.

In this section, we will focus on the use of Basque at the University of the Basque Country (Euskal Herriko Unibertsitatea-Universidad del País Vasco, www.ehu.es) and we will mention briefly the situation at the Universities of Deusto and Mondragon. The University of the Basque Country is the only public university in the BAC and it is the biggest university in the whole of the Basque Country. It is a multicampus university with faculties and colleges in Bizkaia (Bilbao and Leioa), Gipuzkoa (Donostia-San Sebastian and Eibar) and Vitoria-Gasteiz. It has 31 faculties and colleges and almost 50,000 students, about 7500 teaching staff and researchers and over 1600 supporting staff.

First steps

The University of the Basque Country was created in 1980 so as to replace the University of Bilbao (created in 1968). The University of Bilbao already had some groups in the Science faculty (Bizkaia) working on the promotion of Basque at the university and the development of Basque as a scientific language. The first classes through the medium of Basque started in 1977 in Science and in teacher training colleges in 1981.

As Aizpuru (2008) says in these early times there were three positions regarding the use of Basque at the university: (1) Some teachers supported the idea of keeping Basque out of university teaching; (2) Others supported the opposite position and considered that the use of Basque was not only beneficial but also completely necessary; (3) A third position defended bilingualism and the gradual introduction of Basque. This intermediate position was the one generally accepted over the years.

Once the University of the Basque Country was created (1980) some steps were given so as to develop the position of Basque. In 1981 the Basque Language Service started to support the publication of textbooks and the teaching of Basque to teachers, students and supporting staff. Other boards and positions were also created such as the Basque Committees, the Basque Institute and the Vice-rector for Basque. At this time it was not a requirement to speak Basque in order to get a job at the university but it was already an asset taken into consideration.

The University of the Basque Country has developed several plans for the use of Basque at the university. Some of these plans have proposed different possibilities: to use Basque for all the courses in some studies, to use Basque for the first years only in all the studies or to have only compulsory courses in Basque but not necessarily optional courses. The idea is that the University cannot be isolated from the rest of the educational system and Basque society and should also participate in the Basquization process because it is the most important cultural reference in the BAC.

Legal support and current situation

The University of the Basque Country has been developed as a bilingual university and its statutes state that Basque and Spanish are the official languages of the university (2004; BOPV 12-1-2004). These statutes are in accordance with other laws and decrees.[1] The statutes recognize the right to use Basque or Spanish, to teach and learn in Basque or Spanish, and to publish and conduct research in any of the two languages. According to the Statutes, all official documents have to be bilingual and the university will give special attention to the scientific and technical aspects of

Basque language and culture. The Statutes also state that the University of the Basque Country should be a driving force in the process of normalization of the Basque language. The logo of the University of the Basque Country, designed by the Basque sculptor Eduardo Chillida, has the name of the university in Basque and Spanish and the slogan '*eman eta zabal zazu*' (give and spread) in Basque (see Figure 10.1).

The use of Basque at the University is not a future goal but a need the University is facing now because of the demand to study through Basque from students who want to go on having the same language of instruction as in secondary school. As we have seen in Chapter 3, 50.12% of the students in higher secondary education are in model D, that is, they have Basque as the language of instruction. Not all the students who finish secondary school in model D go to the University of the Basque Country to study through the medium of Basque. Some go to other universities, some choose to study through the medium of Spanish and in some cases teaching through the medium of Basque is not possible. The University of the Basque Country also has some students from Navarre who studied through the medium of Basque in primary and secondary school. There is a clear trend towards the increasing use of Basque as the language of instruction as it can be seen in Figure 10.2.

The data indicate that there has been an important increase from 23.46% to 43.90% in 10 years. If this trend does not change, within a few years, over 50% of the students at the University of the Basque Country will be studying in Basque. When considering the total number of students at the university, approximately 35% have half or more of their courses through the medium of Basque.

The use of Basque as the language of instruction at the university has many difficulties because of the large number of courses taught. Just

Figure 10.1 The logo of the University of the Basque Country

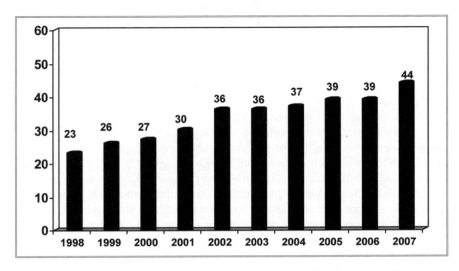

Figure 10.2 Percentage of students learning through Basque in the first year
Source: University of the Basque Country (www.ehu.es)

looking at the undergraduate level, there are almost 25,000 credits taught in the whole university. The use of Basque as the language of instruction when the University of the Basque Country was created in 1980 was marginal and the current situation is completely different. We can see the percentages of compulsory and optional credits taught through the medium of Basque in Table 10.1.

Table 10.1 Percentages of credits that can be studied in Basque. Undergraduate level

	1st cycle Compulsory	2nd cycle Compulsory	Optional[2]
Experimental Sciences	90.77	27.56	71.64
Technical Studies	53.74	23.04	62.51
Health Sciences	91.04	24.34	55.24
Law and Social Sciences	95.40	68.12	174.49
Humanities	81.58	83.11	232.72
Total	76.03	46.13	137.98

Source: University of the Basque Country (www.ehu.es)

When looking at compulsory credits, the data indicate that students can study more credits in Basque in the first cycle (76.03%) which in most cases corresponds to the first two years of their studies than in the second cycle (46.13%). It can also be seen that there are important differences depending on the field. Almost all students who wish to study in Basque can do so in most cases in the first cycle except in the case of Technical Studies such as the different engineering degrees. The percentage for Humanities, 81.58%, is lower than for Law and Social Sciences because Humanities includes Language Studies with other languages (French, English and German) as languages of instruction. We can also see that the possibility of studying in Basque is more reduced in the second cycle in all the studies except in Humanities. That means that students have to take some or all the compulsory courses in Spanish mainly in the case of Experimental Science, Technical Studies and Health Science.

The percentages corresponding to optional courses correspond to the number of credits available in Basque of the total number of optional credits students have to complete. As they are optional courses there are a lot more credits offered than the ones that are required. For example in the case of Humanities, which includes different studies (Philosophy, History, Art, Geography, Translation & Interpretation or Language and Literature Studies), the total number of optional credits needed for all the studies in Humanities is 981 and the number of credits offered in Basque is 2283, that is 232.72%. So, in Humanities, students can make a choice of Basque or Spanish and if they decide to have all the courses in Basque, they can still have some options and take some courses and not others. This is not the case in Experimental Science, Technical Studies and Health Science. If students in these studies take all the optional courses offered in Basque they still need to take courses in Spanish to complete the required number of credits.

The studies offered at the undergraduate level are 79 different degrees and there are differences in the number of credits in Basque within each of the five fields included in Table 10.1. Some studies can be carried out completely in Basque while in others the use of Basque as the language of instruction is very modest.

According to the most recent Master Plan for Basque (Euskararen Plan Gidaria, 2007), the aim of the University of the Basque Country is to offer all compulsory credits at the undergraduate level in Basque provided that there is a reasonable number of students. This aim is complicated by the fact that Spanish Universities are in a process of reviewing all their degrees and there could be important changes in the near future.

Undergraduate studies are aimed mainly at local students. In contrast to other countries, Basque and Spanish students try to get accepted in universities which are close to their family home and in many cases they live with their parents while they study at the university. That means that most of the students who attend model D in secondary school will prefer to have Basque as the language of instruction at the University of the Basque Country or one of the private universities. At the undergraduate level the influence of the language of instruction in secondary school is strong.

As there are still many credits which are not taught in Basque, the criteria to be taken into account when deciding the priority of using Basque in some studies over others is whether enrolment is high enough for courses in Basque or whether another Faculty or college of the University is already offering that degree in Basque.

The development of the European Higher Education Area has very important consequences for postgraduate studies. Master degrees have existed in Spanish universities for years but they have not been part of the official university degrees. Nowadays most official masters are in the process of being designed and in the case of the University of the Basque Country it is difficult to know exactly what the use of Basque could be. It is likely that Masters programs will attract more students from other universities both from Spain and other countries. This means that the use of English will become more important in the future.

Main Challenges of Using the Minority Language as the Medium of Instruction

The challenges faced when using a minority language as the language of instruction at the university are basically the same as when the minority language is used in primary and secondary school. The most urgent needs are to have a sufficient number of teachers who are proficient enough to teach through the medium of Basque and to have enough teaching materials. However in the case of higher education these urgent needs are more complex at least for two reasons:

1. The number of courses existing at the University of the Basque Country undergraduate level and the courses at the graduate level is much larger than the total number of courses in primary and secondary schools.
2. High specialization is required for teaching staff at the university level.

These two factors have important implications for teacher education and the development of teaching materials.

Teaching staff

As compared to primary and secondary education where there are enough teachers qualified to teach through the medium of Basque, the number of lecturers and professors who can teach though the medium of Basque is still a problem at the university. Nowadays only 35.31% of the full time teaching staff at the University of the Basque Country are bilingual and can teach in Basque. The distribution of the percentages is given in Table 10.2.

It can be observed that, in general, the percentages are quite low if we take into account the aims about the use of Basque as the language of instruction and the increasing number of model D students going to the university. The percentages are even lower in Technical Studies and Health Sciences.

The main policy to increase the number of bilingual lecturers and professors is through retirements and new contracts. The majority of those retiring in the next years are monolingual and proficiency in Basque is a requirement for many new jobs. New contracts for Basque speaking staff are not only possible to replace Spanish speaking staff who retire but in some cases, the creation of new jobs is also possible. According to the Master Plan for Basque (Euskararen Plan Gidaria, 2007), the aim is to get to 43% of Basque speaking teaching staff by 2012. This means having an average of 57 Basque speaking new jobs per year. In order to get a 'Basque post' candidates must have obtained the certificate of Basque proficiency.

As compared to primary and secondary schools, there is some financial support for teaching staff who study Basque but there is no specific

Table 10.2 Number and percentages of bilingual staff at the University of the Basque Country

	Number	*(%)*
Experimental Sciences	145	(31.39)
Technical Studies	225	(28.30)
Health Sciences	52	(23.53)
Law and Social Sciences	461	(44.46)
Humanities	157	(36.51)
Total	1040	(35.31)

Source: University of the Basque Country (www.ehu.es)

large-scale plan to teach Basque to professors and lecturers. The high level required on part of the teacher and the specialization of university subjects are added difficulties for the training of teaching staff. Moreover, in many cases it is not a question of changing Spanish posts into Basque posts but of creating Basque language streams.

The University of the Basque Country offers free classes for teaching staff and plans to create a limited number of special workshops as a pilot experience. The aim of these workshops is to work at the lexical and discourse levels on specific areas and to be able to discuss problems and questions arising from the use of Basque for teaching and research.

Apart from the number of bilingual teaching staff there are two other related problems. One is that there are more Basque speaking instructors than Spanish speaking instructors who do not have a PhD. Some of these situations have been created because of the urgent need to hire Basque speaking staff. There are some measures to solve this problem and they include leaves of absence for staff to finish their PhD theses or not to hire teaching staff without a doctorate unless it is absolutely necessary. The second problem is related to the conditions of Basque speaking staff. Due to the limited number of bilingual staff, bilingual instructors often have an additional burden because they have to teach more credits and more different subjects, they have to teach subjects at different faculties or they have to teach mainly undergraduate courses.

Academic staff teaching through the medium of Basque gets support from the Basque Language Service. There are recommendations about the use of Basque, the possibility of getting class notes in Basque corrected and there is access to reference texts and specialized dictionaries.

Supporting staff

A very important sector at the university is supporting staff. Supporting staff is a very mixed group with different qualifications depending on the jobs they do and include librarians, lawyers, secretaries, translators, technicians, computer experts, clerks, etc. The total number of supporting staff at the University of the Basque Country is over 1600. There is an important difference between supporting staff in primary and secondary education and at the university level. First, there is an important difference in the relative number of supporting staff. Schools have a limited number of secretaries, technicians and clerks who do not have much contact with the teachers and students. At the university, the relative number of supporting staff is much higher and teachers and researchers and in some cases students have a lot more contact with them.

Table 10.3 Language profiles for supporting staff (equivalent to CEFR levels)

Profile 1 B1	Be able to get the general meaning of a written or oral text. Be able to take part in very simple conversations
Profile 2 B2	Be able to get and provide information. Be able to take part in meetings conducted in Basque
Profile 3 C1	Be able to write different types of texts. Be able to use linguistic forms correctly both in oral and written language
Profile 4 C2	Be able to understand and produce technical texts. Oral and written fluency similar to that of those who have completed university studies in Basque

Source: Decree 86/1997: BOPV 17-4-1997

Table 10.4 Language profiles of supporting staff (2007)

	Number	*(%)*
No Basque	791	(47.91)
Profile 1 B1	132	(8.00)
Profile 2 B2	446	(27.01)
Profile 3 C1	257	(15.57)
Profile 4 C2	25	(1.51)
Total	1651	(100)

Source: University of the Basque Country (www.ehu.es)

The regulations for the Basquization of supporting staff are the same as for civil servants in the Basque Government, county governments and town halls in the BAC. According to these regulations, supporting staff needs to achieve a specific level of proficiency, a 'linguistic profile' depending on the characteristics of their job. The description of the four profiles, which correspond to CEFR levels, is given in Table 10.3.

The distribution of the supporting staff among the different profiles is given in Table 10.4.

The data indicate that almost half of the staff have not achieved any of the profiles and that only just over 17% have achieved profiles 3 and 4. Supporting staff can get free Basque language classes and learn Basque in their working hours. For example, in the academic year 2007–08, 205 members of staff had Basque classes for two hours per day, 35 had classes for five hours per day and 15 people who already had Profile 2 had two hours per day to try to obtain Profile 3.

According to the Master Plan for Basque (Euskararen Plan Gidaria, 2007), some posts will become bilingual in the next five years. Apart from the general language classes there are special courses and workshops for developing the use of Basque in different sectors of the supporting staff. Supporting staff have an online program 'AZPidazki' to facilitate the use of Basque when writing documents.

Students

Students who have Basque as the language of instruction at the university have also had Basque as the language of instruction in pre-primary, primary and secondary school. Almost all of them were enrolled in model D and are used to Basque as the language of instruction for all the subjects. They take the University entrance test as all the other students but they do not have to take any special test to have Basque as the language of instruction. Undergraduate students can also take an optional subject to get a better knowledge of the specific terminology of their studies. According to the Master Plan for Basque (Euskararen Plan Gidaria, 2007), in the next years there will be a common optional subject about norms and use of the language in standard Basque and another optional subject specific for each degree about terminology and professional use of the language. It is expected that in the near future, students will also have access to benefit from consultation with the Basque language service so as to improve the quality of the texts they produce in Basque.

Materials

The limited number of textbooks and other teaching materials in Basque has been one of the main challenges of teaching through the medium of Basque. Today approximately 40% of the books and 20% of the journals published by the University of the Basque Country are in Basque. There is a wide range of books about different academic topics published by the University of the Basque Country, other Universities and independent publishers but there are still problems to find enough materials in Basque in some fields. The main problems are in experimental sciences, technical studies and health sciences while the fields of Law and Social Sciences and Humanities have more publications in Basque.

Publications in Basque are either original books or translations of textbooks and other teaching material. One of the problems of translating books from other languages is that the translation process and production of the book takes a long time and in some cases by the time the book is published it is no longer up-to-date. Nevertheless, the Master Plan for Basque (Euskararen Plan Gidaria, 2007) considers that it is still necessary to translate some basic textbooks into Basque and proposes to translate 30 more textbooks by the year 2011–12, half of them in Technical Studies. Textbooks translated into Basque are reviewed both for content and language.

The creation of study materials in Basque in electronic format is considered as a more economic and practical way to make the materials in Basque available and some books have already been published.

Research

The use of the Basque language in research is not very common. The first PhD thesis in Basque was defended in 1974 but there are only approximately 15 doctoral theses in Basque each year as compared to approximately 200 in Spanish. PhD theses in English are not very common either and the number is similar or lower to the number of theses in Basque. Research conducted in the Basque Country has to be related to research conducted in other countries and that means that the impact is potentially bigger if it is published in English. Basque is also used in research publications for the general public. There is the ZIO book series which aims at popularizing scientific research. There is also the idea of having a magazine on research for secondary school students in the BAC.

Publications in international journals are in most cases in English and they are valued more than local publications in Basque. Some researchers consider that this is not fair in the case of internal promotion at the University of the Basque Country (Isasi, 2004).

Use of Basque

The University of the Basque Country is not isolated from its sociolinguistic context and as it is the case in other levels of education and in Basque society in general, one of the main challenges it faces is the use of Basque in everyday communication. So far the regulations and plans have considered the use of both Basque and Spanish in all official documents, signs at the university, on the university website and all its resources.

Multilingualism at the University in the Basque Country

The importance of English as a language of global communication and the language of science and technology makes it necessary for Basque universities to go from bilingualism to multilingualism. The University of the Basque Country board approved the Multilingualism Plan in 2005. Its aims are the following:

1. To foster mobility and participation in the European Higher Education Area (EHEA). One of the objectives of EHEA is to increase mobility of students so that an increasing number of students may study in universities in other countries, and to improve their training for the European labor market. In this context, Basque students will have to use languages other than Basque and Spanish to go to other universities and in most cases the language they will need to use will be English. On the other hand, the number of students from other countries is expected to increase in the next years and a multilingual university can offer more possibilities for foreign students.
2. To follow up the multilingualism projects developed in secondary education. As we have already seen in Chapter 5, some schools in the BAC are already using English as an additional language of instruction in the different school models. The University aims at providing the possibility of following up on these projects. In fact, so far many students do not use any English once they are at the university and they lose confidence about their skills in English.
3. To foster the mobility of teaching staff. Academic staff can also benefit from using additional languages at the university in a context of increased international relations and increased mobility.

The Statutes of the University of the Basque Country include the possibility of using additional languages as languages of instruction and some courses are being taught in English from the academic year 2005–06. The idea is that all compulsory courses should be offered in Basque and Spanish but only some courses in English or other languages. It is expected that the use of English at the postgraduate level will be more important in the next years. There are already some courses in English and French in some master degrees. The number of courses taught through the medium of English at the undergraduate level is still quite modest but it is increasing and in the academic year 2008–09 the number of courses taught through English was over 100. Most courses are in economics and business studies, technical studies and experimental sciences. Students can also take some courses through the medium of English from a special program for American students and courses in different languages in the Philology Faculty can be taken as optional courses by other students. There is also one course with French as the language of instruction and there are plans to use more French and German as additional languages of instruction but for a very limited number of courses.

Academic staff who wish to teach through the medium of English or another language (French or German) need to meet one of the following conditions in order to prove their language proficiency: (1) to hold an official certificate of proficiency; (2) to have completed their doctoral thesis in an English, French or German speaking university or (3) to have taught courses in English, French or German at the university level in other countries. Academic staff who do not meet any of these requirements and wish to teach through the medium of English have to pass a specific exam including oral and written tests.

Academic staff teaching through the medium of English can take a specific short language course on interactional oral skills in the classroom so as to help them to communicate with the students. They also get some support to translate and review their teaching materials and for the first two years the number of credits they teach in English or other languages count double for their total number of teaching hours required.

Students who learn through the medium of English not only get the possibility of increased mobility and will be better prepared for the labor market but also learn the specific terminology of their specialization in another language and have easier access to publications and lectures in foreign languages. Still, the number of students who decide to take one or more of the courses taught through the medium of English is very limited. Students do not seem to be ready to make an extra effort to learn through the medium of another language and in many cases they are not confident about their proficiency in English or other languages.

Other Universities in the Basque Autonomous Community

The other two universities in the BAC are University of Deusto (www.deusto.es) and University of Mondragon (www.mondragon.edu). The University of Deusto is the oldest in the BAC and it was founded in 1886. It has approximately 11,000 students distributed in seven faculties in two campuses in Bilbao and Donostia-San Sebastian. The University of Deusto is a private religious university.

The number of subjects in Basque in the different studies at the University of Deusto is very limited. Apart from the studies such as Basque Philology, there are some courses in Basque and Spanish but most courses are only taught in Spanish. There are also a few optional subjects in some studies taught through the medium of English. According to Pagola (2004) there are different aims according to the characteristics of the degrees.

According to the 2nd General Plan for the Basque language (University of Deusto, 2006), all official information and general information for the general public or for students should be bilingual. This plan also aims at having a system of profiles for the posts held by supporting staff aiming at having 50% of the posts in contact with the public with staff who has obtained profile 1 (see Table 10.4). The aim is to offer a minimum of 30% in Basque in all the studies. Teaching staff is encouraged to learn Basque and Basque is going to be an asset for hiring and promotion. The University of Deusto also aims at developing teaching materials for Basque classes and to use more Basque in everyday communication. It has a centre to teach Basque language to students. The University of Deusto aims at developing students' proficiency in Basque, Spanish and English.

The university of Mondragon was created in 1997 and it is a private university which is part of the Mondragon Cooperative Corporation (MCC). MCC is a group of companies which is the biggest corporation in the Basque Country and one of the biggest in Spain. Mondragon University has approximately 4000 students and most of them (about 75%) have studied in model D. Mondragon University has three Faculties: Humanities and Education, Politechnical School and Business School. Basque is the main language of instruction in the Faculty of Humanities and Education. Some studies are through Basque and Spanish in the Polytechnic and Business Schools but Spanish is more common than Basque. The Plan for the Basque language (University of Mondragon, 2006) aims at developing the use of Basque as the language of communication, using more Basque in the interaction with students, the relations with companies, the quality of Basque, the use of Basque for administration and the identification of university staff with the Basque language.

Mondragon University is carrying out a special pedagogical project '*The Mendeberri project*' and one of its aims is that students acquire communicative skills in Basque, Spanish and English. Seventy eight per cent of the teaching staff at Mondragon University is bilingual. According to Arrasate (2004), Mondragon University does not usually produce materials to teach in Basque and uses the materials produced by other universities and publishers.

As we can see these two private universities also go in the same direction as the University of the Basque Country and aim at using more Basque as the language of instruction at the University level along with other languages. At the same time, the universities in the BAC aim at internationalization and fully integration in the European Higher Education Area by using more English.

Adult language learning

University teaching staff, supporting staff, students and any other citizen over the age of 16 can attend Basque schools for adults (_'euskaltegiak'_) to learn Basque (see also Azkue & Perales, 2005). These schools are public and private institutions where Basque is taught as a second language and they also teach literacy skills to speakers of Basque as a first language who had only Spanish as their language of instruction. Nowadays, very few students are in this situation and most students at _'euskaltegiak'_ learn Basque as a second or additional language.

According to the Basque Government Language Policy unit, there were 29,830 students of Basque in official _'euskaltegiak'_ in the BAC in November 2008 and the total number for the whole 2008–09 academic year is estimated to reach 40,000 because students can register at different times during the academic year (El País, 29 November, 2008). This figure has increased for the first time in the last years. The mean age for these students is 35 years old, almost 70% are women and only about 20% work in public institutions. There is an increasing number of foreign adult students of Basque, mainly immigrants.

Basque language courses have financial funding from public institutions and there are different courses according to their intensity. It is also possible to be a full-time student taking a course in a boarding school or _'barnetegia'_ or to spend sometime with a Basque-speaking family in a rural area to practice oral skills. Students who are successful can take part in a public examination to obtain a certificate of Basque that can be useful in the job market. Basque is valued in some jobs as we have seen in the case of school teachers and university supporting staff. Adult learners have different reasons to learn Basque but an integrative orientation to be a fully member of the Basque-speaking community is still very important (Perales, 2004).

A Basque Government Agency, HABE (The Adult Institute for developing literacy and proficiency in Basque) was created in 1983 and guides and coordinates adult Basque schools in the BAC (http://www.habe.euskadi.net). Nowadays materials to teach Basque include not only printed materials but audiovisual and multimedia materials. For example, _'Boga'_ is a multimedia system to learn Basque through the internet and covers all levels (http://www.boga.habe.org/). An example of the materials can be seen in Figure 10.3.

Basque and many other languages (French, English, German, Italian, Portuguese, Russian and Spanish as a foreign language) can be learned in another type of schools for adults, the Official Language Schools. Of these, there are 11 schools in the BAC and the most popular languages are English

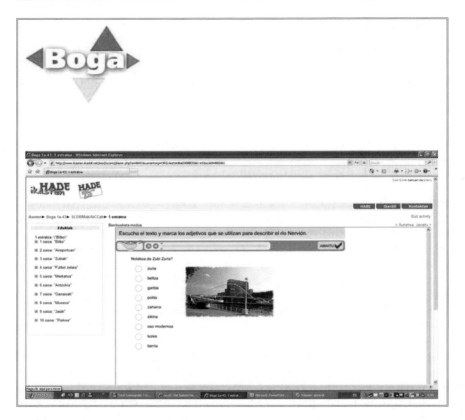

Figure 10.3 Boga

and Basque. According to the Basque Government Department of Education there are about 50,000 students in these schools. These schools offer different levels and organized exams to obtain official certificates. There are also private schools of languages all over the BAC and the main language taught is English both to schoolchildren and adults.

Conclusion

This chapter has focused on the use of the minority language and English at the university. The Basque Country, and particularly the University of the Basque Country has a strong policy to promote the use of Basque. Basque has a relatively strong presence at the university as compared to other universities in regions where minority languages are used. The use of Basque has a strong legal and organizational basis and a very important demand resulting from the increasing use of Basque as the language of instruction in primary and secondary education. The use of English is a more recent phenomenon and not as common as in many other universities around the world.

The use of different languages at the university is very relevant for society not only because these languages can potentially be used by a high number of teaching staff, researchers, supporting staff and students but also because of the impact that students have on society once they finish their studies. In this sense, it is important that the university provides students with the necessary resources for the labor market. For example, the increasing use of Basque and English as languages of instruction in primary and secondary schools make it necessary to prepare university students who will become teachers to be experts in some studies (mathematics, science, history) and at the same to be able to teach through the medium of two or three languages. The increasing use of Basque as a language of instruction and the teaching of some subjects through the medium of English may be positive but perhaps insufficient. A more flexible system without hard boundaries between different studies including minors in different languages or content studies could also be desirable.

There is a need to conduct research on bilingualism and multilingualism at the university so as to see the effect of using other languages as languages of instruction. Research on the use of English at the University in other contexts can also be relevant for the Basque context (Van Leeuwen & Wilkinson, 2003; Wilkinson *et al.*, 2006; Fortanet-Gómez & Räisänen, 2008).

Key Points

- English-medium instruction at the university is spreading in many countries.
- Basque has been used as a language of instruction at the university for many years but it is still a challenge to offer all undergraduate students the possibility to have Basque as the language of instruction.
- Basque has a weaker role in postgraduate studies and research while English is becoming stronger.
- Adults have special courses to learn Basque (and other languages).

Notes

1. The Statutes of the University of the Basque Country are in accordance with the Basic Law for the Normalization of the Use of the Basque Language (1982: BOPV 16-12-1982), the Decree for the Normalization of Basque in the Administration (Decree 86/1997: BOPV 17-4-1997) and the Law for the Basque University System (3/2004: BOPV 12-3-2004).
2. The percentage is over 100 in some optional courses because they correspond to the number of available credits in Basque. In these cases students can even make a choice between different courses in Basque to complete the required credits.

Chapter 11
Conclusions and Future Perspectives

Basque Bilingual and Multilingual Education

This volume has looked at different aspects of bilingual and multilingual education in the Basque Autonomous Community and has reported research on the results of using Basque as the language of instruction and the acquisition of English as a third language. The volume also proposes the '*Continua of Multilingual Education*' as a model that accounts for different types of bilingual and multilingual education as related to the sociolinguistic context in which schools are located.

The Basque educational system shows that it is possible to use a minority language as the language of instruction not only at primary and secondary school but also at the university. We have seen that academic results in the BAC are as good as or even better than those in other areas of Spain. This implies that use of the minority language in the curriculum and even as the main language of instruction does not hinder academic development. These findings confirm the positive outcomes of bilingual education aiming at the development of bilingualism and biliteracy in other parts of the world (Cummins, 2007: xiv–xv). The results regarding the teaching of English as a third language indicate that it is possible to combine a strong position for the minority language in the curriculum with an increasing presence of English in it both at school and the university. Research indicates that bilingualism in Basque and Spanish can have a positive effect on the acquisition of English as a third language and also that different programs such as the early introduction of English, Content and Language Integrated Learning (CLIL) and the use of English as an additional language of instruction are possible. Strengthening the role of English in the curriculum can be advantageous provided that the position of the weakest language, Basque in this case, remains strong. In fact, establishing clear goals for the different languages and integrating them in multilingual syllabuses are necessary steps to establish additive multilingual education. The results of research in the

BAC can be useful for other contexts in which the maintenance of the minority languages and the protection of linguistic diversity have to go along with the use of languages of wider communication.

The current Basque educational system is one of the outcomes resulting from an enormous effort made to reverse language shift by promoting the minority language (see also Azurmendi & Martínez de Luna, 2005, 2006b). The school system has contributed to increasing the number of Basque speakers but it has a limited influence on the language use (Altuna, 2007). Zalbide and Cenoz (2008) compare the situation of Basque in the seventies with the current situation and report the important advancements made regarding the use of Basque as a language of instruction, the official funding and the legal status of Basque-medium instruction, teachers' competence, learning materials in Basque and the standardization of the Basque language. All these achievements are certainly impressive and Basque is in a very good situation as compared to other minority languages. However, the survival of Basque faces a new situation. According to the 2006 Sociolinguistics survey (Basque Government, 2008) 39.7% of the bilingual speakers in the BAC find it easier to use Spanish than Basque, in many cases because Basque is not their first language. As Zalbide and Cenoz (2008) point out, the use of Basque is still very limited in the case of Basque L2 speakers in some domains (home, friends, community) and this situation has implications for the quality of Basque. The problem lies in intergenerational transmission of Basque, that is, stage 6 in the Graded Intergenerational Disruption Scale (Fishman, 1991). The Basque educational system has made an important contribution to the promotion of Basque but as we have seen in this volume, it is also important to promote the use of Basque to a larger extent for non-academic activities either at school or outside school. As Spolsky (2004: 46) says, the school is one of the most important domains of language policy to develop the language competence of young people. Language proficiency acquired at school can certainly improve intergenerational transmission but the sociolinguistic context also has an important influence. This can be seen in the comparison of former students in two Basque-medium schools in different areas of the BAC (Basque Government, 2005ab). Adults who have had Basque as the main medium of instruction (model D) use more or less Basque depending on its use in the social networks and sociolinguistic context. Even when Basque is the language of instruction (model D), some of the research studies reported in this volume highlight the minority and 'less dominant' status of Basque as compared to Spanish in productive vocabulary or cross-linguistic influence (Erriondo *et al.*, 1998; Cenoz, 2001b). The use of a minority language as the language of instruction can have an important effect on its revitalization but this does not necessarily mean that its future as a language used in all domains is secured (see also Hornberger, 2008).

Towards a Multilingual Approach

The characteristics of the Basque educational system and research conducted in the Basque Country and elsewhere indicate that it may not be appropriate to establish hard boundaries when working with bilingual and multilingual education. As we have already seen in the introduction, the Basque educational system combines heritage language learning, second language acquisition, foreign language acquisition, bilingual and multilingual education and folk and elite bi/multilingualism. Research on heritage language learning generally ignores the role of languages of wider communication and research on second/foreign language acquisition has ignored the role of other languages known or being learned by learners. Second/foreign acquisition research, and particularly new proposals to integrate language and content, are not always aware of the important experience that bilingual programs have in this integration. The development of multilingual education in the Basque Country and research focusing on Basque, Spanish and English is a step forward in the direction of linking second/foreign and heritage language acquisition to the socioeducational and sociolinguistic context. The 'Continua of Multilingual Education' also provides a model to study multilingual schools from this holistic perspective. As we have already seen it can be a useful tool to analyze different multilingual schools in different parts of the world.

A related issue is the establishment of hard boundaries between languages as compared to adopting a hybrid and holistic approach in research and school practices in bilingual and multilingual schools. Most bilingual and multilingual schools try to create hard boundaries between languages both in teaching practices and assessment. The strategies used to do this include the following:

- having different teachers for different languages;
- having different classrooms for each language with the linguistic landscape on the walls in only one language;
- establishing rules to use only the target language;
- referring to monolingual native speakers as the model to be achieved in each language;
- planning and assessing languages separately.

Research in second/foreign language acquisition and bilingualism has generally looked at separate languages by examining the process of acquiring one single language or different aspects of the competence acquired in different languages. There have been proposals that question this approach in the assessment of language proficiency and suggest that bilinguals (and multilinguals) should be regarded as such and that their total linguistic repertoire should be taken into account because they are different from monolinguals (Grosjean, 1992, 2008; Cook, 1995).

The long tradition of research on code-switching shows that when languages are in contact, speakers use them in different ways and as a resource (see for example Gafaranga, 2007). However, as Jessner (2006: 130) says *'Most language teachers still treat each curricular language as an isolated unit, that is they do not allow any code-switching or any other mention of the students' mother tongue or other languages in the curriculum'*. According to Jessner, this view is limiting the possibilities of benefiting from the possible advantages of multilingualism as related to metalinguistic awareness and the use of learning strategies. When looking at competence in several languages, Shohamy (2006: 172) proposes a multilingual and multimodal approach understood as the competences derived from hybrids of different languages and the use of multiple codes including not only printed texts but visuals and a variety of symbols. García (2008a) does not believe in clear-cut boundaries between the languages used by bilinguals either and refers to multiple discursive practices as translanguaging. When discussing identities, Jaffe (2007: 51) makes the distinction between understanding bilingualism as two separate monolingualisms and two separate identities or as *'a potentially uneven mixture of codes, practices and competencies distributed across different individuals and different moments and domains of social action'*. Indeed, the boundaries between languages (and identities) are soft in language practices and even more nowadays because new technologies have contributed to softening the boundaries between codes. Multilingualism cannot be separated from the implications that multimodality for language learning in school contexts (see Schultz & Hull, 2007; Cenoz & Gorter, 2008b).

Some practices in the Basque Country go in the direction of approaching multilingual education from a multilingual perspective by integrating different languages in a common syllabus. Some research has also looked at multilingual proficiency, the influence of bilingualism on third language acquisition, attitudes towards multilingualism and the interaction between languages. However, there is still a long way to change the 'monolingual' approach to multilingual education and most teachers and researchers take the ideal educated monolingual as the yardstick against which to measure students' proficiency. The Common European Framework of Reference (Council of Europe, 2002), which is becoming an important reference in the

Basque Country and elsewhere in Europe, is a step towards defining competencies in different languages but still considers languages separately. In many cases, learners of Basque as a second language, who use mainly Spanish outside school, are expected to achieve the same level of communicative competence in Basque as students with Basque as a first language who live in a Basque speaking environment. Similarly, the latter are expected to have the same level of linguistic, sociolinguistic, pragmatic, discourse and strategic competence in Spanish as those who only speak Spanish and have Spanish as the language of instruction. Balanced bilinguals who are highly competent in two languages for any function are exceptional and this is even more the case if we go beyond bilingualism into multilingual competence. Basque students cannot be expected to be ideal native speakers of Basque, Spanish and English but they can be expected to achieve high levels of communicative competence in these and even additional languages and should be regarded as multilingual speakers taking into account their socioeducational and sociolinguistic context.

Future Perspectives

This volume has reported research on bilingual and multilingual education in the Basque Country. As we have seen, there have been a considerable number of studies on different areas and some interesting findings have been reported. The research conducted so far has focused mainly on the outcomes of bilingual and multilingual education and attitudes towards different languages. This type of research is interesting because it provides information about many areas of bilingualism, multilingualism and language acquisition as related to linguistic, sociolinguistic and educational factors. At the same time, the study of multilingual education provides useful information for parents, teachers, language planners and society in general.

However, the scope of this research is somehow limited and it is necessary to conduct research in other directions as well. One possibility is to adopt a more multilingual approach as we have already discussed. This approach could be adopted not only regarding the study of multilingual competence but also multilingual identities in the school context (Pavlenko & Blackledge, 2004). It is necessary to conduct more ethnographic research inside bilingual and multilingual classrooms so as to analyze instructional practices, negotiation of meaning and language processing when language and content are integrated (see for example Lyster, 2007) and to analyze the practices regarding the allocation and functions of different languages in classroom interaction. Another line of research in bilingual and multilingual education is to include a critical interpretative perspective which focuses on the way discourse practices are related to institutional and historical contexts and reflect power relations (Heller, 2007; Martin-Jones *et al.*, 2007). As we have already seen, multilingual education cannot be separated from the socio-political context in which it takes place. Another possibility is to adopt an interdisciplinary approach and to explore new areas in bilingual and multilingual education such as the definition of the use and non-use values of multilingualism by adopting models used in the study of biodiversity (see for example Cenoz & Gorter, 2009 for an application to the study of the linguistic landscape).

This volume shows that bilingual and multilingual education in the Basque Country (and elsewhere) is dynamic, it involves multiple practices and faces different challenges at different times (see also García, 2008a). Nowadays, some of these challenges in the Basque Country are related to the increasing number of immigrants who speak Spanish and other languages. Other challenges are related to the need to acquire communicative competence in Basque and other languages, the use of these languages and the need to maintain and if possible improve academic results. The achievements of the educational system in the BAC cannot be separated from current and future challenges. One of the areas that needs to be examined is the actual use of Basque, Spanish and English for new types of communication (texting, chatting, emailing, etc). The analysis of multilingual and multimodal practices is particularly interesting in the case of minority languages. A gap between language practices at school and out of school with friends and classmates is to be expected, but the extent to which the minority language is used along with others in these practices can have implications for language policy and the use of the language. These practices can also be related to feelings and emotions about the languages (see also Pavlenko, 2005).

Bilingual and multilingual education can take different forms because they are necessarily linked to the sociolinguistic context in which they take place. The Basque educational system has more similarities with other European bilingual areas with other European minority languages used in education in regions such as Catalonia (Muñoz, 2005; Vila, 2008), Friesland (Gorter, 2005; Gorter & Van der Meer, 2008), Wales (Baker, 2003; Lewis, 2008) or Ireland (Harris, 2007, 2008), but it also shares challenges with many other areas where minority languages and languages of wider communication are part of the school curriculum.

The Basque educational system has some specific characteristics related to its sociolinguistic, political, historical and economic context. Its organization, its different possibilities and the research conducted in the Basque

Country can provide useful information for other contexts involving different forms of bilingual and multilingual education. The maintenance and promotion of a minority language, Basque in this case, contributes to the maintenance of linguistic and cultural diversity. There are important ecological, historical, economic, cultural and emotional reasons to go on protecting and promoting Basque and for giving Basque children the opportunity to learn and use Basque along with other languages in schools which aim at multilingualism and multiliteracy.

References

Aarts, R., Extra, G. and Yağmur, K. (2004) Multilingualism in the Hague. In G. Extra and K. Yağmur (eds) *Urban Multilingualism in Europe* (pp. 193–220). Clevedon: Multilingual Matters.

Abutalebi, J., Cappa, S.F. and Perani, D. (2005) What can functional neuroimaging tell us about the bilingual brain? In J.F. Kroll and A.M.B. de Groot (eds) *Handbook of Bilingualism: Psycholinguistic Approaches* (pp. 497–515). New York: Oxford University Press.

Aierbe, P., Etxezarreta, J. and Satrustegi, L.M. (1974) Ikastoletako aurren jakite mailaren azterketa konparatiboa. *Zeruko Argia* 603, 1.

Aierbe, P., Arregi, P., Etxeberria Balerdi, F. and Etxeberria Sagastume, F. (1989) *Urretxu-Legazpi-Zumarraga Eskoletako Euskararen Egoera.* Kilometroak 85.

Aiestaran, J. (2003) Aspects of language contact in Rioja Alavesa. PhD thesis, Bangor University.

Aizpuru, M. (2008) Euskara Euskal Herriko Unibertsitatean. On WWW at www.euskara-errektoreordetza.ehu.es.

Ajzen, I. (1988) *Attitudes, Personality and Behavior.* Chicago, IL: Dorsey Press.

Alcón, E. (2007) Linguistic unity and cultural diversity in Europe: Implications for research on English language and learning. In E. Alcón and M.P. Safont (eds) *Intercultural Language Use and Language Learning* (pp. 23–39). Dordrecht: Springer.

Aldekoa, J. and Gardner, N. (2002) Turning knowledge of Basque into use: Normalization plans for schools. *International Journal for Bilingual Education and Bilingualism* 5, 339–354.

Aliaga, R. (2002) Introducción temprana de la lengua inglesa en las escuelas públicas del País Vasco. In F. Etxeberria and U. Ruiz Bikandi (eds) *¿Trilingües a los 4 años?* (pp. 85–104). Donostia-San Sebastián: Ibaeta Pedagogia.

Altuna, O. (ed.) (2007) Kale neurketaren V. neurketa. *Bat Soziolinguistika aldizkaria* 64 (special issue).

Amorrortu, E. (2001a) Unibertsitate-ikasleen euskalki eta batuarekiko jarrerak. In J. Goikoetxea (ed.) *Euskalkia eta hezkuntza* (pp. 61–80). Bilbao: Mendebalde Euskal Kultur Alkartea.

Amorrortu, E. (2001b) Elkartasuna eta estatusa hizkuntz jarreretan: Euskararen erabilera aurreikusten? *Bat Soziolinguistika aldizkaria* 40, 75–89.

Arano, R.M., Berazadi, E. and Idiazabal, I. (1996) Planteamiento discursivo e integrador de un proyecto de educación trilingüe. In M. Pujol and F. Sierra (eds) *Las Lenguas en la Europa comunitaria* (Vol. II) (pp. 65–88). Amsterdam: Rodopi.

Arano, R.M. and Ugarte, M.J. (2000) Hirugarren hizkuntzaren irakaskuntza arlo baten bidez: Txingudi Ikastolako esperientzia. *Ikastaria* 11, 119–128.

Arrasate, J. (2004) Mondragon Unibertsitatea eta Euskara *Bat. Soziolinguistika aldizkaria* 50, 51–56.

Artigal, J.M. (1993) La importancia del uso en la adquisición de una nueva lengua. In *I Jornadas Internacionales de Educación Plurilingüe* (pp. 99–111). Las Arenas-Getxo, Spain: Fundación Gaztelueta.

Arzamendi, J. and Genesee, F. (1997) Reflections on Immersion Education in the Basque Country. In K. Johnson and M. Swain (eds) *Immersion Education: International Perspectives* (pp. 151–166). Cambridge: Cambridge University Press.

Atxaga, B. (2007) Everything that lives desires to last. In Ons Erfdeel Vzw (ed.) *Standing Tall in Babel*. Rekkem: Ons Erfdeel Vzw.

Azkue, J. and Perales, J. (2005) The teaching of Basque to adults. *International Journal of the Sociology of Language* 174, 73–83.

Azpillaga, B., Arzamendi, J., Etxeberria, F., Garagorri, X. and Lindsay, D. (2001) Preliminary findings of a format-based foreign language teaching method for schoolchildren in the Basque Country. *Applied Psycholinguistics* 22, 35–44.

Azpillaga, B. (2005) Diferencias en la aplicación del programa Hocus y Lotus y sus repercusiones en el aprendizaje de una lengua nueva en educación primaria. PhD thesis, University of the Basque Country.

Azurmendi, M.J., Bachoc, E. and Zabaleta, F. (2001) Reversing language shift: The case of Basque. In J.A. Fishman (ed.) *Can Threatened Languages Be Saved?* (pp. 234–259). Clevedon: Multilingual Matters.

Azurmendi, M.J. and Martínez de Luna, I. (2005) Introduction: Presenting the Basque Case. *International Journal of the Sociology of Language* 174, 1–8.

Azurmendi, M.J. and Martínez de Luna, I. (2006a) Introduction. In M.J. Azurmendi and I. Martínez de Luna (eds) *The Case of Basque: Past, Present and Future* (pp. 13–18). Andoain: Soziolinguistika Klusterra.

Azurmendi, M.J. and Martínez de Luna, I. (eds) (2006b) *The Case of Basque: Past, Present and Future*. Andoain: Soziolinguistika Klusterra.

Azurmendi, M.J. and Luque, J. (2006) Euskararen jabekuntza goiztiarra: Alderdi psikologiko ebolutiboak eta nortasunezkoak. In J. Cenoz and D. Lasagabaster (eds) *Hizkuntzak Ikasten eta Erabiltzen* (pp. 243–264). Bilbao: Euskal Herriko Unibertsitatea.

Azurmendi, M.J., Larrañaga, N. and Apalategi, J. (2008) Bilingualism, identity and citzenship in the Basque Country. In M. Niño-Murcia and J. Rothman (eds) *Bilingualism and Identity* (pp. 35–62). Amsterdam: John Benjamins.

Baetens Beardsmore, H. (1993a) The European school model. In H. Baetens Beardsmore (ed.) *European Models of Bilingual Education* (pp. 121–154). Clevedon: Multilingual Matters.

Baetens Beardsmore, H. (1993b) An overview of European models of bilingual education. *Language, Culture and Curriculum* 6, 197–208.

Baetens Beardsmore, H. (2008) Language promotion by European supra-national institutions. In O. García (ed.) *Bilingual Education in the 21st Century: A Global Perspective* (pp. 197–217). Chichester, UK: Wiley-Blackwell.

Baetens Beardsmore, H. and Swain, M. (1985) Designing bilingual education: Aspects of immersion and 'European school' models. *Journal of Multilingual and Multicultural Development* 6, 1–15.

Baetens Beardsmore, H. and Lebrun, N. (1991) Trilingual education in the Grand Duchy of Luxembourg. In O. García (ed.) *Bilingual Education* (pp. 107–120). Amsterdam/Philadelphia: John Benjamins.

Bahry, S., Niyozov, S. and Shamatov, D.A. (2007) Bilingual education in Central Asia. In J. Cummins and N.H. Hornberger (eds) *Encyclopedia of Language and Education* (Vol. 5: Bilingual Education) (pp. 205–221). New York: Springer.

Baker, C. (1992) *Attitudes and Language.* Clevedon: Multilingual Matters.

Baker, C. (2000) *The Care and Education of Young Bilinguals: An Introduction for Professionals.* Clevedon: Multilingual Matters.

Baker, C. (2003) Biliteracy and transliteracy in Wales: Language planning and the Welsh National Curriculum. In N.H. Hornberger (ed.) *Continua of Biliteracy: An Ecological Framework for Educational Policy, Research and Practice in Multilingual Settings* (pp. 71–90). Clevedon: Multilingual Matters.

Baker, C. (2006) *Foundations of Bilingual Education and Bilingualism* (4th edn). Clevedon: Multilingual Matters.

Baker, C. (2007a) Becoming bilingual through bilingual education. In P. Auer and L. Wei (eds) *Handbook of Multilingualism and Multilingual Communication* (pp. 131–152). Berlin: Mouton de Gruyter.

Baker, C. (2007b) Knowledge about bilingualism and multilingualism. In J. Cenoz and N.H. Hornberger (eds) *Encyclopedia of Language and Education* (Vol. 6: Knowledge about Language) (pp. 315–327). New York: Springer.

Baker, C. and Prys Jones, S. (1998) *Encyclopaedia of Bilingualism and Bilingual Education.* Clevedon: Multilingual Matters.

Ball, P., Beobide, H. and Muñoa, I. (2005) Como enseñar Ciencias Sociales en inglés. *Immersió Lingüística* 7, 91–107.

Balke-Aurell, G. and Lindblad, T. (1982) *Immigrant Children and their Languages.* Department of Education Research, University of Gothenburg.

Balluerka, N. and Gorostiaga, A. (2005) Lehen eta bigarren hizkuntzen ulermen eta adierazpen idatzian eragiten duten faktoreak Euskal Herriko ikasle elebidunengan: hizkuntzen erabilera eta jabetze historia. *Bat Soziolinguistika aldizkaria* 56, 29–42.

Banfi, C. and Day, R. (2004) The evolution of bilingual schools in Argentina. *International Journal of Bilingual Education and Bilingualism* 7, 398–411.

Banfi, C. and Rettaroli, S. (2008) Staff profiles in minority and prestigious bilingual education contexts in Argentina. In C. Hélot and A.M. De Mejía (eds) *Forging Multilingual Spaces* (pp. 140–180). Clevedon: Multilingual Matters.

Basque Government (1995) *Euskararen Jarraipena I. La Continuidad del Euskera I. La Continuité de la Langue Basque I.* Vitoria-Gasteiz: Basque Government.

Basque Government (1997) *Euskararen Jarraipena II. La Continuidad del Euskera II. La Continuité de la Langue Basque II.* Vitoria-Gasteiz: Basque Government.

Basque Government (2003) *Euskararen Jarraipena III. La Continuidad del Euskera III. La Continuité de la Langue Basque III.* Vitoria-Gasteiz: Basque Government.

Basque Government (2004) *Gazteen argazkiak/Retratos de Juventud, 7* (Portraits of Youth). Vitoria/Gasteiz: Eusko Jaurlaritza/Gobierno Vasco.

Basque Government (2005a) Euskararen erabilera eta transmisioa Donostiako Santo Tomas Lizeoko ikasle ohien adibidea. On WWW at http://www.euskara. euskadi.net/r59-738/es/contenidos/informacion/argitalpenak/es_6092/adjuntos/Santo%20Tomas_c.pdf.

Basque Government (2005b) Euskararen erabilera eta transmisioa Olabide Ikastolako ikasle ohien adibidea. On WWW at http://www.euskara.euskadi. net/r59-3693/eu/contenidos/informacion/artik1_1_aizpurua_05_05/eu_8647/adjuntos/OlabideEuskara.pdf.

Basque Government (2008) *IV Inkesta Soziolinguistikoa*. Vitoria-Gasteiz: Basque Government.
Basque News (2007a) Basque News 105. On WWW at http://www.lehendakaritza. ejgv.euskadi.net/r48-457/en/contenidos/noticia/boletin_eusk/en_369/ adjuntos/ingles_105.pdf.
Basque News (2007b) Basque News 106. On WWW at http://www.lehendakaritza. ejgv.euskadi.net/r48-457/en/contenidos/noticia/boletin_eusk/en_369/ adjuntos/ingles_106.pdf.
Beloki, L., Idiazabal, I. and Manterola, I. (2005) Bost urteko haur elebidunen euskarazko ipuin-kontaketak. *Bat Soziolinguistika Aldizkaria* 56, 79–96.
Benson, C. (2004) Trilingualism in Guinea-Bissau and the question of instructional language. In C. Hoffmann and J. Ytsma (eds) *Trilingualism in Family, School and Community* (pp. 166–184). Clevedon: Multilingual Matters.
Berman, R.A. and Slobin, D.I. (1994) *Relating Events in Narrative: A Crosslinguistic Developmental Study*. Hillsdale, NJ: Erlbaum.
Bernaus, M., Andrade, A.I., Kervran, M., Murkowska, A. and Trujillo Sáez, F. (2007) *Plurilingual and Pluricultural Awareness in Language Teacher Education: A training kit*, Strasbourg/Graz: Council of Europe [book + CD-Rom]. On WWW at http://www.ecml.at/mtp2/Lea/html/LEA_E_Results.htm.
Bialystok, E. (1997) The structure of age: In search of barriers to second language acquisition. *Second Language Research* 13, 116–137.
Bialystok, E. and Miller, B. (1999) The problem of age in second language acquisition: Influences from language, structure and task. *Bilingualism, Language and Cognition* 2, 127–145.
Bialystok, E. (2001) *Bilingualism in Development*. Cambridge: Cambridge University Press.
Bialystok, E. (2003) Bilingualism, aging and cognitive control: Evidence from the Simon task. *Psychology and Aging* 19, 290–303.
Bialystok, E. (2005) *Consequences of Bilingualism for Cognitive Development*. New York: Oxford University Press.
Bilbao, J. (1994) Experiencia Trilingüe en Gaztelueta. *Proceedings of the II International Conference on Plurilingual Education*. Vitoria-Gasteiz: 3–4 November 1994.
Bild, E.R. and Swain, M. (1989) Minority language students in a French Immersion programme: Their French proficiency. *Journal of Multilingual and Multicultural Development* 10, 255–74.
Birdsong, D. (2004) Second language acquisition and ultimate attainment. In A. Davies and C. Elder (eds) *Handbook of Applied Linguistics* (pp. 82–105). London: Blackwell.
Blackledge, A. and Creese, A. (2009) *Multilingualism: A Critical Perspective*. London Continuum.
Blum-Kulka, S. (1991) Interlanguage pragmatics: The case of requests. In R. Phillipson, E. Kellerman, L. Selinker, M. Sharwood Smith and M. Swain (eds) *Foreign/Second Language Pedagogy Research* (pp. 255–272). Clevedon: Multilingual Matters.
Blum-Kulka, S., House, J. and Kasper, G. (1989) *Cross-Cultural Pragmatics: Requests and Apologies*. Norwood, NJ: Ablex.
Boix-Fuster, E. and Sanz, C. (2008) Language and identity in Catalonia. In M. Niño-Murcia and J. Rothman (eds) *Bilingualism and Identity* (pp. 11–32). Amsterdam: John Benjamins.
Bongaerts, T. (2005) Introduction: Ultimate attainment and the critical period hypothesis for second language acquisition. *International Review of Applied Linguistics in Language Teaching* 43 (4), 259–267.

Brohy, C. (2001) Generic and/or specific advantages of bilingualism in a dynamic plurilingual situation: The case of French as official L3 in the school of Samedan (Switzerland). *International Journal of Bilingual Education and Bilingualism* 4, 38–49.

Burstall, C. (1975) French in the primary school: The British experiment. *The Canadian Modern Language Review* 31, 388–402.

Byram, M. and Leman, J. (eds) (1990) *Bicultural and Trilingual Education: The Foyer Model in Brussels*. Clevedon: Multilingual Matters.

Candelier, M. (2007) 'Awakening to languages' and educational language policy. In J. Cenoz and N.H. Hornberger (eds) *Encyclopedia of Language and Education* (Vol. 6: Knowledge about Language) (pp. 219–232). New York: Springer.

Carder, M. (2007) *Bilingualism in International Schools*. Clevedon: Mulltilingual Matters.

Carli, A. and Ammon, U. (eds) (2008) What can future applied linguistics do to mitigate disadvantages for non-anglophones? *Aila Review* 20, 1–3.

Carrasquillo, A.L. and Rodriguez, V. (2002) *Language minority students in the mainstream classroom*. Clevedon: Multilingual Matters.

Cenoz, J. (1992) *Enseñanza-aprendizaje del inglés como L2 o L3*. Bilbao: University of the Basque Country.

Cenoz, J. (1998) Multilingual education in the Basque Country. In J. Cenoz and F. Genesee (eds) *Beyond Bilingualism: Multilingualism and Multilingual Education* (pp. 175–191). Clevedon: Multilingual Matters.

Cenoz, J. (2001a) Basque in Spain and France. In G. Extra and D. Gorter (eds) *The Other Languages of Europe* (pp. 45–57). Clevedon: Multilingual Matters.

Cenoz, J. (2001b) The effect of linguistic distance, L2 status and age on cross-linguistic influence in L3 acquisition. In J. Cenoz, B. Hufeisen and U. Jessner (eds) *Cross-linguistic Influence in Third Language Acquisition.* (pp. 8–20). Clevedon: Multilingual Matters.

Cenoz, J. (2001c) Three languages in contact: Language attitudes in the Basque Country. In D. Lasagabaster and J.M. Sierra (eds) *Language Awareness in the Foreign Language Classroom* (pp. 37–60). Bilbao: University of the Basque Country.

Cenoz, J. (2003a) The role of typology in the organization of the multilingual lexicon. In J. Cenoz, B. Hufeisen and U. Jessner (eds) *The Multilingual Lexicon* (pp. 103–116). Dordrecht: Kluwer Academic.

Cenoz, J. (2003b) The additive effect of bilingualism on third language acquisition: A review. *International Journal of Bilingualism* 7, 71–88.

Cenoz, J. (2003c) The intercultural style hypothesis: L1 and L2 interaction in requesting behaviour. In V. Cook (ed.) *Effects of the Second Language on the First* (pp. 62–80). Clevedon: Multilingual Matters.

Cenoz, J. (2003d) The influence of age on the acquisition of English: General proficiency, attitudes and code mixing. In M.P. García Mayo and M.L. García Lecumberri (eds) *Age and the Acquisition of English as a Foreign Language: Theoretical Issues and Field Work* (pp. 77–93). Clevedon: Multilingual Matters.

Cenoz, J. (2004) Teaching English as a third language: The effect of attitudes and motivation. In C. Hoffmann and J. Ytsma (eds) *Trilingualism in Family, School and Community* (pp. 202–218). Clevedon: Multilingual Matters.

Cenoz, J. (2005) English in bilingual programs in the Basque Country. *International Journal of the Sociology of Language* 171, 41–56.

Cenoz, J. (2008a) The Basque language Baskisch. In U. Ammon and H. Haarmann (eds) *Wieser Enzyklopädie der Sprachen Westereuropas*. Klagenfurt: Wieser. 49–62.

Cenoz, J. (2008b) Achievements and challenges in bilingual and multilingual education in the Basque Country. *Aila Review* 21, 13–30.

Cenoz, J. (ed.) (2008c) *Teaching through Basque*. Clevedon: Multilingual Matters (also special issue of *Language, Culture and Curriculum* 21, 1).

Cenoz, J. and Gallardo, F. (2000) Evaluación del proyecto de plurilingüismo. Unpublished research report.

Cenoz, J., Lindsay, D. and Espí, M.J. (1994) Plurilingüismo temprano. Evaluación. Unpublished research report. Ikastolen Elkartea.

Cenoz, J. and Lindsay, D. (1994) Teaching English in primary school: A project to introduce a third language to eight year olds in the Basque Country. *Language and Education* 8, 201–10.

Cenoz, J. and Valencia, J. (1994) Additive trilingualism: Evidence from the Basque Country. *Applied Psycholinguistics* 15, 157–209.

Cenoz, J. and Genesee, F. (1998) Introduction. In J. Cenoz and F. Genesee (eds) *Beyond Bilingualism: Multilingualism and Multilingual Education* (pp. vii–x). Clevedon: Multilingual Matters.

Cenoz, J. and Jessner, U. (eds) (2000) *English in Europe: The Acquisition of a Third Language*. Clevedon: Multilingual Matters.

Cenoz, J. and Gorter, D. (eds) (2005) Trilingualism and minority languages in Europe. *International Journal of the Sociology of Language* 171 (special issue).

Cenoz, J. and Gorter, D. (2006) Linguistic landscape and minority languages. *International Journal of Multilingualism* 3, 67–80.

Cenoz, J. and Gorter D. (eds) (2008a) Applied linguistics and the use of minority languages in education. *Aila Review* 21 (special issue).

Cenoz, J. and Gorter, D. (2008b) The linguistic landscape as an additional source of input in second language acquisition. *IRAL: International Review of Applied Linguistics* 46, 267–287.

Cenoz, J. and Gorter, D. (2009) Language economy and linguistic landscape. In E. Shohamy and D. Gorter (eds) *Linguistic Landscape: Expanding the Scenery* (pp. 55–69). New York: Routledge.

Clyne, M. (1997) Some of the things trilinguals do. *International Journal of Bilingualism* 1, 95–116.

Clyne, M, Hunt, C.R. and Isaakidis, T. (2004) Learning a community language as a third language. *International Journal of Multilingualism* 1, 33–52.

Cobbey, H. (2007) Challenges and prospects of minority bilingual education in China: An analysis of four projects. In A. Feng (ed.) *Bilingual Education in China* (pp. 182–199). Clevedon: Multilingual Matters.

Cook, V. (1992) Evidence for multi-competence. *Language Learning* 42, 557–591.

Cook, V. (1995) Multi-competence and the learning of many languages. *Language, Culture and Curriculum* 8, 93–98.

Cook, V. (2003) Introduction: The changing L1 in the L2 user's mind. In V. Cook (ed.) *Effects of the Second Language on the First* (pp. 1–18). Clevedon: Multilingual Matters.

Cook, V.J., Iarossi, E., Stellakis, N. and Tokumaru, Y. (2003) Effects of the second language on the syntactic processing of the first language. In V.J. Cook (ed.)

Effects of the Second Language on the First (pp. 214–233). Clevedon: Multilingual Matters.

Cook, V. (2007) The goals of ELT: Reproducing native-speakers or promoting multi-competence among second language users? In J. Cummins and C. Davison (eds) *International Handbook of English Language Teaching* (pp. 237–248). New York. Springer.

Cooper, R.L. (1989) *Language Planning and Social Change*. Cambridge: Cambridge University Press.

Cots, J.M. (2007) Knowledge about language in the mother tongue and foreign language curricula. In J. Cenoz and N.H. Hornberger (eds) *Encyclopedia of Language and Education* (Vol. 6: Knowledge about Language) (pp. 15–30). New York: Springer.

Council of Europe (1992) European Charter for Regional or Minority Languages. On WWW at http://www.coe.int/t/e/legal_affairs/local_and_regional_ democracy/regional_or_minority_languages/1_The_Charter/_summary.asp.

Council of Europe (2002) Common European Framework of Reference for Languages. On WWW at http://www.coe.int/t/dg4/linguistic/CADRE_EN.asp.

Coyle, D. (2000) Meeting the challenge: Developing the 3Cs curriculum. In S. Green (ed.) *New perspectives on Teaching and Learning Modern Languages* (pp. 158–182). Clevedon: Multilingual Matters.

Coyle, D. (2007) CLIL: A pedagogical approach from the European perspective. In Van Deussen-Scholl and N.H. Hornberger (eds) *Encyclopedia of Language and Education* (Vol. 4: Second and Foreign Language Education) (pp. 97–111). Berlin-New York: Springer.

Creese, A. and Martin, P. (eds) (2003) *Multilingual Classroom Ecologies*. Clevedon, Multilingual Matters.

Crystal, D. (2000) *Language Death*. Cambridge: Cambridge University Press.

Crystal, D. (2003) *English as a Global Language*. Cambridge: Cambridge University Press.

Cummins, J. (1979) Linguistic interdependence and the educational development of bilingual children. *Review of Educational Research* 49, 222–251.

Cummins, J. (2000) *Language, Power and Pedagogy: Bilingual Children in the Crossfire*. Clevedon: Multilingual Matters.

Cummins, J. (2003) Bilingual education: Basic principles. In J.M. Dewaele, A. Housen and L. Wei (eds) *Bilingualism: Beyond Basic Principles* (pp. 56–66). Clevedon: Multilingual Matters.

Cummins, J. (2007) Introduction to volume 5: Bilingual Education. In J. Cummins and N.H. Hornberger (eds) *Encyclopedia of Language and Education* (Vol. 5: Bilingual Education) (pp. xiii–xxiii). New York: Springer.

Dagenais, D., Armand, F., Walsh, N. and Maraillet, E. (2007) L'Eveil aux langues et la co-construction de connaissances sur la diversité linguistique. *Canadian Journal of Applied Linguistics* 10, 197–219.

Dai, Q and Cheng, Y. (2007) Typology of bilingualism and bilingual education in Chinese minority nationality regions. In A. Feng (ed.) *Bilingual Education in China* (pp. 75–93). Clevedon: Multilingual Matters.

Dalton-Puffer, C. (2007) *Discourse in Content and Language Integrated Learning (CLIL) Classrooms*. Amsterdam: John Benjamins.

Dávila, P. (ed.) (1995) *Lengua, escuela, cultura: El proceso de alfabetización en Euskal Herria: siglos XIX y XX*. Bilbao: University of the Basque Country.

Davidson, C. and Cummins, J. (2007) Assessment and evaluation in ELT. In J. Cummins and C. Davison (eds) *International Handbook of English Language Teaching* (pp. 415–420). New York/Berlin: Springer.

De Angelis, G. (2007) *Third or Additional Language Learning*. Clevedon: Multilingual Matters.

De Graaff, R., Koopman, G.J., Anikina, Y. and Westhoff, G. (2007) An observation tool for effective L2 pedagogy in content and language integrated learning (CLIL). *International Journal of Bilingual Education and Bilingualism* 10, 603–624.

De Keyser, R. (2000) The robustness of critical period effects in second language acquisition. *Studies in Second Language Acquisition* 22, 499–533.

De Keyser, R. and Larson-Hall, J. (2005) What does the critical period really mean? In J.F. Kroll and A.M.B. De Groot (eds) *Handbook of Bilingualism: Psycholinguistic Approaches* (pp. 88–108). Oxford: Oxford University Press.

De Keyser, R. (2006) A critique of recent arguments against the critical period hypothesis. In C. Abello-Contesse, R. Chacón-Beltrán, M. Dolores López-Jiménez and M. Mar Torreblanca-López (eds) *Age in L2 Acquisition and Teaching* (pp. 49–58). Bern: Peter Lang.

De Mejía, A.M. (2002) *Power, Prestige and Bilingualism*. Clevedon: Multilingual Matters.

De Mejía, A.M. (ed.) (2004) Bilingual education in South America. *International Journal of Bilingual Education and Bilingualism* 7 (special issue).

Doiz, A. and Lasagabaster, D. (2004) The effect of the early teaching of English on writing proficiency. *International Journal of Bilingualism* 8, 527–542.

Dörnyei, Z. (2006) Individual differences in second language acquisition. *Aila Review* 19, 42–68.

Doughty, C. and Williams, J. (eds) (1998) *Focus on Form in Classroom Language Acquisition* (pp. 42–63). New York: Cambridge University Press.

Douglas, W. and Bilbao, J. (2005) *Amerikanuak: Basques in the New World*. Reno: University of Nevada Press (reprint).

Dutcher, N. (1998) Eritrea: Developing a programme of multilingual education. In J. Cenoz and F. Genesee (eds) *Beyond Bilingualism: Multilingualism and Multilingual Education* (pp. 259–269). Clevedon: Multilingual Matters.

Echeverria, B. (2005) Language attitudes in San Sebastian: The Basque vernacular as challenge to Spanish language hegemony. *Journal of Multilingual and Multicultural Development* 26, 249–264.

Edwards, J. (2003) The importance of being bilingual. In J.M. Dewaele, A. Housen and L. Wei (eds) *Bilingualism: Beyond Basic Principles* (pp. 28–41). Clevedon: Multilingual Matters.

Edwards, J. (2007) Societal multilingualism: Reality, recognition and response. In P. Auer and L. Wei (eds) *Handbook of Multilingualism and Multilingual Communication* (pp. 447–467). Berlin: Mouton de Gruyter.

Edwards, V. (2004) *Multilingualism in the English-speaking World*. Oxford: Blackwell.

Egiguren, I. (2006) Atzerriko hizkuntza goiztiarraren eragina gaitasun eleaniztunean. PhD thesis, University of the Basque Country.

Elhuyar Kultur Elkartea (1993) *Hiztegi Entziklopedikoa*. Lizarra: Elhuyar.

Ellis, E.M. (2004) The invisible multilingual teacher: The contribution of language background to Australian ESL teachers' professional knowledge and beliefs. *International Journal of Multilingualism* 1, 90–108.

Elorza, I. and Muñoa, I. (2008) Promoting the minority language through integrated plurilingual language planning: The case of the ikastolas. *Language, Culture and Curriculum* 21, 85–101.

Ennaji, M. (2005) *Multilingualism, Cultural Identity and Education in Morocco.* Berlin-New York: Springer.

Enomoto, K. (1994) L2 perceptual acquisition: The effect of multilingual linguistic experience on the perception of a 'less novel' contrast. *Edinburgh Working Papers in Applied Linguistics* 5, 15–29.

Erriondo, L., Isasi, X. and Rodríguez, F. (1993) *Hezkuntza, hizkuntza eta elebiduntasuna.* Bilbao: Udako Euskal Unibertsitatea.

Erriondo, L., Garagorri, X. and Isasi, X. (1998) *Hezkuntzaren Normalkuntza.* Bilbao: Udako Euskal Unibertsitatea.

Espasa-Calpe (1994) *Diccionario Enciclopedico Espasa* (11th edn). Madrid: Mateu Cromo AG.

Etxeberria, F. (1999) *Bilingüismo y Educación en el País del Euskara.* Donostia: Erein.

Etxeberria, F. (2002) Educación trilingüe precoz en el País Vasco y la bicicleta de Cummins. In F. Etxeberria and U. Ruiz Bikandi (eds) *¿Trilingües a los 4 años?* (pp. 165–191). Donostia: Ibaeta Pedagogía.

Etxeberria, F. (2004) Trilinguals at four? Early trilingual education in the Basque Country. In C. Hoffmann and J. Ytsma (eds) *Trilingualism in Family, School and Community* (pp. 185–201). Clevedon: Multilingual Matters.

Etxeberria-Sagastume, F. (2006) Attitudes towards language learning in different linguistic models of the Basque Autonomous Community. In O. García, T Skutnabb-Kangas and M.E. Guzmán (eds) *Imagining Multilingual Schools* (pp. 111–133). Clevedon: Multillingual Matters.

Etxeberria, F. and Elosegi, K. (2008) Basque, Spanish and immigrant minority languages in the Basque school. *Language Culture and Curriculum* 21, 69–84.

European Commission (1995) White paper on education and learning. On WWW at http://europa.eu/documents/comm/white_papers/pdf/com95_590_en.pdf.

European Commission (2005a) A new framework strategy for multilingualism. On WWW at http://europa.eu/languages/servlets/Doc?id=913.

European Commission (2005b) Eurobarometer 237: Europeans and their languages. On WWW at http://ec.europa.eu/public_opinion/archives/ebs/ebs_237.en.pdf.

European Commission (2006) Eurobarometer 243: Europeans and their languages. On WWW at http://ec.europa.eu/public_opinion/archives/ebs/ebs_243_sum_en.pdf.

European Commission (2007 final report) High level group on multilingualism. On WWW at http://ec.europa.eu/education/policies/lang/doc/multireport_en.pdf.

Eurydice (2008) Key Data on Teaching Languages at School in Europe. On WWW at http://eacea.ec.europa.eu/ressources/eurydice/pdf/0_integral/095EN.pdf.

Euskararen Plan Gidaria (2007) University of the Basque Country. On WWW at www.ehu.es.

Eustat (2008) Basque Statistics Office. On WWW at http://www.eustat.es/elem/ele0000000/tbl0000063_i.html.

Extra, G. and Gorter, D. (2001) Comparative perspectives on regional and immigrant minority languages in multicultural Europe. In G. Extra and D. Gorter (eds) *The Other Languages of Europe* (pp. 1–41). Clevedon: Multilingual Matters.

Extra, G. and Yağmur, K. (2004) Demographic perspectives. In G. Extra and K. Yağmur (eds) *Urban Multilingualism in Europe* (pp. 25–72). Clevedon: Multilingual Matters.

Extra, G. and Gorter, D. (2007) Regional and immigrant minority languages in Europe. In M. Hellinger and A. Pauwels (eds) *Handbook of Language and Communication Diversity and Change* (pp. 15–52). Berlin: Mouton de Gruyter.

Feng, A. (ed.) (2007) *Bilingual Education in China*. Clevedon: Multilingual Matters.

Fishman, J.A. (1991) *Reversing Language Shift: Theoretical and Empirical Foundations of Assistance to Threatened Languages*. Clevedon: Multilingual Matters.

Fishman, J.A. (ed.) (2001) *Can Threatened Languages Be Saved? Reversing Language Shift Revisited: A 21st Century Perspective*. Clevedon: Multilingual Matters.

Fishman, J.A. and Lovas, J. (1972) Bilingual education in sociolinguistic perspective. In B. Spolsky (ed.) *The Language Education of Minority Children* (pp. 83–93). Rowley: Newbury House.

Fortanet-Gómez, I., Ch. Räisänen (eds) (2008) *ESP in European Higher Education. Integrating Language and Content*. Amsterdam: John Benjamins.

Franceschini, R., Zappatore, D. and Nitsch, C. (2003) Lexicon in the brain: What neurobiology has to say about languages. In J. Cenoz, B. Hufeisen and U. Jessner (eds) *The Multilingual Lexicon* (pp. 153–166). Dordrecht: Kluwer.

Gabiña, J.J., Gorostidi, R., Iruretagoiena, R., Olaziregi, I. and Sierra, J. (1986) *EIFE: Influence of Factors on the Learning of Basque*. Vitoria-Gasteiz: Eusko Jaurlaritzaren Argitalpen Zerbitzu Nagusia.

Gafaranga, J. (2007) Code-switching as a conversational strategy. In P. Auer and L. Wei (eds) *Handbook of Multilingualism and Multilingual Communication* (pp. 279–313). Berlin: Mouton de Gruyter.

Gallardo del Puerto, F. (2005) *La adquisición de la pronunciación del inglés como tercera lengua*. Bilbao: University of the Basque Country.

Gallardo del Puerto, F. (2007) Is L3 phonological competence affected by the learner's level of bilingualism? *International Journal of Multilingualism* 4, 1–16.

Garagorri, X. (2000) Eleaniztasun goiztiarrari bai, baina ez edonola. *Ikastaria* 11, 97–117.

Garagorri, X. (2002) Hirueletasun goiztiarra ikastoletan 'Eleanitz-Ingelesa' proiektuaren ebaluazioa. In F. Etxeberria and U. Ruiz Bikandi, *¿Trilingües a los 4 años?* (pp. 105–143). Donostia: Ibaeta Pedagogía.

García, O. (2007) Multilingual language awareness and teacher education. In J. Cenoz and N.H. Hornberger (eds) *Encyclopedia of Language and Education* (Vol. 6: Knowledge about Language) (pp. 385–400). New York: Springer.

García, O. (ed.) (2008a) *Bilingual Education in the 21st Century: A Global Perspective*. Chichester, UK: Wiley-Blackwell.

García, O. (2008b) Introducing bilingual education. In O. García (ed.) *Bilingual Education in the 21st Century: A Global Perspective* (pp. 3–17). Chichester, UK: Wiley-Blackwell.

García Azkoaga, I. and Idiazabal, I. (2003) La cohesion nominale dans les textes narratifs des écoliers bilingues basque-espagnol. *Lidil* 27, 75–87.

García Lecumberri, M.L. and Gallardo, F. (2003) English FL sounds in school learners of different ages. In M.P. García Mayo and M.L. García Lecumberri (eds) *Age and the Acquisition of English as a Foreign Language*. (pp. 115–135). Clevedon: Multilingual Matters.

García Lecumberri, M.L. and Gallardo, F. (2006) Ingelezko bokalen pertzepzioa eta ekoizpena atzerriko hizkuntza gisa: jatorrizko kategoria fonetikoen eta hasteko adinaren eragina. In J. Cenoz and D. Lasagabaster (eds) *Hizkuntzak Ikasten eta Erabiltzen* (pp. 159–175). Bilbo: Euskal Herriko Unibertsitatea.

García Mayo, M.P. (1999) Grammaticality intuitions of bilingual and monolingual Basque EFL learners. *Estudios de lingüística aplicada* 29, 71–82.

García Mayo, M.P. (2003) Age, length of exposure and grammaticality judgements in the acquisition of English as a foreign language. In M.P. García Mayo and M.L. García Lecumberri (eds) *Age and the Acquisition of English as a Foreign Language* (pp. 94–114). Clevedon: Multilingual Matters.

García Mayo, M.P. and García Lecumberri, M.L. (eds) (2003) *Age and the Acquisition of English as a Foreign Language: Theoretical Issues and Field Work.* Clevedon: Multilingual Matters.

García Mayo, M.P., Lázaro Ibarrola, A. and Liceras, J.M. (2005) Placeholders in the English interlanguage of bilingual (Basque/Spanish) children. *Language Learning* 55, 445–489.

García Mayo, M.P. (2006) Synthetic compounding in the English interlanguage of Basque-Spanish bilinguals. *International Journal of Multilingualism* 3, 231–257.

Gardner, N. (2000) *Basque in Education in the Basque Autonomous Community.* Vitoria-Gasteiz: Basque Government.

Gardner, N. (2005) *The Basque Language in Education in Spain.* Ljouwert/Leeuwarden: Mercator-Education. On WWW at www.mercator-education.org.

Gardner, N., Puigdevall i Serralvo, M. and Williams, C.H. (2000) Language revitalization in comparative context: Ireland, the Basque Country and Catalonia. In C.H. Williams (ed.) *Language Revitalization: Policy and Planning in Wales* (pp. 311–361). Cardiff: University of Wales Press.

Gardner, R.C. and Lambert W.E. (1972) *Attitudes and Motivation in Second Language Learning.* Rowley: Newbury House.

Gardner-Chloros, P. (2007) Multilingualism and autochthonous minorities. In P. Auer and L. Wei (eds) *Handbook of Multilingualism and Multilingual Communication* (pp. 469–491). Berlin: Mouton de Gruyter.

Garrett, P., Coupland, N. and Williams, A. (2003) *Investigating Language Attitudes: Social Meanings of Dialect, Ethnicity and Performance.* Cardiff: University of Wales Press.

Genesee, F. (1987) *Learning Through Two Languages: Studies of Immersion and Bilingual Education.* Cambridge, MA: Newbury House.

Genesee, F. (1998) A case study of multilingual education in Canada. In J. Cenoz and F. Genesee (eds) *Beyond Bilingualism: Multilingualism and Multilingual Education* (pp. 243–258). Clevedon: Multilingual Matters.

Genesee, F. (2004) What do we know about bilingual education for majority-language students. In T.K. Bathia and W.C. Ritchie (eds) *The Handbook of Bilingualism* (pp. 547–576). London: Blackwell.

Genesee, F. and Lindholm-Leary, K. (2007) Dual language education in Canada and the United States. In J. Cummins and N.H. Hornberger (eds) *Encyclopedia of Language and Education* (pp. 253–266). New York: Springer.

Genesee, F. and Riches, C. (2006) Literacy: Instructional issues. In F. Genesee, K. Lindholm-Leary, W.M. Saunders and D. Christian (eds) *Educating English Language Learners: A Synthesis of Research Evidence* (pp. 109–175). New York: Cambridge University Press.

Gibbons, J. and Ramirez, E. (2004) *Maintaining a Minority Language: A Case Study of Hispanic Teenagers*. Clevedon: Multilingual Matters.

Gibson, M., Hufeisen, B. and Libben, G. (2001) Learners of German as an L3 and their production of German prepositional verbs. In J. Cenoz, B. Hufeisen and U. Jessner (eds) *Cross-linguistic Influence in Third Language Acquisition: Psycholinguistic Perspectives* (pp. 138–148). Clevedon: Multilingual Matters.

Giles, H., Bourhis, R.Y. and Taylor, D.M. (1977) Towards a theory of language in ethnic group relations. In H. Giles (eds) *Language, Ethnicity and Intergroup Relations* (pp. 207–348). New York: Academic Press.

Giles, H. and Byrne, J.L. (1982) An intergroup approach to second language acquisition. *Journal of Multilingual and Multicultural Development* 3, 17–40.

Goikoetxea, N. (2007) *Gaitasun komunikatiboa eta hizkuntzen arteko elkar eragina EAE-ko hezkuntza eleanitzean*. Leioa: University of the Basque Country.

Gonzalez-Ardeo, J. (2001) Engineering students and ESP in the Basque Country: SLA vs. TLA. In J. Cenoz, B. Hufeisen and U. Jessner (eds) *Looking beyond second language acquisition: Studies in tri- and multilingualism*. (pp. 75–95). Tübingen: Stauffenburg.

Gordon, Raymond G., Jr. (ed.) (2005) *Ethnologue: Languages of the world* (15th edn). Dallas, TX: SIL International. On WWW at http://www.ethnologue.com/.

Gorostiaga, A. and Balluerka, N. (2002) The influence of the social use and the history of acquisition of Euskera on comprehension and recall of scientific texts in Euskera and Castilian. *Language Learning* 52, 491–512.

Gorter, D. (2005) Three languages of instruction in Fryslân. *International Journal of the Sociology of Language* 171, 57–73.

Gorter, D. and van der Meer, C. (2008) Developments in bilingual Frisian-Dutch education in Friesland. *Aila Review* 21, 87–103.

Goyeneche, L.F. (1993) *La utilización de la lengua inglesa como vehículo de otras áreas curriculares.I Jornadas Internacionales de Educación Plurilingüe* (pp. 195–204). Las Arenas-Getxo: Fundación Gaztelueta.

Graddol, D. (2006) *English Next: Why Global English may mean the End of English as a Foreign Language*. London: British Council.

Grosjean, F. (1992) Another view of bilingualism. In R.J. Harris (ed.) *Cognitive Processing in Bilinguals* (pp. 51–62). Amsterdam: North Holland.

Grosjean, F. (2008) *Studying Bilinguals*. Oxford: Oxford University Press.

Hamel, R. (2007) Bilingual education for indigenous communities in Mexico. In J. Cummins and N.H. Hornberger (eds) *Encyclopedia of Language and Education* (Vol. 5: Bilingual Education) (pp. 311–322). New York: Springer.

Hamers, J.F. and Blanc, M.H.A. (2000) *Bilinguality and Bilingualism* (2nd edn). Cambridge: Cambridge University Press.

Hammarberg, B. (2001) Roles of L1 and L2 in L3 production and acquisition. In J. Cenoz, B. Hufeisen and U. Jessner (eds) *Cross-linguistic Influence in Third Language Acquisition: Psycholinguistic Perspectives* (pp. 21–41). Clevedon: Multilingual Matters.

Harris, J. (2007) Bilingual education and bilingualism in Ireland North and South (guest editorial). *International Journal of Bilingual Education and Bilingualism* 10, 359–368.

Harris, J. (2008) The declining role of primary schools in the revitalisation of Irish. *Aila Review* 21, 49–68.

Harley, B. (1986) *Age in Second Language Acquisition*. Clevedon: Multilingual Matters.

Harley, B. and Wang, W. (1997) The critical period hypothesis: Where are we now? In A. de Groot and J. Kroll (eds) *Tutorials in Bilingualism: Psycholinguistic Perspectives* (pp. 19–52). London: Lawrence Erlbaum.

Heller, M. (ed.) (2007) *Bilingualism: A Social Approach*. Basingstoke: Palgrave.

Heller, M. and Martin-Jones, M. (eds.) (2001) *Voices of Authority: Education and Linguistic Difference*. Westport, CT: Ablex.

Hélot, C. (2007) Awareness raising and multilingualism in primary education. In J. Cenoz and N.H. Hornberger (eds) *Encyclopedia of Language and Education* (Vol 6: Knowledge about Language) (pp. 371–384). New York: Springer.

Hélot, C. and De Mejía, A-M. (eds) (2008) *Forging Multilingual Spaces*. Clevedon: Multilingual Matters.

Herdina, P. and Jessner, U. (2002) *A Dynamic Model of Multilingualism*. Clevedon: Multilingual Matters.

Hickey, T. (2007) Children's language networks in minority language immersion: What goes in may not come out. *Language and Education* 21, 46–65.

Hirvonen, V. (2008) 'Out on the fells, I feel like a Sámi': Is there linguistic and cultural equality in the Sámi. In N.H. Hornberger (ed.) *Can Schools Save Indigenous Languages?* (pp. 15–41). London: Palgrave.

Hawkins, E. (ed.) (1996) *Thirty Years of Language Teaching*. London: CILT.

Hellekjaer, G.O. and Westergaard, M.R. (2003) An exploratory survey of content learning through English in Nordic Universities. In C. Van Leeuwen and R. Wilkinson (eds) *Multilingual Approaches in University Education* (pp. 65–80). Nijmegen: Valkhof Pers.

Hoffmann, C. (1998) Luxembourg and the European schools. In J. Cenoz and F. Genesee (eds) *Beyond Bilingualism: Multilingualism and Multilingual Education* (pp. 143–174). Clevedon: Multilingual Matters.

Hornberger, N. (1989) Continua of Biliteracy. *Review of Educational Research* 59, 271–296.

Hornberger, N.H. (1991) Extending enrichment bilingual education: Revisiting typologies and redirecting policy. In O. García (ed.) *Bilingual Education* (pp. 215–234). Amsterdam/Philadelphia: John Benjamins.

Hornberger, N.H. (ed.) (2008) *Can Schools Save Indigenous Languages?* London: Palgrave.

Hornberger, N.H. and López, L.E. (1998) Policy, possibility and paradox: Indigenous multilingualism and education in Peru and Bolivia. In J. Cenoz and F. Genesee (eds) *Beyond Bilingualism: Multilingualism and Multilingual Education* (pp. 206–242). Clevedon: Multilingual Matters.

Hornberger, N.H. (2002) Multilingual language policies and the continua of biliteracy: An ecological approach. *Language Policy* 1, 27–51.

Hornberger, N.H. (ed.) (2003) *Continua of Biliteracy: An Ecological Framework for Educational Policy, Research and Practice in Multilingual Settings*. Clevedon: Multilingual Matters.

Hornberger, N.H. (2007) Continua of biliteracy. In A. Creese, P. Martin and N.H. Hornberger (eds) *Encyclopedia of Language and Education* (Vol. 9: Ecology of Language) (pp. 275–290). New York-Berlin: Springer.

Hornberger, N.H. and Skilton-Sylvester, E. (2000) Revisiting the Continua of Biliteracy: International and Critical Perspectives. *Language and Education* 14, 96–122.

Hu, G. (2007) The Juggernaut of Chinese–English bilingual education. In A. Feng (ed.) *Bilingual Education in China* (pp. 94–126). Clevedon: Multilingual Matters.

Hualde, J.I., Lakarra, J.A. and Trask, R.L. (eds) (1995) *On the History of the Basque Language: Readings in Basque Historical Linguistics*. Amsterdam: John Benjamins.

Huguet, A. and Lasagabaster, D. (2007) The linguistic issue in some European bilingual contexts: Some final considerations. In D. Lasagabaster and A. Huguet (eds) *Multilingualism in European Bilingual Contexts: Language Use and Attitudes* (pp. 234–251). Clevedon: Multilingual Matters.

Hyltenstam, K. and Abrahamsson, N. (2003) Maturational constraints in SLA. In C. Doughty and M.H. Long (eds) *The Handbook of Second Language Acquisition* (pp. 539–588). Oxford: Blackwell.

Ibarraran, A., Lasagabaster, D. and Sierra, J.M. (2007) *Inmigración y Aprendizaje del Lenguas en un Contexto Bilingüe*. Bilbao: Lete.

Idiazabal, I. (1998) Modernidad, desarrollo e idiomas minorizados: El case del euskera. In L.E. López and I. Jung (eds) *Sobre las Huellas de la Voz* (pp. 213–243). Madrid: Morata.

Idiazabal, I. and Larringan, L.M. (1997) Transfert de maîtrises discursives dans un programme d'enseignement bilingue basque-espagnol. *AILE: Acquisition et Interaction en Langue Étrangère* 10, 107–126.

Idiazabal, I. and Larringan, L.M. (1999) Aprendizajes interlingüísticos de carácter discursivo en un programa de enseñanza bilingüe. In F. Sierra Martínez and C. Hernández González (eds) *Las Lenguas en la Europa Comunitaria. III, La Adquisición-enseñanza de Segundas Lenguas y-o de Lenguas Extranjeras – Las lenguas de minorías* (pp. 479–496). Amsterdam: Rodopi.

Ikastolen Elkarteko Eleanitz-Ingelesa Taldea (2003) Eleanitz-English: Gizarte Zientziak ingelesez. *Bat Soziolinguistika Aldizkaria* 49, 79–97.

Ikuspegi: Immigrazioaren Euskal Behatokia, Observatorio Vasco de Immigración. (2004) Percepciones, valores y actitudes de la población vasca hacia la immigración extranjera. On WWW at http://www.ikuspegi.org/es/.

Ikuspegi (2007) Immigrazioaren Euskal Behatokia-Observatorio Vasco de Immigración. On WWW at http://www.ikuspegi.org/es/. Trends in International Mathematics and Science Study. On WWW at http://timss.bc.edu/timss2003.html.

Instituto Nacional de Estadística (2007) Demography and population. On WWW at http://www.ine.es/en/welcome_en.htm.

Isasi, X. (2004) Unibertsitario euskaldunen egoera zaila. *Bat Soziolinguistika Aldizkaria* 50, 131–139.

ISEI-IVEI (2002) Evaluación de 6º curso de Educación Primaria 1999.

ISEI-IVEI (2004a) Informe de la evaluación de la Educación Secundaria Obligatoria 2000. Spanish and Basque.

ISEI-IVEI (2004b) Informe de la Evaluación de la lengua inglesa. 2 de ESO 2001.

ISEI-IVEI (2005a) *Evaluación Internacional de Matemáticas y Ciencias. TIMSS 2003. Euskadi. Primer informe de resultados*. Bilbao: Basque Institute for Evaluation and Research in Education.

ISEI-IVEI (2005b) *Evaluación Internacional de Matemáticas y Ciencias. Segundo informe de resultados TIMSS 2003*. Euskadi: Matemáticas

ISEI-IVEI (2005c) *Evaluación Internacional de Matemáticas y Ciencias. Segundo informe de resultados TIMSS 2003*. Euskadi: Ciencias Naturales

ISEI-IVEI (2005d) Level B2 in Basque at the end of obligatory education (4th ESO): Summary of the Spanish version.

ISEI-IVEI (2006) Evaluación de la educación primaria 2004. Resumen ejecutivo. Conclusiones y propuestas de mejora.

ISEI-IVEI. (2007) Trilingual students in secondary school.

ISEI-IVEI (2008) Informe final de la Evaluación PISA 2006.

ISEI-IVEI (2009) Evaluación Internacional de Matemáticas y. Ciencias. TIMSS 2007. Bilbao: Basque Institute for Evaluation and Research in Education.

Jacobs, H., Zingraf, S.A., Wormuth, D.R., Hartfiel, V.F. and Hughey, J.B. (1981) *Testing ESL Composition*. Rowley, MA: Newbury House.

Jaffe, A. (2007) Minority language movements. In M. Heller (ed.) *Bilingualism: A Social Approach* (pp. 50–70). London: Palgrave.

Jaspaert, K. and Lemmens, G. (1990) Linguistic evaluation of Dutch as a third language. In M. Byram and J. Leman (eds) *Bicultural and Trilingual Education: The Foyer Model in Brussels* (pp. 30–56). Clevedon: Multilingual Matters.

Jausoro, N., Martínez de Luna, I. and Dávila, A. (1998) Gazte donostiarren hizkuntzarekiko harremanak. *Bat Soziolinguistika Aldizkaria* 27, 51–81.

Jessner, U. (2006) *Linguistic Awareness in Multilinguals*. Edinburgh: Edinburgh University Press.

Jessner, U. (2008) A DST model of multilingualism and the role of metalinguistic awareness. *Modern Language Journal* 92, 270–283.

Jewitt, C. and Kress, G. (2003) *Multimodal Literacy*. New York: Peter Lang.

Jiang, Q., Liu, Q., Quan, X. and Ma, C. (2007) EFL education in ethnic minority areas in Northwest China: An investigational study in Gansu province. In A. Feng (ed.) *Bilingual Education in China* (pp. 240–255). Clevedon: Multilingual Matters.

Jiménez Catalán, R., Ruiz de Zarobe, Y. and Cenoz, J. (2006) Vocabulary profiles of English foreign language learners in English as a subject and as a vehicular language. *Viewz: Viena English Working Papers* 15, 23–27.

Johnson, R.K. and Swain, M. (eds) (1997) *Immersion Education: International Perspectives*. Cambridge: Cambridge University Press.

Johnstone, R. (2006) Characteristics of immersion programs. In O. García and C. Baker (eds) *Bilingual Education* (pp. 19–32). Clevedon: Multilingual Matters.

Johnstone, R. (2007) *Multilingualism in Scotland: Keynote address at the 5th international conference on Third Language Acquisition and Multilingualism*. Stirling, UK: 3 September 2007.

Kasper, G. and Blum-Kulka, S. (1993) Interlanguage pragmatics: An introduction. In G. Kasper and S. Blum-Kulka (eds) *Interlanguage Pragmatics* (pp. 3–17). Oxford: Oxford University Press.

Kecskes, I. and Papp, T. (2000) *Foreign Language and Mother Tongue*. Mahwah, NJ: Erlbaum.

Kemp, C. (2007) Strategic processing in grammar learning: Do multilinguals use more strategies? *International Journal of Multilingualism* 4, 241–261.

Kenner, C. (2004) *Becoming Biliterate: Young Children Learning Different Writing Systems*. Stoke-on-Trent, UK: Trentham Books.

Keshavarz, M.H. and Astaneh, H. (2004) The impact of bilinguality on the learning of English vocabulary as a foreign language. *International Journal of Bilingual Education and Bilingualism* 7, 295–302.

Kling, J. (2006) Evaluating foreign language skills in communication in management: Application of CEF criteria. In C. Van Leeuwen and R. Wilkinson (eds) *Multilingual Approaches in University Education* (pp. 161–176). Nijmegen: Valkhof Pers.

Kirsch, C. (2006) Young children learning languages in a multilingual context. *International Journal of Multilingualism* 3, 258–279.

Klein, E.C. (1995) Second versus third language acquisition: Is there a different? *Language Learning* 45, 419–465.

Krauss, M. (1992) The World's Languages in Crisis. *Language* 68, 4–10.

Krashen, S.D., Long, M.A. and Scarcella, R.C. (1979) Age, rate and eventual attainment in second language acquisition. *Tesol Quaterly* 13, 573–582.

Khubchandani, L. (2007) Lnaguage policy and education in the Indian subcontinent. In S. May and N.H. Hornberger (eds) *Encyclopedia of Language and Education* (Vol. 4: Second and Foreign Language Education) (pp. 369–381). Berlin/New York: Springer.

Laka, I (1996) A brief grammar of Euskara, the Basque Language. On WWW at http://www.ehu.es/grammar.

Lam, A.S. (2007) Bilingual or multilingual education in China: Policy and learner experience. In A. Feng (ed.) *Bilingual Education in China* (pp. 13–33). Clevedon: Multilingual Matters.

Lambert, W.E., Hodgson, R.C., Gardner, R.C. and Fillenbaum, S. (1960) Evaluational reactions to spoken language. *Journal of Abnormal and Social Psychology* 60, 44–51.

Lambert, W.E. (1974) Culture and language as factors in language and education. In F.E. Aboud and R.D. Meade (eds) *Cultural Factors in Learning and Education: 5th Western Washington Symposium on Learning*. Bellingham, Washington.

Larrañaga, N. (1995) Euskalerriko gaztetxoek euskararekiko dituzten jarrerak eta beren eragina euskara ikasi eta erabiltzean. PhD thesis, University of Deusto.

Larringan, L.M. and Idiazabal, I. (2005) Euskararen kalitatea aztertzeko marko teorikoa eta metodologia. *Ikastaria* 14, 9–29.

Lasagabaster, D. (1998) *Creatividad y conciencia metalingüística: Incidencia en el aprendizaje del inglés como L3*. Bilbao: University of the Basque Country.

Lasagabaster, D. (2000) Three languages and three linguistic models in the Basque Educational System. In J. Cenoz and U. Jessner (eds) *English in Europe: The Acquisition of a Third Language* (pp. 179–197). Clevedon: Multilingual Matters.

Lasagabaster, D. (2001) University students' attitudes towards English as an L3. In J. Cenoz, B. Hufeisen and U. Jessner (eds) *Looking Beyond Second Language Acquisition* (pp. 43–50). Tübingen: Stauffenburg.

Lasagabaster, D. (2003) *Trilingüismo en la enseñanza: Actitudes hacia la lengua minoritaria, la mayoritaria y la extranjera*. Lleida: Milenio.

Lasagabaster, D. (2007) Language use and language attitudes in the Basque Country. In D. Lasagabaster and A. Huguet (eds) *Multilingualism in European Bilingual Contexts: Language Use and Attitudes* (pp. 65–89). Clevedon: Multilingual Matters.

Lasagabaster, D. and Doiz, A. (2003) Maturational constraints on foreign-language written production. In M.P. García Mayo and M.L. García Lecumberri (eds) *Age and the Acquisition of English as a Foreign Language* (pp. 136–160). Clevedon: Multilingual Matters.

Lenneberg, E.H. (1967) *Biological Foundations of Language*. New York: Wiley.

Lewis, G. (2008) Current challenges in bilingual education in Wales. *Aila Review* 21, 69–86.

Llurda, E. (ed.) (2005) *Non-Native Language Teachers: Perceptions, Challenges and Contributions to the Profession*. New York: Springer.

Lo Bianco, J. (2007) Bilingual education and socio-political issues. In J. Cummins and N.H. Hornberger (eds) *Encyclopedia of Language and Education* (Vol. 5: Bilingual Education) (pp. 35–50). New York: Springer.

Long, M. (2005) Problems with supposed counter-evidence to the Critical Period Hypothesis. *International Review of Applied Linguistics* 43, 287–317.

López, L. E. (2006) Cultural diversity, multilingualism and indigenous education in Latin America. In O. García, T. Skutnabb-Kangas and M.E. Guzmán (eds) *Imagining Multilingual Schools* (pp. 238–261). Clevedon: Multillingual Matters.

López, L.E. and Sichra, I. (2007) Intercultural bilingual education among indigenous peoples in Latin America. In J. Cummins and N.H. Hornberger (eds) *Encyclopedia of Language and Education* (Vol. 5: Bilingual Education) (pp. 295–309). New York: Springer.

Lukas, J.F. (1994) *Trebetasun eta Errendimendu Matematikoa Testuinguru Elebidunetan*. Bilbao: Universidad del País Vasco/Euskal Herriko Unibersitatea.

Luque, J. (2003) Euskararen irakaskuntza eta jabekuntza-ikaskuntza estrategiak (2–4 urtekoek) D ereduan. *Bat Soziolinguistika aldizkaria* 49, 111–128.

Lyster, R. (2007) *Learning and Teaching Languages through Content*. Amsterdam: John Benjamins.

Mackey, W.F. (1970) A typology of bilingual education. *Foreign Language Annals* 3, 596–608.

MacWhinney, B. (2000) *The Childes Project: Tools for Analyzing Talk* (3rd edn) (Vols 1 and 2). Mahwah, NJ: Lawrence Erlbaum Associates. On WWW at http://childes.psy.cmu.edu/.

Madariaga, J.M. (1994) *Estudio de la influencia de los factores actitudinales y motivacionales en la adquisición del euskera*. Bilbao: Universidad del País Vasco/Euskal Herriko Unibersitatea.

Maffi, L. (2000) Language preservation vs. language maintenance and revitalization: Assessing concepts, approaches, and implications for language sciences. *International Journal of the Sociology of Language* 142, 175–190.

Mägiste, E. (1984) Learning a third language. *Journal of Multilingual and Multicultural Development* 5, 415–421.

Magnan, S. (ed.) (2008) *Mediating Online Discourse*. Amsterdam: John Benjamins.

Manzanos, C. and Ruiz Pinedo, I. (eds) (2005) *La infancia immigrante en las escuelas de Vitoria-Gasteiz*. Vitoria-Gasteiz: UPV.EHU/ Denon Eskola.

Marsh, C. (2007) Language awareness and CLIL. In J. Cenoz and N.H. Hornberger (eds) *Encyclopedia of Language and Education* (Vol. 6: Knowledge about Language) (pp. 233–246). New York: Springer.

Martin-Jones, M. (2007) Bilingualism, education and the regulation of access to language resources. In M. Heller (ed.) *Bilingualism: A Social Approach* (pp. 161–182). London: Palgrave.

Martin-Jones, M., De Mejía, A.M. and Hornberger N.H. (eds) (2007) *Encyclopedia of Language and Education. Vol 3: Discourse and Education*. NewYork/Berlin: Springer.

Martínez, J. (1997) Factores organizativos y de inte'res para favorecer la educación trilingüe de los alumnos. *Ikastaria* 9, 131–151.

Martínez de Luna, I. (2006) Hizkuntzen erabilera ikertzen eskolako testuinguran. Andoain: Soziolinguistika Klusterra (Unpublished document).

Martínez de Luna, I. and Suberbiola, P. (2008) Measuring student language use in the school context. *Language Culture and Curriculum* 21, 59–68.

May, S. (2004) Māori-medium education in Aotearoa/New Zealand. In J.W. Tollefson and A.B.M. Tsui (eds) *Medium of Instruction Policies: Which agenda? Whose agenda?* (pp. 21–41). Mahwah, NJ: Lawrence Erlbaum Associates.

May, S. and Hill, R. (2005) Maori-medium education: Current issues and challenges. *International Journal of Bilingual Education and Bilingualism* 8, 377–403.

May, S. (2007) Bilingual/Immersion education: What the research tells us. In J. Cummins and N.H. Hornberger (eds) *Encyclopedia of Language and Education* (Vol. 5: Bilingual Education) (pp. 19–34). New York: Springer.

Mayer, M. (1969) *Frog, Where Are You?* New York: Dial Press.

McCarty, T.L., Romero, M.E. and Zepeda, O. (2006) Reimagining multilingual America: Lessons from native American youth. In O. García, T. Skutnabb-Kangas and M.E. Guzmán (eds) *Imagining Multilingual Schools* (pp. 91–110). Clevedon: Multillingual Matters.

McCarty, T.L. (2007) Bilingual education by and for American-Indians, Alaska natives and native Hawaiians. In J. Cummins and N.H. Hornberger (eds) *Encyclopedia of Language and Education* (Vol 5: Bilingual Education) (pp. 239–251). New York: Springer.

McLaughlin, B. and Nayak, N. (1989) Processing a new language: Does knowing other languages make a difference? In H.W. Dechert and M. Raupach (eds) *Interlingual Processes* (pp. 5–16). Tübingen: Gunter Narr.

Mercosur Educacional (2007) Proyectos y programas de la educación básica que se implementan en Paraguay. On WWW at http://www.sic.inep.gov.br/index.php?option=com_docman&task=cat_view&gid=125&Itemid=34&lang=es.

Melià, B. (2004) El español y las lenguas indígenas en el Paraguay Congreso internacional lengua española. Rosario 2004 17-20 noviembre. On WWW at http://congresosdelalengua.es/rosario/ponencias/aspectos/melia_b.htm.

Met, M. (1998) Curriculum decision-making in content-based language teaching. In J. Cenoz and F. Genesee (eds) *Beyond Bilingualism: Multilingualism and Multilingual Education* (pp. 35–63). Clevedon: Multilingual Matters.

Ministerio de Educación y Ciencia (2007) Panorama de la Educación. Indicadores de la OCDE 2007. Informe español. Madrid.

Mohanty, A.K. (2006) Multilingualism of the unequals and predicaments of education in India: Mother tongue or other tongue. In O. García, T. Skutnabb-Kangas and M.E. Guzmán (eds) *Imagining Multilingual Schools* (pp. 262–283). Clevedon: Multillingual Matters.

Mohanty, A. (2007) Multilingual education in India. In J. Cummins and N.H. Hornberger (eds) *Encyclopedia of Language and Education* (Vol. 5: Bilingual Education) (pp. 165–174). New York: Springer.

Moore, D. (2006) *Plurilinguismes et école*. Paris: Didier.

Mugertza, K. and Aliaga, R. (2005) El multilingüismo y el multiculturalismo en el sistema educativo vasco. In D. Lasagabaster and J.M. Sierra (eds) *Multilingüismo y Multiculturalismo en la Escuela* (pp. 97–112). Barcelona: ICE/Horsori.

Muñoz, C. (2000) Bilingualism and trilingualism in school students in Catalonia. In J. Cenoz and U. Jessner (eds) *English in Europe: The Acquisition of a Third Language* (pp. 157–178). Clevedon: Multilingual Matters.

Muñoz, C. (2005) Trilingualism in the Catalan Educational System. _International Journal of the Sociology of Language_ 171, 75–93.

Muñoz, C. (ed.) (2006a) _Age and the Rate of Foreign Language Learning_. Clevedon: Multilingual Matters.

Muñoz, C. (2006b) The effects of age on foreign language learning: The BAF project. In C. Muñoz (ed.) _Age and the Rate of Foreign Language Learning_ (pp. 1–40). Clevedon: Multilingual Matters.

Muñoz, C. (2008a) Age-related differences in foreign language learning: Revisiting the empirical evidence. _IRAL: International Review of Applied Linguistics_, 46.

Muñoz, C. (2008b) Symmetries and asymmetries of age effects in naturalistic and instructed L2 learning. _Applied Linguistics_ 29, 578–596.

Murtagh, L. (2007) Out-of-school use of Irish, motivation and proficiency in immersion and subject-only post-primary programmes. _International Journal of Bilingual Education and Bilingualism_ 10, 428–453 (special issue edited by J. Harris).

Nation, R. and McLaughlin, B. (1986) Novices and experts: An information processing approach to the 'good language learner' problem. _Applied Psycholinguistics_ 7, 41–56.

Nayak, N., Hansen, N., Krueger, N. and McLaughlin, B. (1990) Language-learning strategies in monolingual and multilingual adults. _Language Learning_ 40, 221–44.

Nikolov, M. (1999) 'Why do you learn English?' 'Because the teacher is short': A study of Hungarian children's foreign language learning motivation. _Language Teaching Research_ 3, 33–56.

Norton, B. and Toohey, K. (eds) (2004) _Critical pedagogies and language learning_, Cambridge: Cambridge University Press.

Niño-Murcia, M. and Rothman, J. (2008) Spanish-contact bilingualism and identity. In M. Niño-Murcia and J. Rothman (eds) _Bilingualism and Identity_ (pp. 11–32). Amsterdam: John Benjamins.

Odlin, T. and Jarvis, S. (2004) Same source, different outcomes: A study of Swedish influence on the acquisition of English in Finland. _International Journal of Multilingualism_ 1, 123–140.

OECD (2003) _PISA Assessment Framework_. On WWW at http://www.pisa.oecd.org/dataoecd/46/14/33694881.pdf.

OECD (2007) _PISA 2006 Science Competencies for Tomorrow's World_ (Vols 1 and 2). On WWW at http://www.pisa.oecd.org/.

O'Laoire, M. (2005) Three languages in the schools in Ireland. _International Journal of the Sociology of Language_ 171, 95–113.

Okita, Y. and Jun Hai, G. (2001) Learning of Japanese Kanji character by bilingual and monolingual Chinese speakers. In J. Cenoz, B. Hufeisen and U. Jessner (eds) _Looking Beyond Second Language Acquisition: Studies in Tri- and Multilingualism_ (pp. 63–73). Tübingen: Stauffenburg.

Ó Riagáin, P. (2007) Relationships between attitudes to Irish, social class, religion and social identity in the Republic of Ireland and Northern Ireland. _International Journal of Bilingual Education and Bilingualism_ 10, 369–393.

Oroz, N. and Sotés, P. (2008) Bilingual education in Navarre: Achievements and challenges. _Language Culture and Curriculum_ 21, 21–38.

Pagola, R.M. (2004) Hizkuntza Politika Deustuko Unibertsitatean. _Bat Soziolinguistika aldizkaria_ 50, 51–56.

Paulston, C.B. and Heidemann, K. (2006) Language policies and the education of linguistic minorities. In T. Ricento (ed.) *Language Policy: Theory and Method* (pp. 292–310). London: Blackwell.

Pavlenko, A. (2002) Poststructuralist approaches to the study of social factors in second language learning and use. In V. Cook (ed.) *Portraits of the L2 User* (pp. 277–302). Clevedon: Multilingual Matters.

Pavlenko, A. and Blackledge, A. (eds) (2004) *Negotiation of Identities in Multilingual Contexts*. Clevedon: Multilingual Matters.

Pavlenko, A. (2005) *Emotions and Multilingualism*. Cambridge: Cambridge University Press.

Penfield, W. and Roberts, L. (1959) *Speech and Brain Mechanisms*. Princeton, NJ: Princeton University press.

Perales, S. (2004) La adquisición de la negación en inglés por hablantes bilingües en euskera-castellano. PhD thesis, University of the Basque Country.

Perales, J. (2004) Euskara helduaroan ikasteko motibazioa: Hainbat gogoeta. *Uztaro* 50, 23–43.

Pinto, M.A. and Titone, R. (1995) Tre test di abilità metalinguistiche: Il Tam-1, il Tam-2, il Tam-3. *Rassegna Italiana di Linguistica Applicata* 27, 45–224.

Poulisse, N. and Bongaerts, Th. (1994) First language use in second language production. *Applied Linguistics* 15, 36–57.

Ransdell, S., Barbier, M.L. and Niit, T. (2006) Metacognitions about language skill and working memory among monolingual and bilingual college students: When does multilingualism matter. *International Journal of Bilingual Education and Bilingualism* 9, 728–741.

Riemersma, A. and De Jong, S. (2007) Frisian: The Frisian language in education in the Netherlands. Ljouwert: Mercator-Education.

Ringbom, H. (2007) *Cross-linguistic Similarity in Foreign Language Learning*. Clevedon: Multilingual Matters.

Robertson, B. (2001) Gaelic in Scotland. In G. Extra and D. Gorter (eds) *The Other Languages of Europe* (pp. 83–101). Clevedon: Multilingual Matters.

Robinson, P. (ed.) (2002) *Individual Differences and Instructed Language Learning*. Amsterdam: John Benjamins.

Ruiz Bikandi, U. (2002) Hirugarren hizkuntzu goiztiarra ala zentzuzkoa? In F. Etxeberria and U. Ruiz Bikandi (eds) *¿Trilingües a los 4 años?* (pp. 145–164). Donostia-San Sebastián: Ibaeta Pedagogia.

Ruiz Bikandi, U. (2005) La reflexió interlingüística: Ajudar a pensar en/amb/sobre tres llengües. *Articles de Didáctica de la Llengua i de la Literatura* 38, 51–66.

Ruiz de Zarobe, Y. (2005) Age and third language production: A longitudinal study *International Journal of Multilingualism* 2, 105–112.

Ruiz de Zarobe, Y. (2006) Garapen kognitiboa eta adina ingelesaren jabekuntzan atzerriko hizkuntza gisa. In J. Cenoz and D. Lasagabaster (eds) *Hizkuntzak Ikasten eta Erabiltzen* (pp. 177–191). Bilbao: Euskal Herriko Unibertsitatea.

Ruiz de Zarobe, Y. and Jiménez Catalán, R.M. (eds) (2009) *Content and Language Integrated Learning: Evidence from Research in Europe*. Bristol: Multilingual Matters.

Safont, M.P. (2005) *Third Language Learners. Pragmatic Production and Awareness*. Clevedon: Multilingual Matters.

Sagasta, P. (2001) *La Producción Escrita en Euskara, Castellano e Inglés en el Modelo D y en el Modelo de Inmersión*. Leioa: Universidad del País Vasco.

Sagasta, M.P. (2002) *La Producción Escrita en Euskara, Castellano e Inglés en el Modelo D y en el Modelo de Inmersión*. Bilbao: University of the Basque Country.

Sagasta, M.P. (2003) Acquiring writing skills in a third language: The positive effects of bilingualism. *International Journal of Bilingualism 7*, 27–42.

Sagasta, M.P. and Etxeberria, L. (2006) Hizkuntzen arteko elkarmenpekotasuna: Hizkuntza transferentziak euskaratik gaztelerara. In J. Cenoz and D. Lasagabaster (eds) *Hizkuntzak Ikasten eta Erabiltzen* (pp. 61–89). Bilbao: Euskal Herriko Unibertsitatea.

Sainz, M. (2001) *Azalpenezko Testu Entziklopedikoaren Azterketa eta Didaktika*. Donostia: Erein.

Sainz, M. (2006) Euskarazko ikasleen hasierako formazioaren eragina: Beren usteak eta konpetentziak. In J. Cenoz and D. Lasagabaster (eds) *Hizkuntzak Ikasten eta Erabiltzen* (pp. 137–156). Bilbao: Euskal Herriko Unibertsitatea.

Sainz, M. and Ruiz Bikandi, U. (2006) Hizkuntza eskolan: Aldaketak egoera berriaren aurrean. *Jakin* 154, 77–90.

Sanders, M. and Meijers, G. (1995) English as L3 in the elementary school. *ITL Review of Applied Linguistics* 107–8, 59–78.

Santiago, K. (1995) Ikaste-estrategietan esku-hartzea: 8. mailan gauzatutako esperientzia. *Tantak* 13, 47–64.

Santiago, K., Lukas, J.F., Moyano, N., Lizasoain, L. and Joaristi, L. (2008) A longitudinal study of academic achievement in Spanish: The effect of linguistic models. *Language, Culture and Curriculum* 21, 48–58.

Sanz, C. (2000) Bilingual education enhances third language acquisition: Evidence from Catalonia. *Applied Psycholinguistics* 21, 23–44.

Scott, M. (1996) *Wordsmith Tools*. Oxford: Oxford University Press.

Schmitt, N., Schmitt, D. and Clapham, C. (2001) Developing and exploring the behaviour of two new versions of the Vocabulary Levels Test. *Language Testing* 18, 55–88.

Schola Europea (2008) Annual report of the Secretary-General to the Board of Governors of the European schools. On WWW at http://www.eursc.eu/index.php?id=134.

Schoonen, R., van Gelderen, A., De Glopper, K., Hulstijn, J., Snellings, P., Simis, A. and Stevenson, M. (2002) Linguistic knowledge, metacognitive knowledge and retrieval speed in L1, L2 and EFL writing. In S. Ransdell and M-L. Barbier (eds) *New Directions for Research in L2 Writing* (pp. 101–122). Dordrecht: Kluwer Academic Publishers.

Schultz, K. and Hull, G. (2007) Literacies in and out of school in the United States. In B.V. Street and N.H. Hornberger (eds) *Encyclopedia of Language and Education* (Vol. 2: Literacy) (pp. 239–250). New York: Springer.

Seidlhofer, B. (2005) English as a lingua franca. *ELT Journal* 59, 339–341.

Seidlhofer, B. (2007) *Common property: English as a lingua franca in Europe*. In J. Cummins and C. Davison (eds) *International Handbook of English Language Teaching* Part 1 (pp. 137–153). New York: Springer.

Seikkula-Leiono, J. (2007) CLIL Learning: Achievement levels and affective factors. *Language and Education* 21, 328–341.

Septien, J.M. (2006) *Un Escuela sin Fronteras. La Enseñanza del Alumnado Immigrante en Alava*. Vitoria-Gasteiz: Ararteko.

Sercombe, P.G. (2007) Small worlds: The language ecology of the Penan in Borneo. In A. Creese, P. Martin and N.H. Hornberger (eds) *Encyclopedia of*

Language and Education (Vol. 9: Ecology of Language) (pp. 183–192). New York: Springer.

Shohamy, E. (2006) Imagined multilingual schools: How come we don't deliver? In O. García, T. Skutnabb-Kangas and M.E. Guzmán (eds) *Imagining Multilingual Schools* (pp. 171–183). Clevedon: Multillingual Matters.

Shohamy, E. (2007) *Language Policy: Hidden agendas and New Approaches*. London: Routledge.

Sierra, J. and Olaziregi, I. (1989) *EIFE 2: Influence of Factors on the Learning of Basque*. Vitoria-Gasteiz: Eusko Jaurlaritzaren Argitalpen Zerbitzu Nagusia.

Sierra, J. and Olaziregi, I. (1991) *EIFE 3: Influence of Factors on the Learning of Basque*. Vitoria-Gasteiz: Eusko Jaurlaritzaren Argitalpen Zerbitzu Nagusia.

Sierra, J. (1995) Evaluación de las experiencias de inglés en la Comunidad Autónoma del País Vasco. In M. Siguán (ed.) *La Enseñanza de la Lengua por Tareas* (pp. 233–250). Barcelona: ICE/Horsori.

Sierra, J. (1996) Los modelos de enseñanza bilingüe y el rendimiento escolar en educación primaria. Paper read at the III European Conference on Immersion Programmes. Barcelona: September, 1996.

Sierra, J. (1997) Hirugarren hizkuntza gure irakas-sisteman. *Jakingarriak* 36, 26–29.

Singleton, D. and Ryan, L. (2004) *Language Acquisition: The Age Factor*. Clevedon: Multilingual Matters.

Skutnabb-Kangas, T. (2000) *Linguistic Genocide in Education or Worldwide Diversity and Human Rights?* Mahwah, NJ: Lawrence Erlbaum.

Skutnabb-Kangas, T. and McCarty, T.L. (2007) Key concepts in bilingual education: Ideological, historical, epistemological and empirical foundations. In J. Cummins and N.H. Hornberger (eds) *Encyclopedia of Language and Education* (Vol. 5: Bilingual Education) (pp. 3–17). New York: Springer.

Snow, C. and Hoefnagel-Höhle, M. (1978) The critical period for language acquisition: Evidence from second language. *Child Development* 49, 1114–1128.

Sotés, P. and Arnau, J. (1996) Diferencias individuales en el uso y adquisición del euskara en un programa de inmersión. In M. Pérez Pereira (ed.) *Estudios sobre la adquisición del castellano, catalán, eusquera y gallego* (pp. 695–709). Santiago de Compostela: Universidade de Santiago de Compostela.

Sotés, P. (1996) La comunicación profesor/a-alumnos al comienzo de un programa de inmersión al euskera. PhD thesis, University of Barcelona.

Spolsky, B. (2004) *Language Policy*. Cambridge: Cambridge University Press.

Stuijt, M. and Sanchez, D. (1998) *The Basque Language in Education in France*. Ljouwert/Leeuwarden: Mercator-Education (www.mercator-education.org).

Swain, M. (1995) Three functions of output in second language learning. In G. Cook and B. Seidlhofer (eds) *Principle and Practice in Applied Linguistics: Studies in Honour of H.G. Widdowson* (pp. 125–144). Oxford: Oxford University Press.

Swain, M., Lapkin, S., Rowen, N. and Hart, D. (1990) The role of mother tongue literacy in third language learning. *Language, Culture and Curriculum* 3, 65–81.

Swain, M. and Lapkin, S. (1982) *Evaluating Bilingual Education: A Canadian Case Study*. Clevedon: Multilingual Matters.

Swain, M. and Johnson, R.K. (1997) Immersion education: A category withing bilingual education. In R.K. Johnson and M. Swain (eds) *Immersion Education: International Perspectives* (pp. 1–16) Cambridge: Cambridge University Press.

Ten Thije, J.D. and Zeevaert, L. (eds) (2007) *Receptive Multilingualism*. Amsterdam: John Benjamins.

Thomas, J. (1988) The role played by metalinguistic awareness in second and third language learning. *Journal of Multilingual and Multicultural Development* 9, 235–46.

Thomas, W.P. and Collier, V.P. (1997) School effectiveness for language minority students. Washington DC: National Clearinghouse for English Language Acquisition (www.ncela.gwu.edu/pubs/resource/effectiveness/index.html).

Thomas, W.P. and Collier, V.P. (2002) *A national study of school effectiveness for language minority students' long term academic achievement*. Santa Cruz, CA: Center for Research on Education, Diversity and Excellence (CREDE).

Torrance, E.P. (1990) *The Torrance Tests of Creative Thinking: Norms-technical manual*. Bensenville, IL: Scholastic Testing Service Inc.

Torres-Guzman, M.E. and Etxeberria, F. (2005) Modelo B/Dual language programs in the Basque Country and the USA. *International Journal of Bilingual Education and Bilingualism* 8, 506–528.

Tragant, E., Muñoz, C. (2000) La motivación y su relación con la edad en un contexto escolar de aprendizaje de una lengua extranjera. In C. Muñoz (ed.) *Segundas Lenguas: Adquisición en el Aula* (pp. 81–105). Barcelona: Ariel.

UNESCO (2002) Universal declaration on cultural diversity. On WWW at http://www.unesco.org/education/imld_2002/unversal_decla.shtml.

Urrutia, H., Candia, L., Martínez, M.D. and Milla, F. (1998) *Bilingüismo y Rendimiento Académico en la Comunidad Autónoma Vasca*. Bilbao: Jóvenes por la Paz.

Urrutia, H. (2005) Usos y actitudes sociolingüísticos en la Comunidad Autónoma Vasca. In Urrutia, H. and Fernández, T. (eds) *La Educación Plurilingüe en España y América* (pp. 239–278) Madrid: Dykinson.

Valencia, J. and Cenoz, J. (1992) The role of bilingualism in foreign language acquisition: Learning English in the Basque Country. *Journal of Multilingual and Multicultural Development* 13, 433–49.

Valero, M.(2000) Lectoescritura en tres lenguas. *Ikastaria* 11, 129–134.

Valero, M. and Villamor, J.L. (1997) Experiencia de immersión trilingüe. *Ikastaria* 9, 57–64.

Van Gelderen, A., Schoonen, R., De Glopper, K., Hulstijn, J., Snellings, P., Simis, A., and Stevenson, M. (2003) Roles of linguistic knowledge, metacognitive knowledge and processing speed in L3, L2 and L1 reading comprehension: A structural equation modelling approach. *International Journal of Bilingualism* 7, 7–25.

Van Leeuwen, C. and Wilkinson, R. (eds) (2003) *Multilingual Approaches in University Education: Challenges and Practices*. Nijmegen: Valkhof Pers.

Vila i Moreno, F.X. (2008) Language-in-education policies in the Catalan language area. *Aila Review* 21, 31–48.

Wagner, D.A., Spratt, J.E. and Ezzaki, A. (1989) Does learning to read in a second language always put the child at a disadvantage? Some counterevidence from Morocco. *Applied Psycholinguistics* 10, 31–48.

Wei, L., Dewaele, J.M. and Housen A. (2002) Introduction: Opportunities and challenges of bilingualism. In L. Wei, J.M. Dewaele and A. Housen (2002) *Introduction: Opportunities and Challenges of Bilingualism* (pp. 1–12). Berlin/New York: Mouton de Gruyter.

Wilkinson, R. and Zegers, V. (2006) Assessing incipient linguistic competences: An institutional perspective. In R. Wilkinson, V. Zegers and C. van Leuuwen (eds) *Bridging the assessment gap in English-medium higher education* (pp. 61–76). Nijmegen: AKD-Verlag Bochum.

Wilkinson, R., Zegers, V. and van Leuuwen, C. (eds) (2006) *Bridging the Assessment Gap in English-medium Higher Education*. Nijmegen: AKD-Verlag Bochum.

Williams, C. (2001) Welsh in Great Britain. In G. Extra and D. Gorter (eds) *The Other Languages of Europe* (pp. 59–81). Clevedon: Multilingual Matters.

Williams, S. and Hammarberg, B. (1998) Language switches in L3 production: Implications for polyglot speaking model. *Applied Linguistics* 19, 295–333.

Wolfe-Quintero, K., Inagaki, S. and Hae-Young, K. (1999) *Second Language Development in Writing: Measures of Fluency, Accuracy and Complexity*. Honolulu: University of Hawaii.

Yang, J. (2005) English as a third language among China's ethnic minorities. *International Journal of Bilingualism and Bilingual Education* 8, 552–567.

Ytsma, J. (2001) Towards a typology of trilingual primary education. *Journal of Bilingual Education and Bilingualism* 4, 11–22.

Yu, L. (2007) English-Chinese bilingual education in China. In J. Cummins and N.H. Hornberger (eds) *Encyclopedia of Language and Education* (Vol 5: Bilingual Education) (pp. 175–189). New York: Springer.

Zalbide, M. (2000) Irakas-sistemaren hizkuntz normalkuntza: Nondik norakoaren ebaluazio-saio bat. *Eleria* 5, 45–61.

Zalbide, M. and Cenoz, J. (2008) Bilingual education in the Basque Autonomous Community: Achievements and challenges. *Language, Culture and Curriculum* 21, 5–20.

Zobl, H. (1993) Prior linguistic knowledge and the conservation of the learning procedure: Grammaticality judgments of unilingual and multilingual learners. In S.M. Gass and L. Selinker (eds) *Language Transfer in Language Learning* (pp. 176–96). Amsterdam: John Benjamins.

Zuazo, K. (1995) The Basque Country and the Basque Language: An overview of the external history of the Basque Language. In J.I. Hualde, J. Lakarra and L. Trask (eds) *Towards a History of the Basque Language* (pp. 5–30). Philadelphia, PA: John Benjamins.

Author Index

Subject Index